Leisure, Recreation and Tourism

Dr Robert Prosser

Lecturer in Recreation and Tourism Studies
The University of Birmingham

Collins Educational
An imprint of HarperCollins*Publishers*

Collins Educational, 77–85 Fulham Palace Road
London W6 8JB
An imprint of HarperCollins*Publishers*

First published 1994

Printed and bound by G. Canale & C. S.p.A., Borgaro T.se (Turin), Italy

ISBN 0 00 326645 1

References

Baud-Bovy, M and Lawson, F (1977) *Tourism and Recreational Development*, Butterworth Heinemann.
Bishop, J and Coalter, F (1988) 'Leisure and the public and voluntary sectors', Leisure Studies Association.
BTA (1992) *Selling Britain to the World*, Annual Report 1991/92, British Tourist Authority.
BTA (1993) Annual Report 1992/93, British Tourist Authority.
Chapman, K (1979) *People, Pattern and Process*, Edward Arnold.
Comedia (1991) *Out of Hours*, Comedia.
Countryside Commission (1986) *Access Study* (CCP216), Countryside Commission.
Countryside Commission (1992a) *Parish Paths Partnership: An Outline*, Countryside Commission.
Countryside Commission (1992b) *Pennine Way Survey 1990: Use and Economic Impact* (CCP361), Countryside Commission.
Dartmoor NPA (1977) *Structure Plan 1977*, Dartmoor National Park Authority.
Edwards, J (1992) *Fit For the Future*, Countryside Commission.
ETB (1991) Annual Report, English Tourist Board.
Johnston, R J (ed.) (1991) *Dictionary of Human Geography*, Blackwell.
Leisure Studies Association (1992) Conference Proceedings, Sheffield, September.
Lentell, (1991) Lecture given at Leisure Studies Association Conference.
Maslen, A (1991) 'Rough guide to young Britain', *Leisure Management*, January.
Open University/Countryside Commission (1985) *The Countryside Handbook*, Croom Helm.
Ryan, C (1991) *Recreational Tourism*, Routledge.
Shoard, M (1987) *This Land is Our Land*, Paladin.
Social Trends (1987, 1988, 1991, 1992), Central Statistical Office, HMSO.
Standeven, J (1991) 'Against the tide', *Leisure Management*, August.
TRRU (1987) *Outdoor Activities in Scotland: A Survey*, Tourism and Recreation Research Unit.
Tucker, D (1991) 'Themes and schemes', *Leisure Management*, February.
White, J (1992) *Leisure: The Cornerstone of Local Government*, Wrekin District Council.
WTO (1990, 1991) *Yearbook of Tourism Statistics*, World Tourism Organisation.

Acknowledgements

Every effort has been made to contact the holders of copyright material, but if any here have been inadvertently overlooked the publishers will be pleased to make the necessary arrangements at the first opportunity.

Photographs and publicity material
The publishers would like to thank the following for permission to reproduce photographs and publicity material:

Aerofilms Ltd, Fig. 6.17; Airtours, Fig. 10.14; Alton Towers, Fig. 9.18; Beamish: The North of England Open Air Museum, Fig. 9.17; John Birdsall Photography, Figs 3.6, 4.2, 4.5, 4.9 6.3, 6.5, 6.6, 6.7; J. Allan Cash Ltd, Fig. 10.25; The CBSO Society Ltd, Managers of the City of Birmingham Symphony Orchestra, Fig. 4.21; Champneys, Fig. 5.1; Churchtown Outdoor Adventure Centre, Fig. 2.8; Coventry Racquet Centre, Figs 5.2, 5.3; Stuart Currie, Fig. 7.17; Prodeepta Das, Figs 3.8, 6.11; Dean Heritage Museum Trust, Fig. 9.14 (right); Ted Ditchburn/Daily Telegraph, Fig. 9.2 (top); Stuart Gill, Fig. 9.12; John Harlow/Daily Telegraph, Fig. 9.2 (bottom); Martyn Hayhow/The Guardian, Fig. 7.7; David Hollis Fig. 2.7; Inspirations Holidays, Fig. 10.24; Roshini Kempadoo/Format, Figure. 3.7; Kuoni Travel Ltd, Fig. 10.27; Mansfield District Council, Fig. 6.7; James McEvoy, Fig. 9.15; John Mills Photography, Fig. 5.5; Noble Caledonia Ltd, Fig. 10.17; Northern Ireland Tourist Board, Figs 4.1, 9.16; Robert Prosser, Figs 1.2, 1.3, 1.4, 1.6, 1.8, 2.2, 2.5, 3.2, 4.6, 4.8, 4.15, 4.16, 4.18, 4.19, 5.7, 5.8, 6.1, 6.2, 6.12, 6.13, 6.15, 7.1, 7.2, 7.9, 8.1, 8.2, 8.3, 8.4, 8.6, 8.11, 8.12, 8.13, 8.15, 8.16, 8.17, 8.19, 8.21, 8.24, 9.9, 10.2, 10.3, 10.6, 10.8, 10.9, 10.11, 10.19, 10.26, 10.32, 10.33, 10.35, 10.36, 10.38, 10.39; Ramblers Association, Fig. 7.15; Carl Royle, Fig. 7.20; South Tyneside District Council, Fig. 9.14 (left); Tomorrow's Leisure plc, Figs 5.4, 5.6; Tony Stone Worldwide, Figs 2.1, 2.10; La Trinité, Fig. 6.20; The Walt Disney Company, Fig. 9.19; Watermeadows Swimming and Fitness Centre, Fig. 6.18; West Air Photography, Fig. 9.5; World Expeditions, Fig 10.27; Wyndley Leisure Centre, Fig. 6.9.

Cover picture
Rollercoaster at Alton Towers. Source: Tony Stone Worldwide.

Maps
Birmingham City Council, Fig 4.19 (top); Butterworth-Heinemann, Oxford, UK, Fig. 10.30 (from an article first published in *Tourism Management*, Vol. 14, No. 4); Denali National Park, Fig. 10.37; Fraser Island Recreation Board, Fig. 10.26; Kingsbury Water Park, Fig. 8.4; Ordnance Survey, Fig. 4.19 (bottom) reproduced from the 1974 Ordnance Survey 1:1250 Plan SP0686 NW map with the permission of the Controller of Her Majesty's Stationery Office; Saltwells Nature Reserve, Fig. 6.15; South-East London Green Chain Working Party, Fig. 6.16.

Contents

Skills matrix
(distribution of numbered tasks)

Chapter	Understanding of text/ newspaper extracts and classification	Graphical/mapping methods and annotated diagrams	Analysis of data from tables, graphs, maps and diagrams	Analysis of photographs	Statistical analysis	Values enquiry	Data collection and project work	Essay writing
1	1, 3, 4			2		8	5, 6, 7	9
2	4	3	1, 2, 5	7				6
3		8	2, 3, 6, 9	1	7	4		5
4	6, 13, 14, 15, 16, 26	1, 11a	7, 8, 9, 10, 11b, 12, 21, 22, 23, 24, 25			17	2, 3, 4, 5, 19, 27	18, 20
5	2, 4, 5, 7	6	1				8	3
6	2, 3, 6, 7, 8, 9, 11, 21, 23, 24	18b	1a, 4, 5, 10, 12, 13, 14, 15, 16, 17, 18a	20		1b, 3, 24	19, 25	22
7	6, 8	9, 10, 19	1, 2, 3, 4, 5, 11, 13, 14, 15, 16			17	12, 20	7, 18
8	4, 6, 7, 8, 9, 10, 12, 13, 15		2, 3	5				1, 11, 14, 16
9	1, 2, 3, 6, 8, 9, 13	4, 14	10, 16	5, 6, 12			11, 15, 18, 19	7, 17
10	1, 2, 9, 10, 11, 13, 16, 20a, 20b, 20c, 22, 23, 26, 27	20d	3, 4, 5, 6, 7, 8, 18, 25	19			14, 15	12, 17, 21, 24, 28

To the student

As you will discover through this book, 'leisure' is a general term used to cover sport, recreation and tourism. There are leisure, recreation and tourism components in geography, economics, business studies and sports science courses; increasingly there are full courses in leisure studies, recreation studies and tourism studies. This book provides a sound foundation across this broad field, whether you are studying at Advanced level or introductory undergraduate level.

The materials are presented through a framework of ideas, concepts and models which are then explored and demonstrated through examples and case studies. It is very important that you pay as close attention to the range of visual resources – photographs, graphs, diagrams and so on – as you do to the written text, for these resources complement and extend the text. Furthermore, through a variety of questions and activities, your attention is focused on such resources and how to make best use of them. This development of learning and response skills should improve your assignment and examination performance in projects, essays, data-response and decision-making exercises.

Leisure studies cross the boundaries of several subjects, but this book is essentially geographical in its approach. Geography is concerned with how space is organised and the effects of this organisation, in both natural and human systems. So, the materials examine the spatial organisation and impacts of recreation opportunities and behaviour: who provides what, where, for whom, and why; who does what, where, with whom, and why. Three fundamental dimensions recur – the 'three p's': participation, policy and provision.

As you work through the various chapters it will become evident that there are direct and valuable connections with other parts of your courses. For example, in urban and social geography, the CBD, service hierarchies and catchment areas, urban regeneration strategies, open space and land-use policies are important topics which are discussed in this book. In the field of economic geography, aspects such as locational decision-making, product cycles, cost–benefit analysis, transport networks, market forces versus social benefits are all introduced. Specific examples are used; with the support of the suggested activities, they help and encourage you to draw parallels with your own localities, regions and experiences. For instance – location and use of local parks or leisure centres; leisure use of CBDs; footpath networks and usage; holiday patterns etc. There are ample ideas and suggestions, too, for coursework projects and fieldwork assignments (individual and group) based upon the concepts, models and issues set out in the book.

Leisure is about 'having fun' – so as the Americans say, 'Enjoy!'. The so-called 'leisure industry' is today the largest in the world, and who knows, there may even be a job at the end of it!

Robert Prosser

1 The varied world of leisure

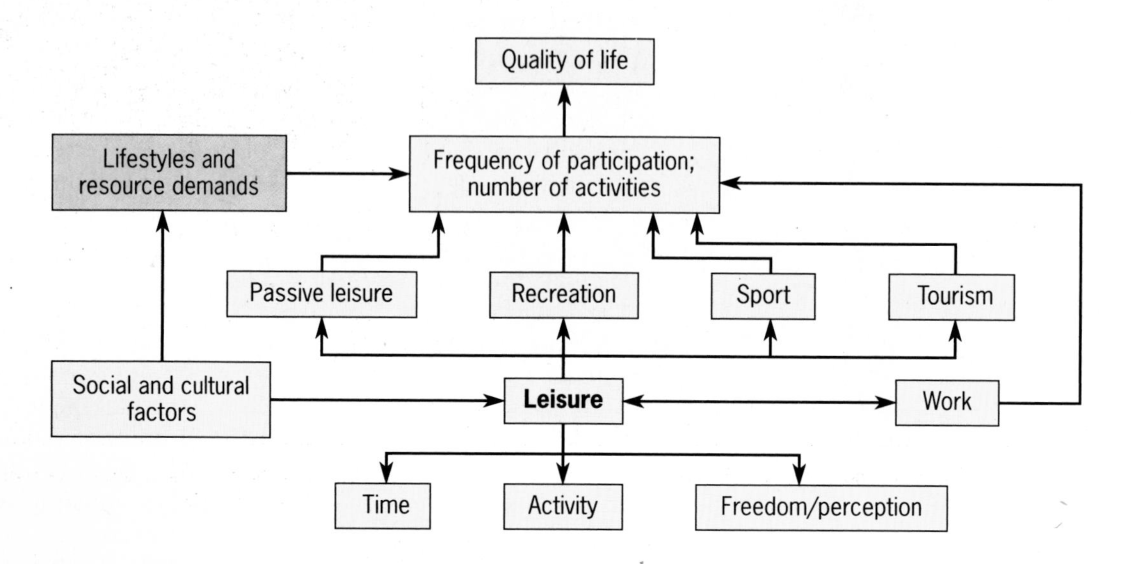

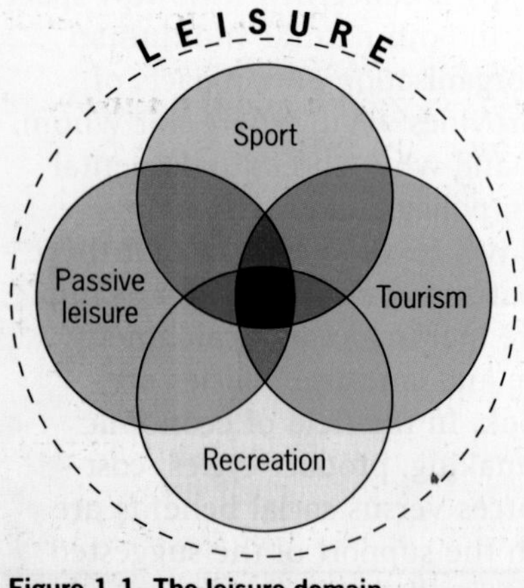

Figure 1.1 The leisure domain

1.1 Introduction

Leisure is one of those words we all use, think we know its meaning, but find difficult to define. It is used in this book as a broad term which encompasses passive leisure, **recreation**, sport and **tourism** (Fig. 1.1). Passive leisure may be simply sitting around, relaxing. Recreation involves some form of activity. Sport involves activity within a formal setting of rules etc. Tourism is activity/ experience which involves travel away from the home environment. However, as the Venn diagram in Figure 1.1 suggests, the distinctions are not clear-cut. For instance, your recreation may include going to watch a sporting event, such as an athletics meeting, but if you watch the athletics at home in front of the TV, it could be defined as 'passive leisure'; if you play pitch-and-putt golf while on holiday, then your activity can be seen as both tourism and recreation (Fig. 1.2). Equally, the same activity can be sport or recreation: competition swimming is a sport, while casual swimming in a leisure pool is a recreational activity.

?

1 Under the headings of each of the four components of leisure, make lists of things you have enjoyed doing during the past year.

Figure 1.2 When recreation and tourism mix: playing mini-golf while on holiday at the seaside

Figure 1.3 'Sun-sea-sand' seekers on Miami Beach, Florida

Figure 1.4 'Wilderness' seekers on a canoe trek in the Everglades National Park, Florida

Recreation and tourism

This book focuses particularly upon recreation and tourism, with some references to sport. Throughout, the emphasis is first upon the resource demands and environmental impacts of the leisure 'explosion', and second upon the decision-making processes involved in both the **demand** for and the **supply** of leisure opportunities and experiences. While most of the materials refer to the United Kingdom, the sections on tourism have a global perspective.

Chapter 1 encourages you to think carefully about what 'leisure' means, and how it relates to the idea of 'work'. Chapters 2 and 3 examine the implications of people wanting to go out and enjoy themselves (i.e. the demand for leisure) and how opportunities are organised and supplied. As the world is becoming increasingly urbanised (in the UK some 80 per cent of us live in towns and cities), Chapters 4 and 5 help you to understand how the urban leisure system works. Chapters 6, 7 and 8 tackle the issues created by the rapidly growing popularity of outdoor activities, from a Sunday afternoon picnic to 'the wilderness experience', particularly in terms of resource ownership and **access**. Chapter 9 turns the spotlight upon the changing patterns of holidaymaking in the UK, while Chapter 10 shows how global tourism, as one of the world's largest industries, carries with it enormous benefits, as well as rising social, economic and environmental costs.

?

2 Look carefully at the photographs in Figures 1.3 and 1.4 and analyse them in terms of these definitions: *time* (When are these activities pursued? How long do they last?); *activity* (What are people doing?); *freedom and perception* (How much choice and freedom do the people have? What satisfaction do they gain, and what feelings do they experience – relaxation, excitement, challenge, being with family or friends, getting fit etc?).

1.2 What do we mean by 'leisure'?

Here are four apparently quite different definitions of leisure:

As time: time free from work and other obligations.

As activity: things you choose to do in your spare time.

As freedom: the relatively freely-chosen non-work area of life.

As perception: relatively self-determined experiences that occur in those parts of your life when you are free from 'work', that you see as 'leisure', and you enjoy across a wide range of intensity and commitment.

From these various elements, we can suggest a single, straightforward definition of leisure: *relatively freely-chosen action within time and space.*

Figure 1.5 Japan's new leisure world (*Source*: *Time* magazine, 5 July 1993)

TRAVELER'S ADVISORY

By Jeffery C. Rubin

ASIA

JAPAN. Two grand attractions are opening their doors this month. In the Tokyo suburb of Funabashi, the world's largest indoor ski area, the $360 million Lalaport Ski Dome, begins operation July 15. Its centerpiece is a 25-storey artificial mountain that offers 490-m-long runs on ultra-fine powder produced fresh nightly by snow machines. Open 10 a.m. to 10 p.m. daily; 9 a.m. to 10 p.m. Sundays. On the southern island of Kyushu, the Seagaia Ocean Dome, a 36,000-sq-m indoor seashore, complete with surf and powdered-marble sand, opens July 30. The $860 million attraction is the biggest of its kind anywhere and allows visitors to surf, swim, and sunbathe under a retractable roof. Open daily 9 a.m. to 10 p.m. Two hours of dome skiing (without equipment rental) will cost $53; a day at the artificial beach, $38.

Time: 5 July 1993

Work ethic versus leisure ethic?

It is clear that leisure experiences must involve the feelings of choice, freedom and pleasure. Equally, it is difficult to define 'leisure' clearly without considering the idea of 'work'. In traditional societies 'work' means the direct production of the necessities of life – food, clothing and shelter. When we use the word 'work' we mean, most commonly, 'earning a living'. But this narrow definition ignores the vast range of unpaid work, such as running a home and family. Thus, a more useful definition of work is: *productive activities, paid or unpaid, which are expected to be completed, and to which there is some contract or obligation.*

The 'earning a living' element of work then may be described as 'labour' or 'employment'.

Work seems to involve limited choice or freedom, and for many people, limited pleasure or satisfaction – think of the 'jobs' you have to do at home, or the Saturday job you have! Yet western society gives high status to the concept of work, based on Victorian religious and moral **values**: work is 'good' and leisure is a 'reward' only to be enjoyed when you have earned it (e.g. 'You can go out to play when you have finished your homework.'). This has been called the 'Victorian work ethic'. Other religions and cultures also value hard work (e.g. the famous Japanese 'work ethic').

From this viewpoint, we gain self-fulfilment, esteem and status through work, while loss of work brings about a sense of failure and loss of status. Those who choose not to work are condemned by mainstream society, e.g. the 'New-Age travellers' whose summer gatherings cause so much outcry.

Yet **attitudes** are changing: those who enjoy high-status lifestyles now give comparable importance to both work and leisure. Across the world, people are beginning to use their wealth to embrace this leisure ethic (Fig. 1.5). Executive residential developments are built around marinas and golf courses (Fig. 1.6). Being healthy and participating in leisure activity is becoming fashionable right through the life cycle, as the tongue-in-cheek review in Figure 1.7 illustrates. The economic potential of this emerging 'leisure ethic' is enormous, as industry, the advertising world and the media have realised. In the early 1990s we in the UK spend approximately 16 per cent of our total expenditure on leisure.

?

3 Select any *two* of the age phases in Figure 1.7. For each, choose a *different* activity, and write a résumé of it in the same form and style as the original.

4 For the activities in Figure 1.7, list the resources they require, and who normally supplies them.

Figure 1.6 The leisure lifestyle: houses built around a golf course, Phoenix, Arizona

Seven ages of the sporting life

Skateboards

Age: 5–13

Fashion rating: five star.
Social rating: two star.
Required attributes: common sense.
Comment: Devotees report great satisfaction from these brakeless 'coffins on wheels' which are said (presumably by the manufacturers) to reflect the new quest for self expression in sport. The differing leisure preferences of embryonic sporting man and his sister become increasingly apparent between the ages of five and eight. She tends to become more introverted, contenting herself with a single, special friend. He opts for the gang and the chance to assert himself aggressively. The skateboard — which transforms streets into adventure playgrounds — was made for him.

Soccer

Age: 13–18

Fashion rating: three star.
Social rating: three star.
Required attributes: Good physical co-ordination and a good eye for the ball. Soccer involves short, sharp bursts, interspersed with periods of relative inactivity.
Comment: Not the best way to keep fit — but better than nothing, especially at this age when sporting man does not have to struggle to keep fit. In soccer even the midfield players, on whom the largest demands are made, are only active for short periods of time. Stop watch checks have shown that these players rarely possess the ball for more than three minutes in a 90 minute match. Soccer will enhance muscular strength and endurance.

Tennis

Age: 18–25

Fashion rating: three star.
Social rating: five star.
Required attributes: co-ordination and eye, plus a strong racket hand and arm and the strength to withstand sudden spurts of explosive effort.
Comment: Tennis will not keep sporting man fit unless he plays vigorously and regularly, and seeks partners who will keep him on the move. At the age of 18, however, sporting man seeks a game played by two sexes. But his appetite for mixed doubles does little to develop his tennis. He may become more interested in holding a glass in the bar (and finding a drinking partner) than a racket on the court. This, at the very time when he should be exercising more.

Squash

Age: 25–35

Fashion rating: five star.
Social rating: three star.
Required attributes: Joints that can twist and turn without protest and good levels of fitness. The popular idea that an all-out game is the ideal therapy for tired business persons and frustrated workers is dangerously misleading.
Comment: Sociologically, squash remained an upper class game until the Seventies, perhaps because sports clubbing was not recognised as a habit of your actual working man. Municipal sports centres changed all that. The explosive growth of the game has also been helped by the quickening pace of life. Many young people have much less time to devote to more consuming passions. Squash is ideal for them.

Jogging

Age: 35–45

Fashion rating: three star.
Social rating: Nil.
Required attributes: Minimal.
Comment: The joy of jogging is that it can be done at your own pace, at your own convenience, with minimal disruption to business or domestic routine, and without having to compete against anyone else. Without jogging, I am sure I would be in the tranquilliser queue. I do not achieve the same kind of mental tranquillity from swimming – perhaps because the open air holds more appeal than the chlorinated, enclosed atmosphere of the swimming pool. But swimming is a possible alternative to jogging. In fact, swimming is arguably the best form of sporting activity available to the middle-aged.

Golf

Age: 45–55

Fashion rating: five star.
Social rating: one star.
Required attributes: Endless patience, love of walking and inane conversation.
Comment: Another game enjoying a boom thanks to TV coverage of big events like the British Open and the US Masters. For the sporting man and woman golf is the first big concession to middle age. They reason that they may as well take it up while "still young" to ensure a reasonable degree of competence in their fifties. They don't recognise until it is too late that this new refuge from domestic responsibilities is treacherous, addictive and time consuming. An average round involves a four mile walk and takes between three and four hours.

Bowling

Age: 55 plus

Fashion rating: four star.
Social rating: four star.
Required attributes: two arms and two legs.
Comment: Yet another game elevated by the small screen, crown green bowling is enjoying a boom among middle-aged and elderly men and women. Ideal for the person who still yearns for the thrill of competition, or who is seeking a sport they can enjoy with their spouse. But the odds are usually stacked in the male partner's favour. It might not look like it from the sidelines, but it can take quite a lot of strength to propel a wood across the green. But in the seventh sporting age it would be as well to supplement bowling with brisk walks. Bowling is hardly stenuous.

Figure 1.7 Newspaper report on the sport-as-leisure life cycle (*Source*: *Guardian*, 1 January 1990)

Figure 1.8 The freedom of open space: Chugach National Forest, Alaska

1.3 So – are we having fun yet?

It is clear that 'leisure' is a very broad concept. It is more than simply 'things I do in my spare time'. Leisure is about how you feel about an experience. It is about *choice, fun, freedom, being in control, doing your thing, getting away from it all, feeling good,* and so on (Fig. 1.8). Some people get this type of satisfaction from their work as well as through leisure, but for others, freedom, success, self-esteem etc. are all achieved through their leisure. Leisure, then, is a crucial component in our **quality of life**.

Social and cultural factors

Two important understandings about leisure behaviour are first, that it is socially and culturally moulded (e.g. 'the Swinging Sixties') and second, that it is strongly influenced by fashion. For instance, in 1985, mountain bikes were a rarity; by 1991 they were seen as 'crucial' urban transport, and **Country Park** managers were laying out special biking tracks to control erosion and reduce tensions with other park users. But in 1995, will the tracks lie unused and will all the bikes be jumble-sale offerings? Our attitudes to and expectations from leisure change over time. For instance, many traditional 'bucket-and-spade' seaside **resorts** have declined over the past 30 years; cinemas have been crippled by the home electronics revolution.

The fundamental issue is, therefore, that (*a*) allocating resources to leisure – money, space, people – and (*b*) managing leisure are especially difficult because of:

- the incredible *range* of activities engaged in by *increasing numbers* of people;
- *swings of fashion* and popularity over time; and
- the *inequalities in society* which result in unequal opportunities for leisure.

Lifestyles and resource demands

The model in Figure 1.9 uses two variables: the frequency of participation (how often) and numbers of activities (how many) to illustrate the diversity of leisure consumption and some of its implications.

?

This preparatory exercise will help you with Chapters 2 and 3.

5 For a Friday evening to Sunday evening, keep a diary of your out-of-home leisure activities, i.e. behaviour and experiences that you think of as leisure. For each episode, record:

a The activity or activities engaged in.
b Where you were and the **facilities** and resources used, both your own (hockey stick; snooker cue) and those provided for you.
c Who provided the resources or facilities.
d If it was free (in which case – who *does* fund it?) or if there was a charge.
e How far you travelled to take part.
f The transport you used – who provided it, and paid for it.
g Who you were with.
h Why you did it, e.g. relaxation, fitness, meeting people etc.

6 Analyse this brief spell in your leisure life in terms of the model in Figure 1.9. If this weekend is not typical, then place yourself within the model and suggest reasons for your placement.

7 Compare your leisure lifestyle with others in your group and place them on the model. Do your placements correspond to where other group members placed themselves on the model, and if not, why not?

8 The model suggests that the more leisure activities you take part in, the better your quality of life. What are the values and attitudes behind this suggestion? (Look again at the leisure–work relationships on p. 8).

9 Essay: All definitions of 'leisure' include the concepts of 'freedom' and 'choice'. Outline the main factors that influence the degree of freedom and choice you have in your leisure life.

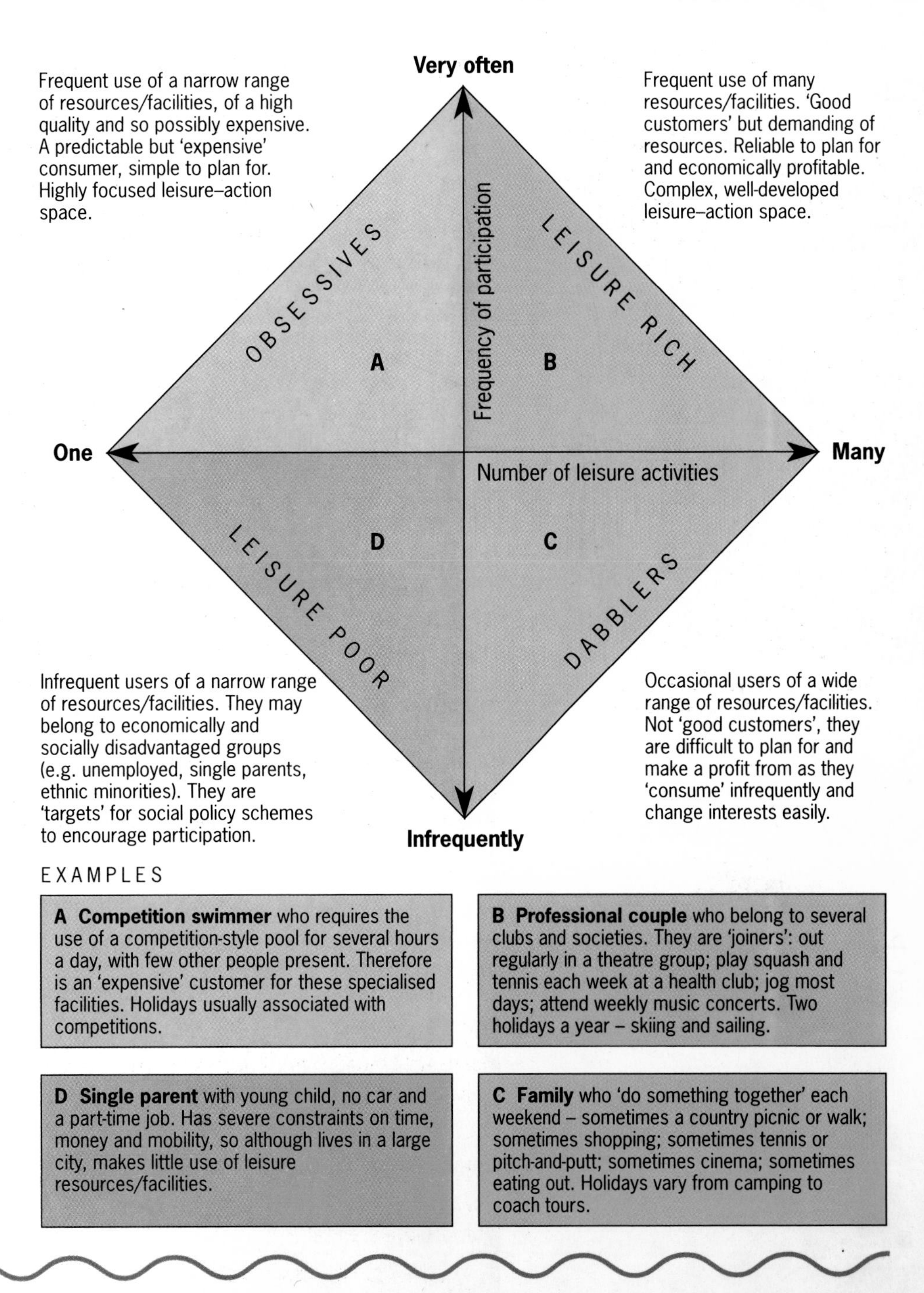

Figure 1.9 Leisure lifestyles and resource demands

Summary

- Leisure includes passive leisure, recreation, sport and tourism.
- All leisure makes some demands upon time and resources.
- Leisure can be studied in terms of time, activity, freedom and perception.
- There is an important relationship between the concepts of leisure and work.
- Social and cultural factors play a major part in leisure participation and resource allocation for leisure.
- Leisure has an important impact upon the quality of life.

2 Leisure demand and supply

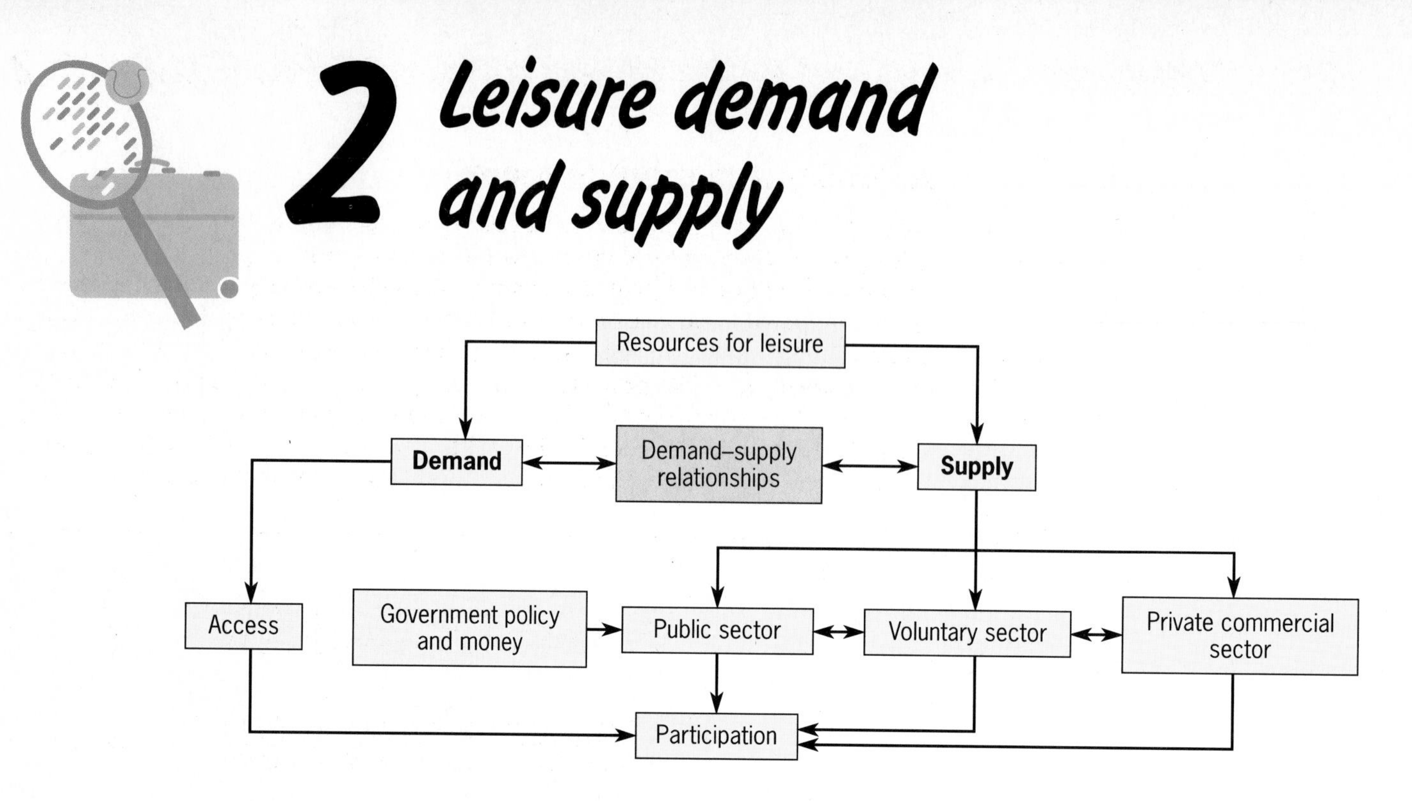

2.1 Introduction

All forms of **leisure** make some demands upon resources, from small patches (your 'personal space' on a beach and a tiny piece of sea to wade in) to high-tech arenas. It is clear that leisure must compete for these resources with other potential uses and users: houses, factories, roads, farms, wildlife etc. (Fig. 2.1). The issues surrounding this competition provide one of the central strands running through this book. A second strand is the concept of **access**, what it is, who controls it and provides it, and on what terms. Whether you want to walk the dog, practise windsurfing, lie on a beach, or work out at a 'popmobility' session, you require access to natural or human-made resources and **facilities**.

Figure 2.1 Recreation must compete for resources and space: Central Park, New York

2.2 Resource management

When demands are made on resources, those who own and/or control them will respond. They either deny access ('Keep out – private property'; 'Trespassers will be prosecuted') or adopt strategies and policies to make the resources available on certain terms ('Entry – £3.50'; 'Stay on footpath'; 'Open Sundays') (Fig. 2.2). We can think of this process of the provision of **supply** to meet **demand** while protecting ownership rights as a sequence of concepts, summarised as a 'concepts cascade', with one idea spilling over into the next – as in Figure 2.3. You may find it helpful to refer back to this diagram as you study the complexities of the issues and case studies throughout this book.

Figure 2.2 Access control, Mt Rainier National Park, USA. A firm but light-hearted way of saying 'Keep off the grass'. The sign is protecting fragile mountain meadows.

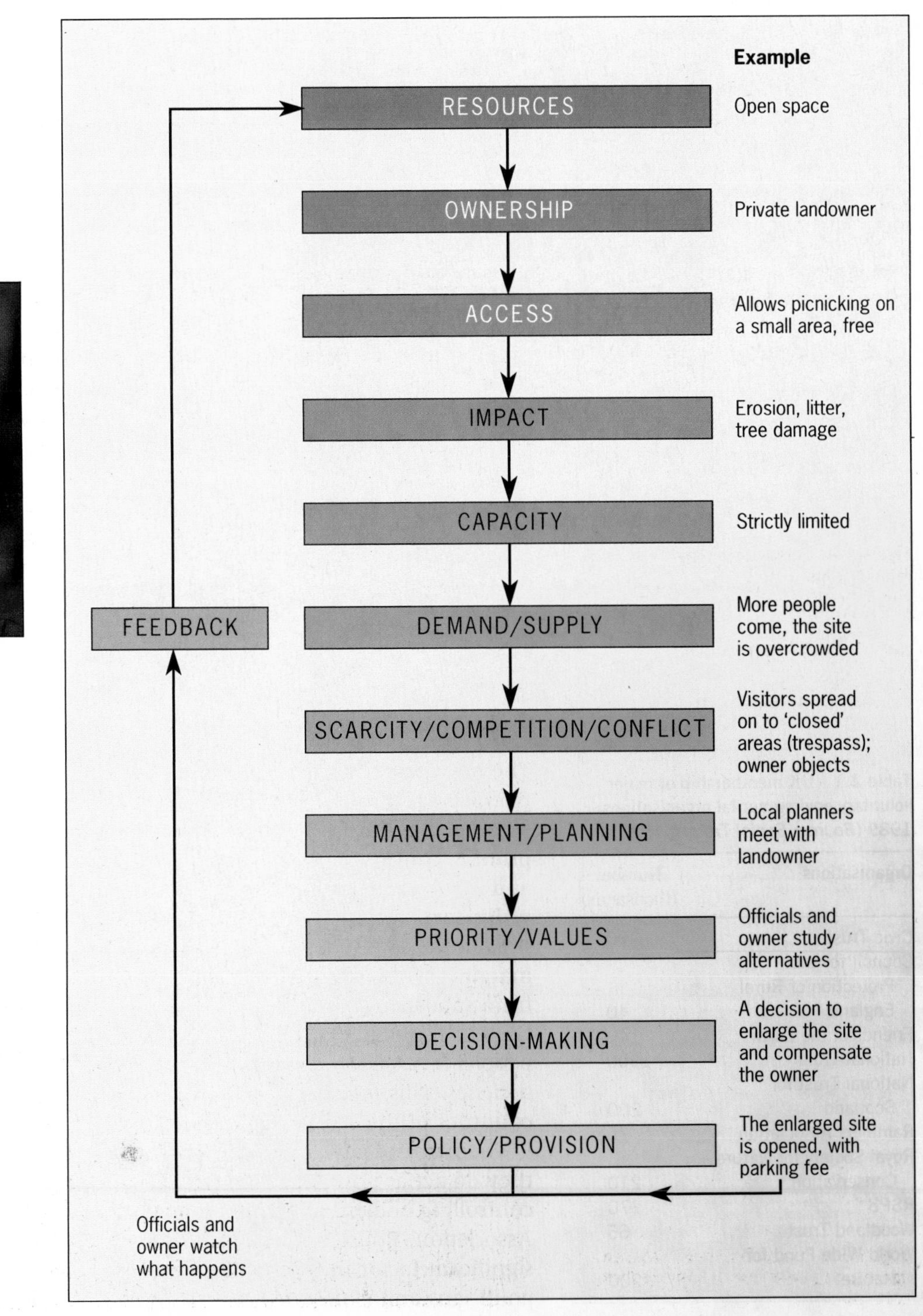

Figure 2.3 A concepts cascade for resource management

Demand–supply relationships

The basic demand–supply relationships are summarised in Figure 2.4. In response to increases in demand, suppliers create additional provision. They also have to react to decreases in demand. We must remember too, that suppliers may make efforts to increase demand (i.e. the number of people who participate).

?

1 Study the graphs in Figure 2.4. For each of the graphs in turn, describe in not more than two sentences the trends and demand–supply relationships shown.

2 To which of the graphs does the following statement apply? 'In 1990 there were 974 golf courses in England, and 195 of them had been built since 1970. There are over a million golfers in the country, half of whom do not belong to a club, and have little hope of joining one. An average waiting list of between 5 and 10 years is not unusual. In some clubs there's a 25-year queue.'

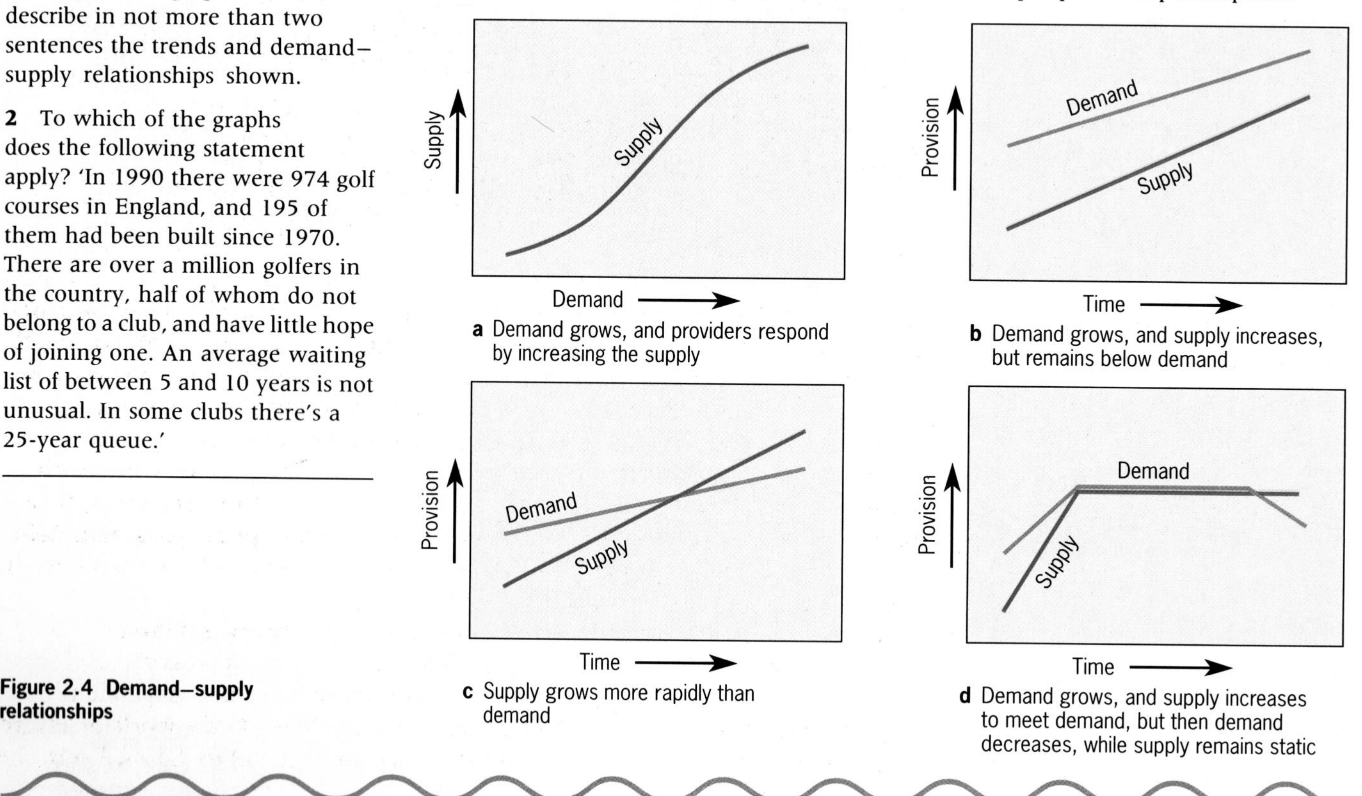

Figure 2.4 Demand–supply relationships

2.3 Supply: providers of leisure resources and facilities

The providers of our opportunities for leisure fall into two major categories: the **private sector** and the **public sector**. The private sector then divides into two sub-types, according to their motivations – the **commercial sector**, whose primary concern is making a profit (from farmers who charge rent for caravans and tents, to major holiday companies such as Thomas Cook Ltd) and the **voluntary sector** (which consists of groups who organise themselves to provide specific types of leisure activity, where social benefit outweighs profit margins). This voluntary sector contains a vast assemblage of clubs and societies, from suburban tennis clubs and choirs to national bodies such as the Caravan Club or National Trust. In Birmingham alone, a city of approximately 1 million people, it has been estimated that there are at least 3000 voluntary clubs and societies. This mixture of public and private enterprise can be found in most countries of the world (Fig. 2.5).

Voluntary organisations may not provide leisure opportunities directly, but they do act as powerful political lobbies and as communications networks, controlling bodies etc., e.g. Ramblers Association (Table 2.1), Football Association, Royal Yachting Association. The size of their membership is a significant factor in their ability to exert influence (e.g. on resource owners, politicians and planners).

Table 2.1 UK membership of major voluntary environmental organisations, 1989 (*Source: Social Trends*, 1991)

Organisations	Number (thousands)
Civic Trust	290
Council for the Protection of Rural England	40
Friends of the Earth	140
National Trust	1900
National Trust for Scotland	200
Ramblers Association	75
Royal Society for Nature Conservation	210
RSPB	770
Woodland Trust	66
World Wide Fund for Nature	200

Figure 2.5 Private enterprises advertising leisure opportunities on Hinchinbrook Island, a National Park in Queensland, Australia

?

3 Draw a simple tree diagram to represent leisure providers. Make your diagram large enough to add notes as you study the rest of this chapter.

4 The Ramblers Association is included in Table 2.1. One of its main objectives is to increase access to the countryside.

a Suggest what leisure opportunities it is likely to campaign for.

b Who is likely to oppose such increased provision?

5 Look at Table 2.2. Make a list of possible reasons why some sports receive more support than others. Discuss your list with your group.

The public sector

The public sector covers leisure provision and **management** by local and central government. Since 1945, government influence has expanded within the sphere of Welfare State policies, with its attempts to improve the **quality of life** for all sections of society. Social fairness, and not financial profit, has been the primary intention. At least, this was the case until the late 1980s, since when the financial rules have been tightened (see pp. 45–6 on compulsory competitive tendering [CCT]). None the less, when you use the local park or youth club, borrow a book from a library, go for a swim, picnic in a **Country Park**, take pottery classes or practise guitar in a local arts centre, or pedal your mountain bike across the hills of a **National Park**, your enjoyment will owe much to the local authorities and central government.

Much government input is indirect, through a separate organisation. Government provides money and guidelines, and sets up 'quangos' (quasi-autonomous non-governmental organisations) – semi-independent bodies to distribute the money and implement the policies. In the world of leisure, the two principal quangos are the Arts Council and the Sports Council (Fig. 2.6 and Table 2.2).

Other government money is allocated to local authorities, who add more money themselves to provide facilities such as parks, libraries, pools, leisure centres, picnic sites, footpaths etc. (Table 2.3).

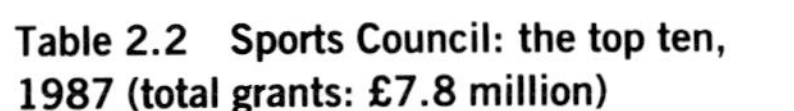

Table 2.2 Sports Council: the top ten, 1987 (total grants: £7.8 million)

Rank	Sport	Amount (£'000)
1	Rowing	440
2	Skiing	405
3	Cycling	332
4	Sailing	321
5	Gymnastics	302
6	Hockey	290
7	Judo	278
8	Squash	260
9	Fencing	250
10	Skating	237

Table 2.3 Estimated local authority expenditure on, and income from, leisure and recreation, England and Wales, 1985–6 (*Source: Social Trends*, 1987)

	Expenditure (£ millions)	Income (£ millions)
Urban parks and open spaces	314	44
Indoor sports halls and leisure centres	221	104
Swimming pools	138	46
Theatres, halls and arts centres	103	42
Art galleries and museums	59	9
Community halls, public halls	51	15
Central or departmental catering	32	35
Outdoor sports facilities	33	9
Country parks, amenity areas, picnic sites and nature reserves	27	6
Promotion of tourism	30	5
Golf courses	14	13
Allotments	5	3
Other leisure and recreation facilities and administration	324	

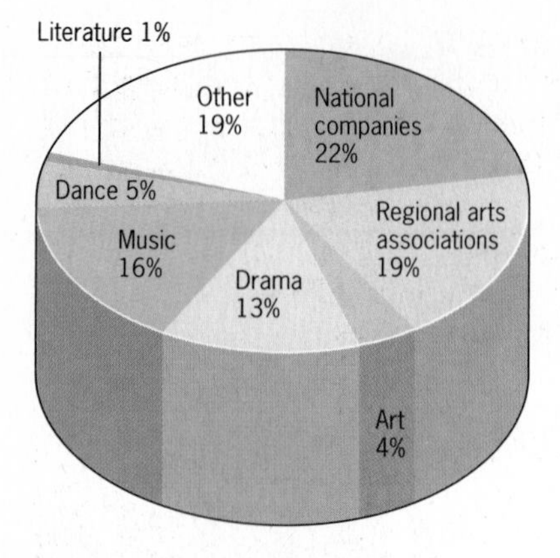

Total expenditure £182 million

Note: 'National companies' are English National Opera, National Theatre, Royal Opera, Royal Ballet, Royal Shakespeare Company

'Others' includes local arts centres and community projects

Figure 2.6 Arts Council support in the UK, 1990, percentage of total expenditure (*Source*: *Social Trends*, 1992)

Figure 2.7 Clent Hills Country Park: a partnership between the private and public sectors provides free access for informal outdoor recreation

Figure 2.8 Holidays for those with special needs

Today, many facilities are the result of partnership between the private and public sectors. For instance, much of the land of the Clent Hills Country Park, in the West Midlands (Fig. 2.7), belongs to the National Trust, a voluntary organisation. But the park is managed by the Worcester and Hereford County Council Recreation Services Department – the local authority – with further support from the Countryside Commission (a quango). Within cities, a common strategy is for the council to provide the land and a private developer to build and run the facility, say a leisure centre or convention centre (see case study on central Birmingham, pp. 35–7).

In contrast to **recreation**, **tourism** development has been dominated by the private commercial sector: travel agents, tour operators, hotels, airlines, **resorts** etc. Do not forget, however, that public sector policies have provided tourist attractions such as National Parks and heritage sites, and voluntary bodies such as the Caravan Club provide support systems for their members.

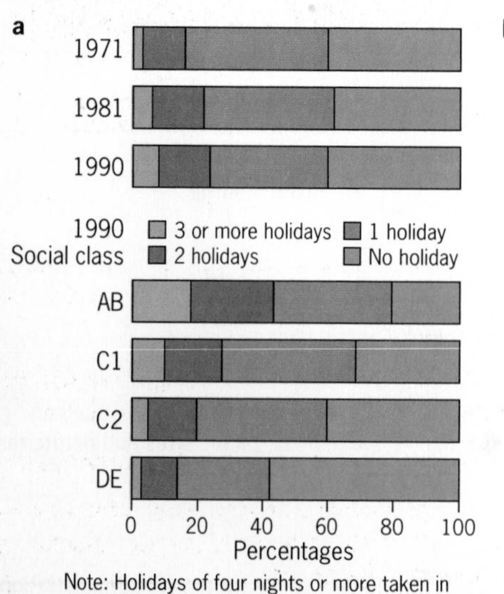

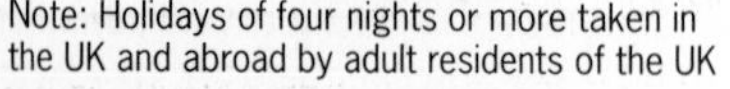
Note: Holidays of four nights or more taken in the UK and abroad by adult residents of the UK

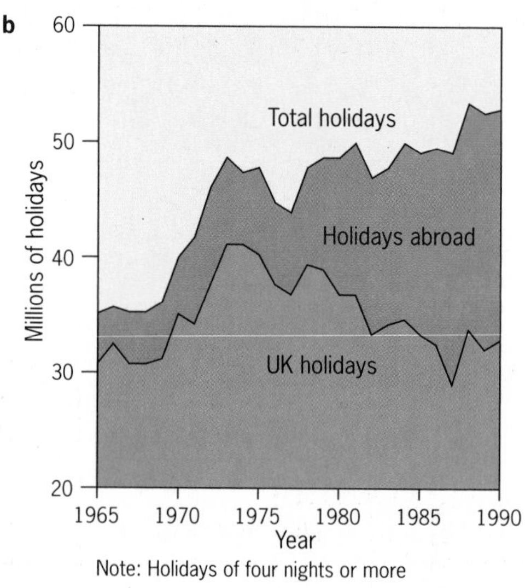

Note: Holidays of four nights or more

Figure 2.9 Holiday patterns in the UK a Number of holidays per year: by social class; b Holidays taken by UK residents: by destination (*Source*: *Social Trends*, 1991)

?

6 Essay: Look at Figure 2.6. Discuss whether you agree that over 20 per cent of all Arts Council spending should go to a small number of national companies, or whether more should be spent on community-based activities.

Furthermore, many thousands of holidays are provided under various social support and welfare programmes, for people who qualify as 'in need' (Fig. 2.8). Yet should we not ask ourselves why approximately four in every ten people in the UK do not take a holiday during the year? (Fig. 2.9). This figure has changed little over the past 20 years.

Finally, we must remember that the government plays a crucial role in the provision of leisure opportunities through the operation of *planning law and policy*, which aims to control the allocation of resources for specific and appropriate purposes (Fig. 2.10).

Figure 2.10 This attractive coastline in Devon is given some protection from resort development by the Heritage Coasts strategy and local planning controls

?

7 Place tracing paper over Figure 2.10 and draw an outline sketch.

a Mark on your sketch where a developer would locate: a cluster of holiday cottages; a small boat marina.

b State: why you have chosen these locations; what the environmental impacts would be; why local planners and conservationists might reject such proposals.

Summary

- Leisure opportunities depend upon who controls the required resources and on what terms these resources are made available.
- Leisure opportunities depend upon the balance between demand and supply.
- The three providers of leisure opportunities are the public sector, the private commercial sector and the private voluntary sector. Each has its own reasons and motivations for provision.

3 Leisure organisation and participation

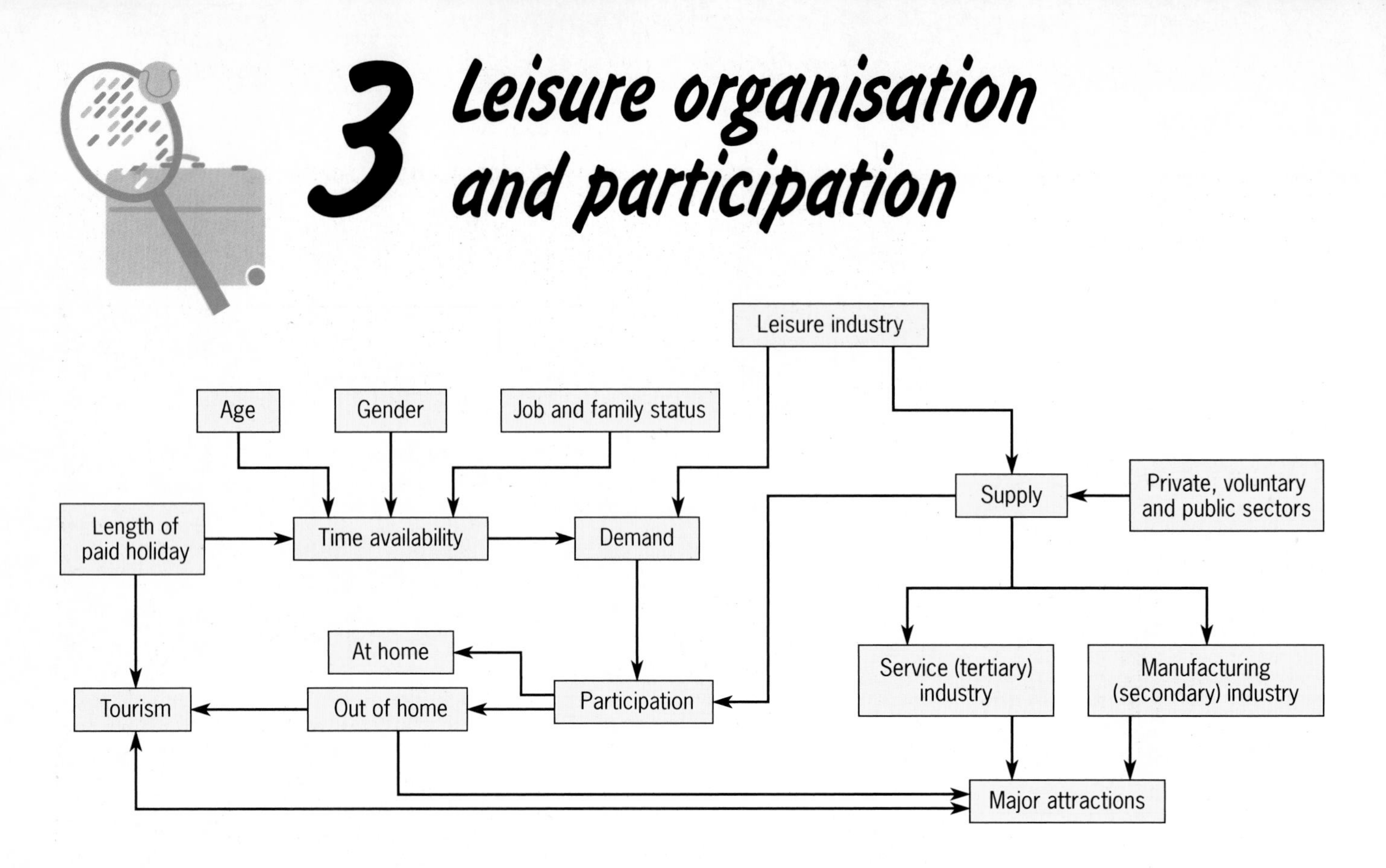

3.1 Introduction

Market researchers claim that **leisure** is the largest industrial sector in the world, yielding almost 10 per cent of global **GNP**. It is also one of the most rapidly growing industries (e.g. between 1970 and 1990, growth rates of **investment** and revenue grew at an average annual rate of 7 per cent). If these claims seem surprising, just think what the umbrella term 'the leisure industry' covers (Fig. 3.1).

Figure 3.1 The leisure industry

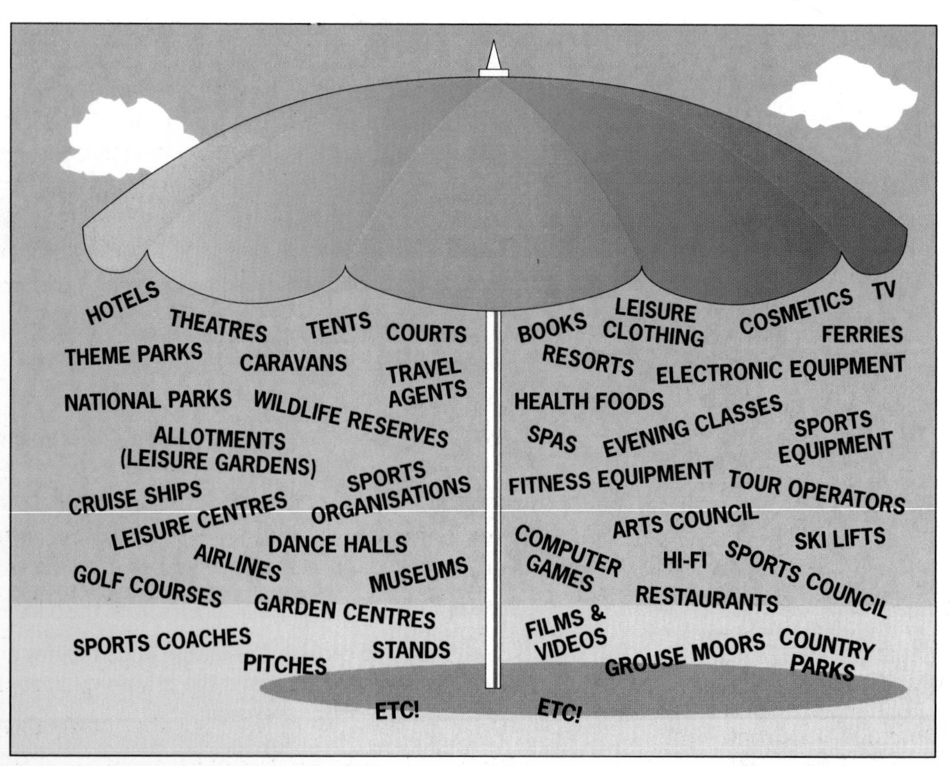

?

1 Analyse the swimming pool in Figure 3.2 in terms of leisure as (*a*) a service industry and (*b*) a manufacturing industry. (Look carefully at *all* the aspects of the pool, including the water quality, equipment and the participants.)

2 Describe the trends shown in Figure 3.3 and suggest reasons for the difference between the 'libraries etc.' category, which maintained its growth, and all the other categories, which shifted from growth to decline.

3 Study Figure 3.4 and describe the relative importance of UK tourism as indicated by percentage employment.

Figure 3.2 **The provision of this private sector swimming pool involves both the service (tertiary) and manufacturing (secondary) dimensions of the leisure industry**

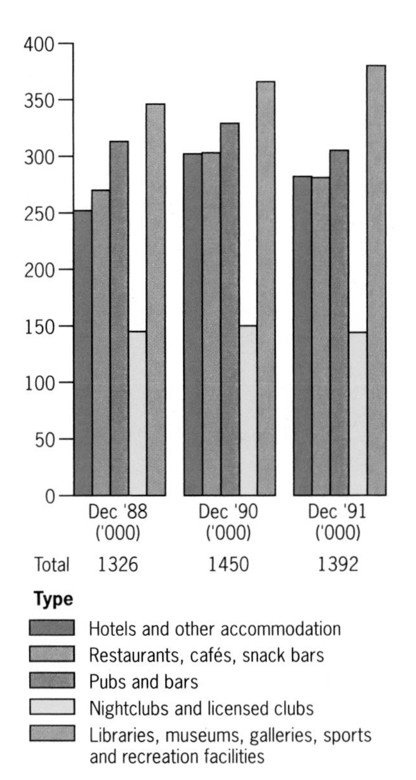

Figure 3.3 Leisure industry employment in the UK, 1988–91 (*Source*: Department of Employment)

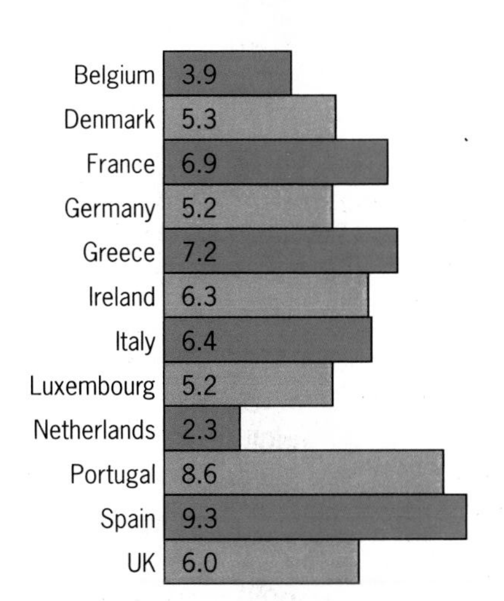

Figure 3.4 Employment in tourism in the EC, percentage of population, 1988 (*Source*: Commission of the European Communities, *Eurostat, Tourism in Europe, Trends*, 1989)

3.2 The leisure industry

The leisure industry behaves as a consumption industry in that we consume leisure goods and services as part of our leisure experience. Thus, organised by the **private** and **public sectors**, it is both a **tertiary**, **service industry** and a **secondary**, **manufacturing industry**. As a service industry it manages and provides us with **access** to parks, pools, pubs etc., and as a manufacturing industry it builds those pools and pubs, designs and makes sports and leisure clothing, sun-tan cosmetics etc. (Fig. 3.2).

This is an important understanding, for as you examine any case study you can apply to it the principles of economic geography about location, resources, decision-making, cost–benefit, profit etc. This is especially true of the private sector, although it applies increasingly to the public and **voluntary sectors** where cost factors have become crucial, e.g. increased charges at leisure centres and rising club membership fees.

Changing trends

The scale and character of the UK leisure industry are summed up in Figure 3.3, with approximately 1.4 million people employed in a wide range of jobs. The figures tell us also that, because our leisure spending comes out of 'disposable income', in times of recession and economic hardship we cut back on such spending. Thus, 1991 saw a decline in leisure spending and employment for the first time in a decade (−4 per cent), a trend which continued into 1992.

This sensitivity is echoed in the **tourism** element of the industry: the UK annual income from overseas visitors is around £9 billion, with 28 per cent of this from business travel. In 1991, the combination of economic recession and the Gulf War reduced the number of North American visitors by 27 per cent and from the rest of the world by 17 per cent from the previous year.

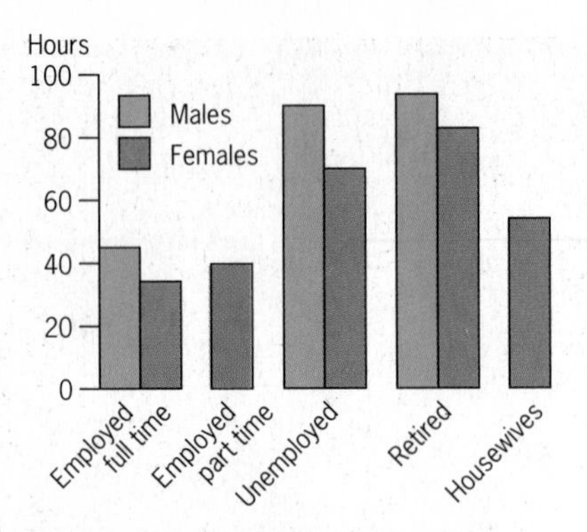

Figure 3.5 Leisure time in a typical week, by gender and employment status, Great Britain, 1990–1 (*Source: Social Trends*, 1992)

Figure 3.6 Retired people can enjoy leisure facilities at off-peak times

3.3 Leisure participation in the UK

The basic factor underlying our leisure behaviour is time. For instance, a common reason given for ceasing to use a leisure centre is – 'Oh, I don't have the time any more'. This person has a more demanding job, has got married, or has started a family etc. Your age, gender, and job status are important factors influencing time availability (Fig. 3.5).

Equally important is when the free time occurs and in what time blocks (e.g. the difference between weekdays and weekends, Table 3.1). This influences participation patterns, and hence the policies that leisure facility owners and managers adopt. For instance, a full round of golf may take 3 hours, plus travelling time. For many people, such a time block is available only at weekends. As a result, such **facilities** show heavily peaked patterns of use – overcrowded at weekends, underused on weekdays. Groups such as the active retired are clearly advantaged in this way: they can enjoy less-crowded and possibly cheaper activities at off-peak times (Fig. 3.6).

Table 3.1 Who has free time, and when (*Source: Social Trends*, 1992)

Free time (hours)	Employed full-time (Male)	Employed full-time (Female)	Part-time (Female)	Housewives	Retired
Per weekday	4.7	3.2	4.7	7.1	12.2
Per weekend day	10.4	8.5	8.0	9.0	13.1

Note: Categories chosen according to available data.

There are many people (such as nurses, security guards, hotel porters, factory workers) involved in a range of jobs that involve shifts and irregular patterns of work. For instance, hospital shifts run round the clock (usually three 8-hour shifts), whereas a factory may only have two shifts, morning and evening (Fig 3.7).

The activity requiring the biggest time-block is, of course, going away on holiday, and one factor influencing the growth of tourism has been the increase in the length of paid holiday leave. In 1971, over 80 per cent of employees in the UK were entitled to less than 3 weeks paid holiday; by 1991, around 90 per cent had at least 4 weeks, significantly more, for example, than is common in the USA. Remember, however, that four in every ten people do not actually go away (Fig. 2.9). In contrast, more people are taking at least two holidays a year and more are likely to go abroad.

Patterns of participation

There are two apparently opposing trends in leisure participation. At-home leisure is growing because of increasing availability of space in many homes, the trend towards DIY for home improvements, and what is called 'the electronics revolution': 99 per cent of UK households now have TV, two-thirds have video-cassette recorders (encouraging and encouraged by the explosion in video rental outlets), one in five have compact disc players and computers. Our out-of-home leisure lifestyles too, have undergone a revolution: more of us are taking part in an ever-widening range of activities.

Table 3.2 provides a glimpse of what it was like to be young in 1950. Tables 3.3 and 3.4 bring the picture up to date across all age ranges. Some important points to notice are: (*a*) the low percentages who take part in most activities; (*b*) the wide range of activities; (*c*) the differences between males and females (Fig. 3.8). This diversity and the overall trend of increasing participation levels create problems for those who make the resources available and who manage them.

?

4 Study Figure 3.5 and reply to the questions attached to each of the following statements. To each reply, add a sentence describing the **values** and **attitudes** it exemplifies.

a Women are disadvantaged in available leisure time. Why is this, how might it influence their leisure participation and what might be done to improve matters?

b The unemployed have plenty of free time. Does this mean they experience plenty of leisure activities and high-quality leisure lives? If not, why not?

c The retired group has the most free time. What distinctive leisure **demands** might they have, and what does this mean for the private and the public sector providers?

Figure 3.7 When do shift workers have time for leisure?

Figure 3.8 A disco, held in the afternoon to allow young Asian women to participate

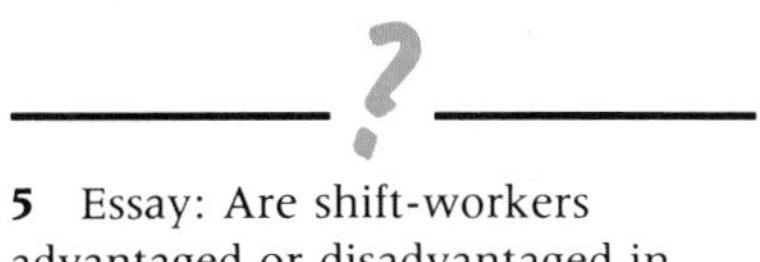

5 Essay: Are shift-workers advantaged or disadvantaged in terms of their opportunities for leisure participation?

Table 3.2 Youth leisure in Birmingham, 1950 (age 14–20 years)

Activity	Males rank	Females rank
Cinema	1	1
Youth organisation	2	3
Dancing	4=	2
Church	6	4
Watching football	3	7
Cycling	4=	5
Cafés and Milk-bars	7	6
Theatre	10	8
Speedway	8	9
Rambling and hiking	9	10

(Ranking based on a sample 1000 people, and recording participation at least once a week.)

Interrogating a database

Tables 3.3 and 3.4 are at first glance, simply a mass of figures. But such sets of figures provide a database from which we can get valuable information, by asking it specific questions. Here is one way it might be done:

1 QUESTION: What are the most popular leisure activities?

2 FINDING AN ANSWER: Use columns (f) and (k) from Tables 3.3 and 3.4. By combining the information from the two tables, make two ranking lists – male and female – of the top ten activities.

3 WHAT DO THE FIGURES TELL US? From your ranking lists, some important understandings emerge. First, people lead very different leisure lives, shown by the fact that participation levels for any single activity are generally low. Second, people engage in a wide range of activities of quite different types, with distinct resource demands and impacts. Third, informal, social activities dominate. Fourth, there is a generally low level of participation in physical activity and sport. Fifth, males and females enjoy quite different patterns of leisure activity, with women tending to have a narrower range and lower levels of participation.

4 TAKING THE QUESTIONING BEYOND THE FIGURES: These findings lead us to questions such as: Why are so few activities popular with a majority of the population? How much time and money commitment are needed? What resources and facilities are required and who provides them? What are the environmental demands and impacts of these activities? What factors might prevent an individual from taking part in any particular activity and what might be done to change this? Which activities attract the private **commercial sector** and what is and should be the role of the public sector?

You can follow a similar sequence(1–4) through other opening questions, e.g. you might want to examine differences by age group.

You may also be able to apply relevant statistical techniques to the figures (e.g. Spearman rank correlation).

3.4 The role of major attractions

The diversity of our leisure demands, and who provides opportunities for visitors' enjoyment, are highlighted in Tables 3.5 and 3.6. Such favoured attractions are very expensive to develop and run, especially as our expectations continue to rise (e.g. a more terrifying 'white-knuckle' ride, a more realistic

Table 3.3 Participation in selected social and cultural activities in Great Britain: by gender and age, 1987 (*Source: Social Trends*, 1988)

	Males					Females				
(a)	(b)	(c)	(d)	(e)	(f)	(g)	(h)	(i)	(j)	(k)
Age	16–19	20–29	30–59	60 or over	All 16 or over	16–19	20–29	30–59	60 or over	All 16 or over
Percentage engaging in each activity in the 4 weeks before interview										
Going to the cinema	24	16	6	1	8	28	16	7	1	8
Visiting historic buildings	6	9	11	7	9	8	11	11	7	10
Going to the theatre/opera/ballet	2	5	5	3	4	4	7	8	4	6
Going to museums/art galleries	3	5	4	3	4	2	5	4	2	4
Amateur music/drama	6	5	4	3	4	7	3	3	2	3
Going to fairs/amusement arcades	4	4	5	2	4	7	6	6	2	5
Going out for a meal	41	56	50	35	47	50	57	51	35	47
Going out for a drink	71	87	68	41	65	72	73	52	18	47
Dancing	19	13	9	5	9	32	18	11	5	12

Table 3.4 Participation in sports and physical exercise in Great Britain: by gender and age, 1987 (*Source: Social Trends*, 1988)

	Males					Females				
(a)	(b)	(c)	(d)	(e)	(f)	(g)	(h)	(i)	(j)	(k)
Age	16–19	20–29	30–59	60 or over	All 16 or over	16–19	20–29	30–59	60 or over	All 16 or over
Percentage participating in each activity in the 4 weeks before interview										
Pedal cycling	28	12	10	5	10	14	8	8	2	7
Track and field athletics	4	1	–	0	1	2	–	–	0	–
Jogging, cross-country/road running	18	17	7	–	8	10	5	2	–	3
Soccer	40	22	5	–	10	2	1	–	0	–
Rugby Union/League	4	2	–	0	1	0	0	0	0	0
Walking at least 2 miles	N/A	N/A	N/A	N/A	24	N/A	N/A	N/A	N/A	22
Cricket	7	5	2	–	2	–	–	–	0	–
Tennis	6	4	2	–	2	4	2	2	–	1
Netball	–	–	–	0	–	6	1	–	0	1
Basketball	7	1	–	0	1	4	–	–	0	–
Golf, pitch and putt, putting	9	9	7	4	7	1	1	1	1	1
Swimming or diving	24	20	14	3	13	24	20	14	3	13
Fishing	7	5	4	1	4	1	1	–	0	–
Yachting or dinghy sailing	1	1	1	–	1	1	1	–	–	–
Other watersports	4	3	2	–	2	2	1	1	0	1
Horse riding, show jumping, pony trekking	1	–	1	–	–	6	3	1	–	1
Badminton	11	6	4	–	4	12	4	3	–	3
Squash	8	8	4	–	4	4	3	1	0	1
Table tennis	14	5	3	1	4	6	2	1	–	1
Snooker, pool, billiards	62	49	23	6	27	23	11	3	–	5
Darts	33	25	13	3	14	11	7	4	1	4
Tenpin bowls or skittles	4	3	2	–	2	4	2	2	–	1
Lawn or carpet bowls	2	1	2	4	2	1	1	1	1	1
Self defence	5	3	1	–	1	1	1	–	0	–
Weight training/lifting	22	17	5	–	7	9	5	2	–	2
Gymnastics	1	–	–	–	–	1	–	–	0	–
Keep fit, yoga, aerobics, dance exercise	5	6	5	3	5	24	20	12	5	12
Skiing	2	1	1	–	1	5	1	–	0	1
Ice skating	4	1	–	–	1	5	1	–	0	1
Motor sports	3	2	1	0	1	–	–	–	0	–

N/A = Not available

6 By comparing Table 3.2 with Tables 3.3 and 3.4, columns (b) and (g), describe the principal changes in the leisure of young people since 1950, and suggest reasons for such changes.

7 By analysis of Tables 3.3 and 3.4, test the hypothesis that levels of leisure participation fall off with age.

Table 3.5 The 'attractions' market, 1989 (*Source*: Leisure Consultants, *Attractions Report*, 1990)

Category	Number	Visitors (millions)
Museums and galleries	776	69
Historic buildings	638	65
Gardens	138	13
Wildlife attractions	131	24
Other attractions[a]	619	116
Total	**2302**	**287**

a 'Other' includes theme parks, amusement parks, country parks, workplaces, steam railways etc.

exhibit etc.). This, along with constantly shifting fashion (in 1992 Alton Towers overtook Madame Tussaud's and the Tower of London as the top fee-charging attraction), has caused problems for the commercial sector (e.g. several safari parks have closed since 1990) and for the voluntary sector (e.g. the National Trust has been reviewing its pricing policy for historic houses and gardens). In the public sector, reduced financial support from central government and rising costs have forced museums, art galleries etc. to charge entrance fees (Table 3.6 notes the effect of this on visits to the London Science Museum).

Two final points relating to demand for and **supply** of major attractions are worth noting: first, the dominance of London, and second, the huge amount of traffic generated by these large visitor numbers. These raise further questions: Are people who live away from London 'disadvantaged' in terms of their leisure opportunities? As at least 80 per cent of visits are made by car, what implications are there for transport policy (e.g. should more major attractions be dispersed away from London and the South-East, and should regional policies take into account the location of these major attractions)?

Table 3.6 The UK top 16 leisure attractions, 1990 (*Source: Social Trends*, 1992)

Name	Location	Provider sector	Attendance (millions)	Admission
Blackpool Pleasure Beach	Resort	Private	6.5	Free
Albert Dock, Liverpool	Urban	Public	6.0	Free
British Museum	London	Public	4.8	Free
Strathclyde Country Park, Motherwell	Urban fringe	Public	4.2	Free
National Gallery	London	Public	3.7	Free
Palace Pier, Brighton	Resort	Public	3.5	Free
Pleasure Beach, Great Yarmouth	Resort	Partnership	2.6	Free
Madame Tussaud's	London	Private	2.5	Charge
Tower of London	London	Public	2.3	Charge
Alton Towers[a]	Rural	Private	2.1	Charge
Tate Gallery	London	Public	1.6	Free
Pleasureland, Southport	Resort	Public	1.5	Free
Natural History Museum	London	Public	1.5	Charge
Chessington World of Adventures	London	Private	1.5	Charge
Blackpool Tower	Resort	Partnership	1.4	Charge
Science Museum[b]	London	Public	1.3	Charge

Note: These are specific facilities, not broad destinations such as resorts, towns or National Parks.

a In 1992, Alton Towers had overtaken Madame Tussaud's and the Tower of London as the most popular attraction charging admission.

b 1988 figure was 2.4 million, but admission charges were introduced in 1989.

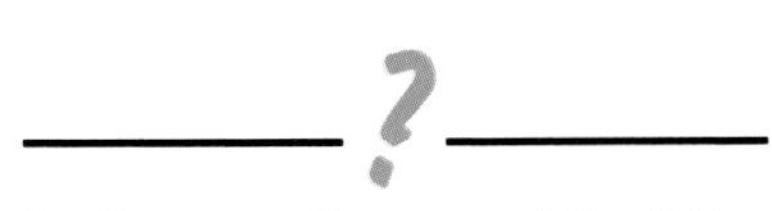

8 On an outline map of the UK, plot the location of:

a the attractions listed in Table 3.6 (the London attractions may be clustered close together).

b for those outside London, the main population centres likely to provide the bulk of the visitors, if you think the catchment is regional rather than national.

9 Suggest three alternative ways the 16 attractions in Table 3.6 can be divided into groups, including one way which is not a column heading for the table. Then construct the three lists under your headings.

Summary

- The leisure industry is both a service and a manufacturing industry.
- The industry has grown rapidly and is now a major employer in the UK.
- Time availability has a significant influence upon leisure participation, and this availability varies across age, gender and social grouping and according to job type.
- Out-of-home leisure is growing in scale and diversity, but few activities are engaged in by a majority of the population.
- A small number of major attractions dominate visitor patterns, with London dominating the location of these attractions. The major attractions are provided by both the private and public sectors.

4 Leisure in urban environments

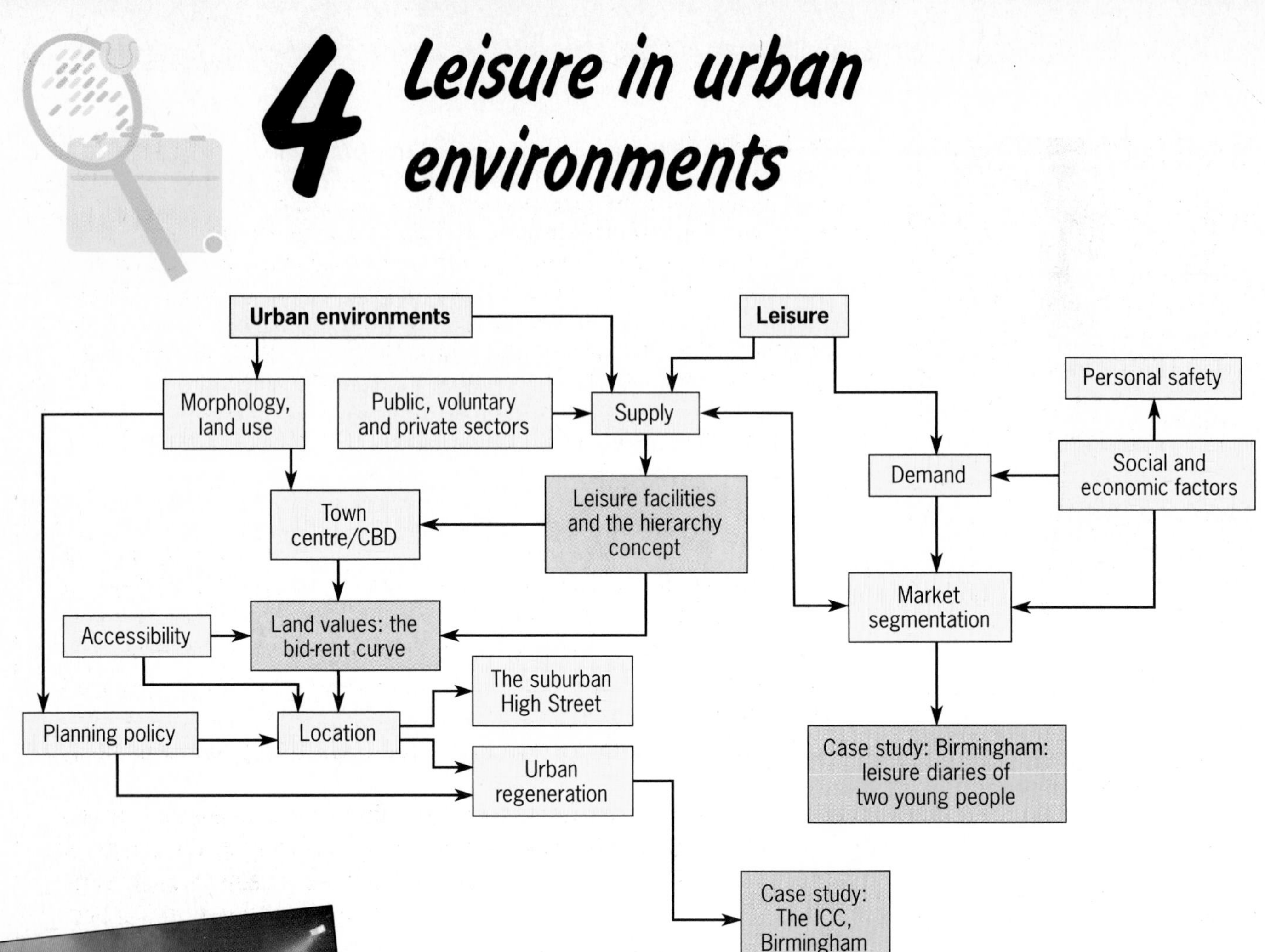

Figure 4.1 The 'Paradise Lost' nightclub, Belfast

Study Figure 4.2.

1 Concern for personal safety during the journey to and from an urban leisure facility is important. For your nearest town centre, produce a map showing areas where you would feel:
(*a*) unsafe (*b*) safe. (You might like to distinguish between daytime and evenings.)

4.1 Introduction

Approximately 80 per cent of the UK's population lives in or on the fringes of urban areas. Thus, for most of us, towns and cities are where we spend our working and **leisure** lives. This chapter will show that resources and **facilities** for leisure activities and experiences are a significant element in land-use patterns, urban morphology (shape and form) and planning policy. For instance, where are professional football stadiums located, and why? What influence does their presence have upon the locality and the lives of the people living nearby? As shopping becomes more of a leisure activity, how does this influence the location and layout of retail centres? So, opportunities for leisure influence our **quality of life**. Because cities concentrate people, so they also encourage the clustering of leisure facilities. Urban dwellers, therefore, should be 'advantaged' in terms of leisure opportunities.

4.2 Young people and leisure

The use an individual makes of leisure facilities depends upon many factors: age, gender, education, mobility, income, culture, stage and status in the family life cycle, personality, interests. For example, a study of young women in Belfast who were regular attenders of a disco club (Fig. 4.1) during 1991–2 found that the main factors influencing their attendance were: money, social class, parental approval, their friends and the **accessibility** of the club. The main reasons they went were: the presence of boys, the music and the opportunity to dance. They also felt it was a relatively 'safe' place to go, especially in pairs and groups.

Figure 4.2 The geography of safety

?

2 Construct a questionnaire which examines the safety issue. You should include questions about:
a age
b gender
c usual mode of transport
d where, when and why you feel unsafe
e company – alone; pair; group.

3 As a group compare your questionnaires, and following your discussions, construct a single questionnaire. (Consider whether you intend to produce a computer database.)

4 Each individual in the group should complete the questionnaire and then, as a group, you should collate and analyse the results (graphs and maps may be useful).

5 From your results suggest ways in which your journeys to and from leisure facilities could be made safer.

6a From Figure 4.3, list the facilities used and who provides them.
b Note what leisure facilities are not used.
c In your opinion, does the account in Figure 4.3 tell of a 'typical' youth lifestyle? If not, suggest reasons why, and how other young people might spend their leisure time.

Market segments

The leisure industry sees the population in terms of 'market segments', based upon particular variables (age, gender, education etc., as mentioned above). For instance, 'Dinkies' ('Double-income-no-kids') are targeted as a group with distinctive interests and spending patterns. Each segment has a distinctive leisure lifestyle, with different interests, mobility, spending power and so on. Thus, the 'youth market' is identified as having active leisure lives, and hence possessing considerable spending potential. This is why the major brewery companies have restyled many of their pubs to attract young people – with music, 'pop' decor etc. Young women in particular have been 'targeted'.The extract in Figure 4.3 claims to summarise 'typical' youth leisure in the early 1990s.

Drinking is the major leisure activity for young people, filling most of the large amount of free time available to them. The pub is seen as a place to meet up with friends and relax. Most go drinking at least twice a week and will end up in the pub after sports activities or visits to the cinema. A typical evening out for a 16–24-year-old will start with the pub and progress to local nightclubs, often with discos or entertainment, with the evening sometimes being rounded off by a curry.

Socialising at the weekend follows the typical routine of meeting friends in a pub, after spending Saturday browsing in the shops or going to a football match. Shopping for clothes is seen as a pleasure, particularly for girls, who enjoy browsing. Sundays are dreaded, particularly by those living at home. Most admit to not doing a lot on Sundays. They want to be active to escape boredom. An evening in is something to be avoided, but will be spent mainly watching TV or listening to music.

Young people living at home frequently complain there are not enough facilities for them, yet are uncertain about what they would like to see available. They feel there are enough sports facilities, but not enough clubs for under 21s. During the week the most popular sporting activity is swimming, with girls also choosing aerobics, or work-outs at the gym, and boys playing football. Cricket, tennis and golf are often mentioned, but not snooker or pool. Cinema-going retains its popularity. Hanging around street corners and getting into trouble with the police still seems to have some appeal.

Most try to go abroad for a holiday every year, although some have to miss out when they leave home and their domestic responsibilities increase. The annual holiday is something that even younger people living at home will save for. For them the summer holiday is 'one long drinking session', with Spain their favoured destination. Those living away from home prefer the relaxation of Greece and Italy, with America becoming more popular. A realistic cost including the holiday and the associated items like clothes is £1000.

Figure 4.3 Is this your life? (*Source*: Maslen, 1991)

Birmingham: leisure diaries of two young people

The diary extracts in Figure 4.4 allow us to look more closely at the ways in which young people enjoy their leisure. Siobhan and Mike, two young adults who live in Birmingham (Fig. 4.5), have recorded their out-of-home leisure activities over a weekend. They have engaged in a range of activities in a range of settings with no round trips of more than 20km. Table 4.1 analyses their leisure experiences in terms of the **demands** made on resources and facilities, and their providers.

Mike
aged 20

October

28 Friday night

Took Sandra to see 'Fatal Attraction' at the 'Odeon'.
Then had a curry at the 'Taj'.

29 Saturday. Met Alan and Wayne in town. Bought Springsteen's new CD at 'Our Price'. Went round dozens of shops to get Wayne a jacket - no luck. A quick pie and pint and off to the Villa. Lost 2-1! Dancing and drinking with Sandra at 'The Dome' - expensive but good music. Chinese take-away on the way home.

30 Sunday

Played football for the office team in the local park in the morning.
Played darts and had a couple of pints in 'The Station' pub at night.

Siobhan
aged 19

October

27

Friday night
An aerobics session with Anne straight after work at the new Leisure Centre near home.
Anne, Steve, Leon and I went to Ronnie Scott's Jazz Club.

28

Saturday. Went to the Central Library to get some books for my Accounting course, and that new Jeffrey Archer novel.
Dad and I sailed all afternoon in the dinghy racing at our Sailing Club. In the evening Steve took me to the University Students Union 'Hop'.

29

Sunday
Mum, Dad and I took the dogs for a walk in the Clent Hills Country Park.
Went to tea at Gran's.
Church in the evening, then a fellowship meeting.

30

Figure 4.4 The leisure diaries of two young people

Figure 4.5 Mike and Siobhan – two typical young leisure users?

7 Compare and contrast the leisure lives of Siobhan and Mike. You will find it useful to refer again to Question 9 in Chapter 3, p. 23 to make a list of the measures you will use.

8 In what ways might their leisure lives change if they were:
a married
b unemployed
c lived in a rural area?

9 What other factors might influence how they spend their free time?

10 What 'messages' would the two diaries send you if you were:
a a leisure services officer in a local authority?
b a market researcher in a **commercial** leisure company?

Table 4.1 An analysis of leisure activities

A MIKE

Activity	Venue	Location	Provider/owner	Free/pay
Watching film	Cinema	Major radial road	Private commercial company	Entrance charge
Eating out	Restaurant	Suburban High Street	Private enterprise	Pay for meals
Shopping	Various shops	City centre	Private commercial companies	Free entry
Eating out	Pub	Inner suburb	Private commercial company	Free entry; payment for consumption
Watching professional sport	Football stadium	Inner suburb	Private company	Entrance fee
Dancing, social entertainment	Nightclub	City centre	Private commercial company	Entrance fee
Eating out	Fast food outlet	Major radial road	Private enterprise	Pay for meals
Playing sport – football	Public park pitch	Outer suburb	Local authority	Free to individual. Team rents pitch
Recreational game and social entertainment	Pub	Outer suburb	Private commercial company	Free entry

B SIOBHAN

Activity	Venue	Location	Provider/owner	Free/pay
Physical exercise – aerobics	Leisure centre	Suburb	Local authority	Payment session
Listening to music and social entertainment	Club	City centre	Private enterprise	Entrance fee
Selecting reading material	Library	City centre	Local authority	Free
Outdoor activity – sailing	Reservoir	Urban fringe	Private club – voluntary sector; renting private water space	Free on day but annual subscription
Dancing and social entertainment	University club	Suburb	Private club with public funding	Entrance fee and guest fee. Annual subscription
Outdoor activity – walking	Country Park	Urban fringe	Local authority and National Trust (public and voluntary sectors)	Free
Visiting relatives	Family home	Inner suburb	Local authority (public sector)	Free
Religious service	Church	Outer suburb	Voluntary sector – Church institution	Free
Discussion	Church meeting room	Outer suburb		

Leisure facilities and the hierarchy concept

Two important ideas put forward by urban geographers are:

1 That the larger the city, the greater the number, variety and quality of services available.

2 That within a city there will be a number of service centres offering a different number, range and quality of services.

Following from these ideas, urban settlements and service centres have been grouped into a set of levels called a hierarchy. Centres of the highest level offer the full range of goods and services including the highest quality and most specialised, known as 'high-order' goods and services. Medium-sized centres offer only up to 'middle-order' level, while small centres contain only 'low-order' goods and services. Equally important, high-order goods and services are few and far between and attract custom from long distances, while at the other extreme, low-order facilities occur frequently and attract only local custom.

This general hierarchy model has been used most commonly to study retail and professional services, but it can also be applied to leisure. For example, we can use this starting hypothesis: *high-order facilities are few in number, large in size and widely spaced, with large threshold populations and extensive* ***catchment areas***. So, Table 3.6 shows the broad scatter of the top attractions, but with the dominance of London. Think too, of the location of the highest-order sporting facilities: London has Wembley for football, Twickenham for Rugby Union, Wimbledon for tennis, and Edinburgh, Cardiff, Belfast and Dublin are all bases for high-order facilities and events (Fig. 4.6).

Do not forget, however, that one element of UK government regional development policies for many years has been to give grant-aid support to help disperse major facilities (e.g. the Sheffield athletics stadium; the aid that was promised to Manchester in their unsuccessful bid for the Olympic Games in 2000).

Figure 4.7 suggests an urban model based on our starting hypothesis. The **Central Business District (CBD)** contains a cluster of high-order facilities whose sphere of influence is city-wide, and indeed may extend to the surrounding region. Major suburban centres contain middle-order facilities with a district catchment area, while residential neighbourhoods are dotted with low-order 'local' facilities.

?

11 To test the usefulness of the leisure model (Fig. 4.7), apply it to a town or city with which you are familiar by studying the distribution of dance and disco clubs. (For a large city you may be able to examine one sector or transect, extending outwards from the CBD, and use one residential neighbourhood.)

a Plot the venues (Yellow Pages or advertisements in the local newspaper can be useful) on a base map and decide whether they are 'high-', 'middle-' or 'low-' order facilities.

b Describe the resulting pattern. Say whether it has a spatial and hierarchical structure similar to that suggested by the model in Figure 4.7.

12 Does the model work for other leisure activities – e.g. swimming pools, libraries, leisure centres, parks? (Check this using the Yellow Pages.) If not, can you suggest reasons why the model works for some activities and not for others?

Figure 4.6 All over the world, major cities are the location of high-order leisure facilities. The famous Opera House occupies a spectacular site in the centre of Sydney, Australia

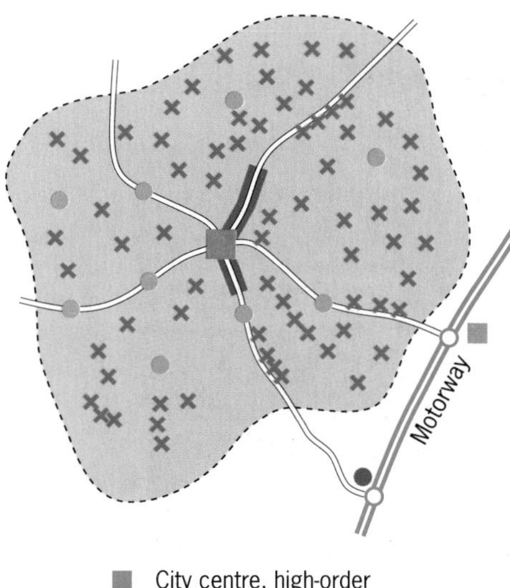

- ■ City centre, high-order facilities
- ● Suburban, middle-order facilities
- × Neighbourhood low-order facilities
- ■ High-order peripheral facilities
- ● Middle-order peripheral facilities
- Middle-order facilities along radial road

Figure 4.7 The urban leisure hierarchy: a model

Figure 4.8 The 'Dome' nightclub, Birmingham: a high-order facility in an accessible location on a radial road at the edge of the CBD, which can be seen in the background

The model diagram shows two significant modifications to this simple pattern: first, there are linear strips of middle-order facilities along main roads (e.g. hotels, clubs) and, second, there are high-grade facilities in peripheral locations – near bypasses or motorway junctions – to take advantage of land availability and accessibility.

We can take dance and disco clubs as an example of how this model works. The city centre has large, high-quality, expensive nightclubs, with perhaps one or two located along a radial road or accessible fringe site (Fig. 4.8). In suburban centres, moderately priced and equipped venues are found, often attached to larger pubs. In residential districts, local pubs may have disco or 'live music' nights, or a community centre or youth club might have 'disco nights'.

The key understanding is that the location and distribution of leisure facilities are not haphazard – there is a pattern. This pattern depends upon a number of factors: history of the area; land values; government policy; local planning policy; transport networks; population distribution; commercial company decisions; fashion etc. The materials in Chapters 4–6 explain these issues.

4.3 Leisure and the town centre

We have already seen how attractive a town or city centre is for leisure providers and for people out to enjoy themselves. The clustering of a range of high-order facilities in a relatively small and accessible area attracts large numbers of people from a wide catchment zone. Yet for many years the CBD in UK cities has been known as 'the dead heart of the city', a 'nine-to-five' district, largely deserted after the commuters go to their homes. This criticism has also been aimed at American 'downtown' areas, but is less true for city centres in countries such as France and Spain. Yet, since the 1940s, planners in the UK have experimented with schemes to bring residential communities back to central areas. Most have failed through a combination of high land costs and people's preferences to live in more spacious neighbourhoods. (Though do remember that there are enclaves of very wealthy people who do cluster in the 'upmarket' districts of the centres of big cities.)

Figure 4.9 Outside a town-centre pub

Figures 4.10–4.13 show four of the key findings of the 1990 study.

13 Study Figure 4.10. How could a wider clientele be attracted to the town-centre pub?

14 Refer to Figure 4.11. Should we be thinking about the '18-hour centre' not the 'nine-to-five centre'? For example, are there alternative leisure uses for underused or disused churches? What about voluntary group and 'street' activities/events?

15 Figure 4.12 describes typical town-centre evenings. What are the main reasons for this youth domination of town-centre evening leisure?

16 Refer to Figure 4.13. Could libraries be offering a wider range of services and could they stay open later? And where are the best locations (e.g. inside new shopping malls, or separately)?

17 State the **values** and **attitudes** implied by your answers to questions 13–16.

18 Essay: Discuss the potential and problems of the leisure use of town centres. NB: You need to outline the activities and behaviour being covered; the issues and problems; the possible alternatives and solutions; and those who are in positions to take decisions about these issues/problems. It will be useful too, to compare *your* experiences and perceptions of a local town or city centre, and to find out what policies the council has towards it.

On the other hand, in cities large enough to support them, theatres, cinemas, concert halls, indoor arenas, specialist clubs etc. focus their main activities in the evenings. However, many facilities continue to adopt office and shop hours – e.g. many museums, libraries, galleries and cafés close in the evenings and at weekends, despite evidence of changing lifestyles. In medium-sized cities and towns, all too often, evening entertainment is limited to the occasional cinema, and a scattering of pubs, mediocre disco clubs, fast-food outlets and 'ethnic' restaurants. And these have become increasingly geared towards the 'youth market'. Town centres in the evenings, therefore, are perceived by many people as 'no-go' areas, patrolled by large groups of noisy youths moving from pub to pub (Fig. 4.9). This has become something of a social issue. There is little doubt that such perceptions do restrict the use of town centres and hence mean that owners and managers of leisure facilities are more reluctant to stay open.

A study carried out in 1990 illustrates these issues. The survey covered 12 town centres in the UK – Basingstoke, Greenwich, Luton, Reading, Middlesbrough, Preston, Southend, Stirling, Gloucester, Swansea, Hounslow and Manchester. The researchers propose that councils and developers need to be more imaginative in the ways existing buildings are used, how safety can be improved, the ways streets can be lit and used for activities. Such schemes would then attract a wider range of people and activities into town centres.

> Pubs dominate British evening social life. A typical comment – 'I don't drink, so there's nothing for me in the town at night.' For Muslim communities in particular, this creates real problems. Also, town-centre pubs seem mostly themed or targeted at young drinkers, with loud music, flashing lights and mostly standing space rather than lounges or snug rooms. There *has* to be an alternative to the typical British town-centre pub, which at present serves a narrow but high-spending section of the community.

Figure 4.10 Extract from study – the dominance of pubs (*Source*: Comedia, 1991)

Figure 4.11 Extract from study – time patterns and leisure provision (*Source*: Comedia, 1991)

> Much entertainment and leisure provision is still geared to traditional time patterns even though lifestyles have changed dramatically. . . . In some town-centre pubs the high point of the day is about 4p.m. when people have done their shopping . . . tea-dances for the elderly in the afternoon rather than in the evening are popular. . . . Yet for young people there is little interest in going to a nightclub until 11p.m.; that's when the evening starts.

Figure 4.12 Extract from study – town-centre 'danger zones' (*Source*: Comedia, 1991)

> Town centres are seen as dangerous places, dominated by rowdy youths, aged 18–25, and so to be avoided. 'In Stirling, Preston and Middlesbrough, Thursday, Friday and Saturday evenings in the town centre are dominated by droves of young people going from pub to pub, or club to club, in large groups – the 'Friday Night Millionaires'. . . . In Middlesbrough on a Saturday night there can be hundreds of young people on the streets and in the pubs until very late, but making hardly any trouble at all. Yet . . . most other sections of the community feel obliged to stay out of the town.' Women in particular, feel threatened in town centres, both on the streets and in many pubs and clubs.

Figure 4.13 Extract from study – the importance of public libraries (*Source*: Comedia, 1991)

> Public libraries are key facilities: 'The widest cross-section of the local population can be seen – young, old, men and women, students, folklorists and eccentrics – able to borrow, study, chat, in some places drink coffee, meet and wait for people without feeling obliged to spend money . . . and feel safe.'

Does who you are affect your use of city centres?

The conclusions from another study, the 1987 Bradford Youth Survey, show how leisure use is linked with family and social background: 'Their leisure lifestyles are dominated by those commercialised and home-based leisure pursuits favoured by their parents – alcohol consumption in pubs, discos and nightclubs, TV and video, listening to tapes and records etc. There seems little gender difference in patterns of consumption except that young women enter the leisure sphere of "going out" on different terms than young men. Put simply, women never go out alone into city centres or elsewhere and hence are dependent upon **access** to parental cars and lifts from friends. In the Asian community, leisure was more home-based because of fears of racism, and the family was an important social group within which leisure took place, especially for Asian women. There were also clear differences along class lines, with young people unemployed or on government schemes experiencing more restricted leisure lifestyles and being more dependent upon parents.' (Leisure Studies Association, 1992)

?

19 Design a survey to test the following hypothesis: gender and cultural background are the most important factors influencing the leisure use of town centres by young people. NB: You may find it useful to complete this survey design and to carry out the survey as a class or set exercise. Also, look again at Questions 1–5.

4.4 Leisure as a competitor for space in the city

Factors that influence the location of leisure facilities in urban areas are: land values, the availability of suitable sites and the planning policies of local authorities. These factors interact and we can see the results of this interaction in any town or city in the UK.

Land values: the bid-rent curve

One explanation for the hierarchy model of Figure 4.7 is given by economic geographers through the bid-rent curve (Fig. 4.14). This states that land values, as measured by the rent which can be obtained for a site, fall as distance from a central point (the PLVI = peak land value intersection) increases. This simple curve is modified by subsidiary peaks along radial roads and at suburban centres. This idea is based upon accessibility: the more people that have ready access to a site, the more valuable that site is for businesses that rely on customers coming to them. So, leisure facilities that need or wish to attract large numbers of people either have to compete for the most accessible sites (e.g. high-grade nightclubs) or have been placed there by historical events (e.g. civic concert halls built in the nineteenth century; older professional football grounds).

20 Essay: To what extent can the leisure facilities hierarchy shown in Figure 4.7 be explained in terms of the bid-rent curve? You will find it useful to look again at your results from Questions 6 and 7.

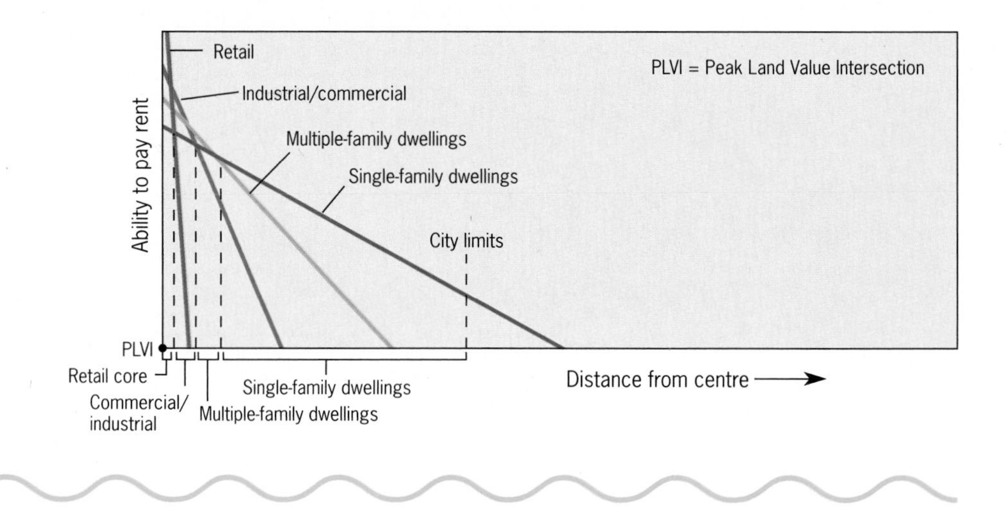

Figure 4.14 The bid-rent curve and land-use patterns (*Source*: Chapman, 1979)

Figure 4.15 Hagley Road, Birmingham. A major radial road to the city centre, originally lined by elegant nineteenth-century houses. Planning policy has zoned this strip for commercial use. Thus today there is a linear development of hotels, wine bars, pubs, restaurants, clubs etc.

Availability of land and buildings; planning policy

Other factors which influence location are the availability of land – clearly related to who owns it – and of suitable existing buildings (e.g. cinemas converted into bingo halls) and above all, planning policy. City development and structure plans are based on **zoning** principles: the city is subdivided into areas according to preferred land uses. Any landowner or developer wishing to bring a 'non-conforming' land use into an area faces the difficult task of justifying their proposal before gaining planning permission. In this way, planning policy has a significant influence upon the distribution of leisure facilities, e.g. semi-continuous strips of pubs, restaurants, clubs and hotels along some radial roads leading to a city centre, which are zoned for commercial use (Fig. 4.15).

Leisure in the suburban High Street

The outcome of the interaction between planning policy and competition for space and place (i.e. location) is easily visible in the typical suburban High Street, where lines of commercial, professional and personal service businesses include a range of leisure-based enterprises. Figure 4.16 illustrates a number of the key features to look out for in such a High Street: (*a*) the *range* and *level* of leisure facilities and services; (*b*) the relatively small site size and hence restriction upon provision; (*c*) accessibility problems caused by traffic congestion and lack of parking space; (*d*) the interspersion of leisure-based facilities among buildings with other uses; (*e*) the predominance of the commercial sector in this relatively high-rental location.

21 Look at Figure 4.16 carefully.

a Divide the leisure-related facilities into not more than four categories and place each facility into one of your categories.

b Describe the pattern of leisure provision in Harborne High Street. Compare this with a suburban High Street with which you are familiar and suggest what range and character of leisure provision appears to be typical of such High Streets.

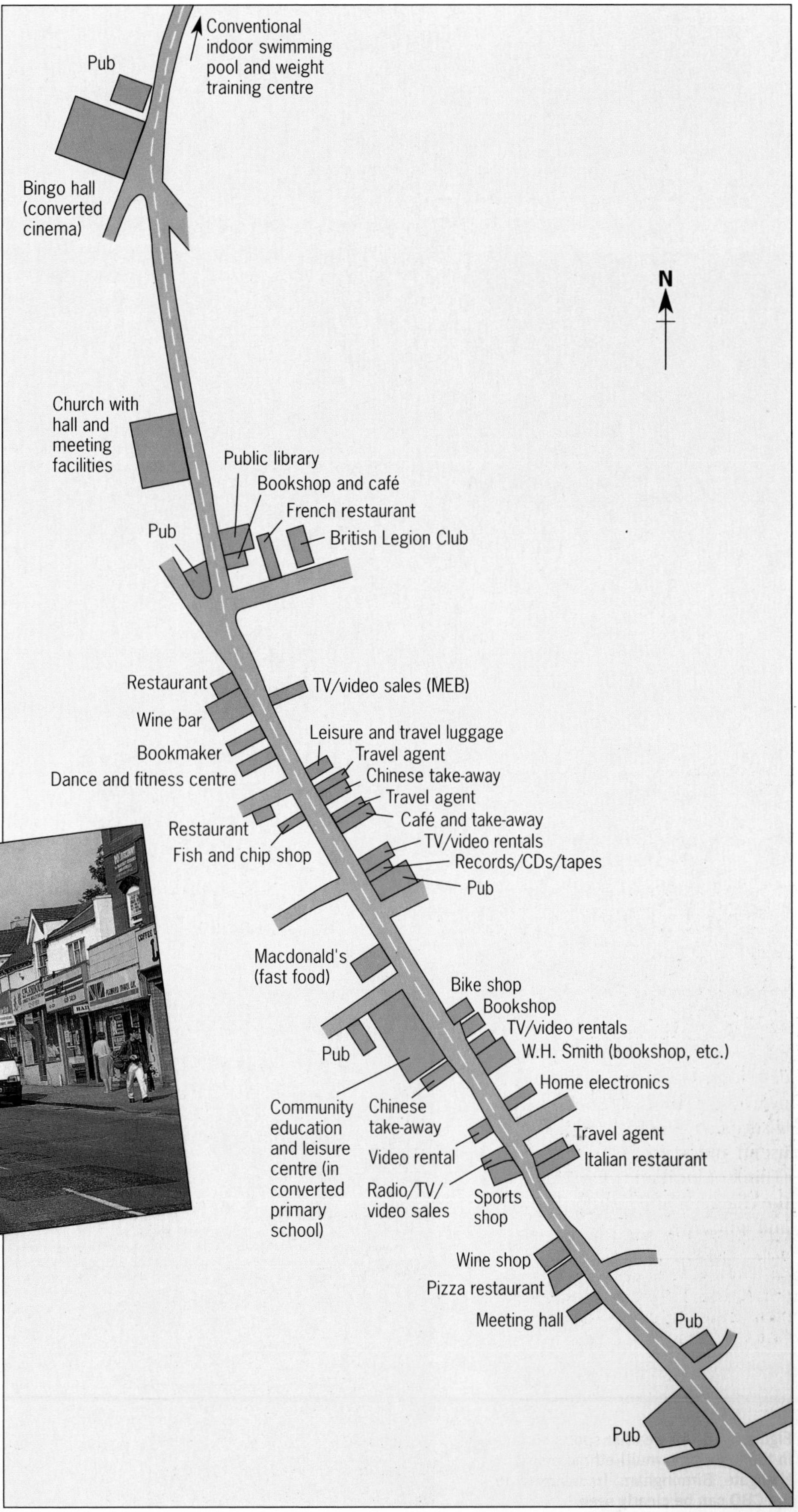

Conventional indoor swimming pool and weight training centre
Pub
Bingo hall (converted cinema)
N
Church with hall and meeting facilities
Public library
Bookshop and café
French restaurant
British Legion Club
Pub
Restaurant
TV/video sales (MEB)
Wine bar
Leisure and travel luggage
Bookmaker
Travel agent
Dance and fitness centre
Chinese take-away
Travel agent
Restaurant
Café and take-away
Fish and chip shop
TV/video rentals
Records/CDs/tapes
Pub
Macdonald's (fast food)
Bike shop
Bookshop
TV/video rentals
Pub
W.H. Smith (bookshop, etc.)
Home electronics
Community education and leisure centre (in converted primary school)
Chinese take-away
Video rental
Radio/TV/ video sales
Travel agent
Italian restaurant
Sports shop
Wine shop
Pizza restaurant
Meeting hall
Pub
Pub

Figure 4.16 Harborne High Street, Birmingham, June 1993. A large suburban High Street along a radial road from the city centre. Originally it was a residential street – the buildings have been modified or replaced. Sites are small and parking is limited. The leisure-related facilities are scattered along the frontage, and shown on the map.

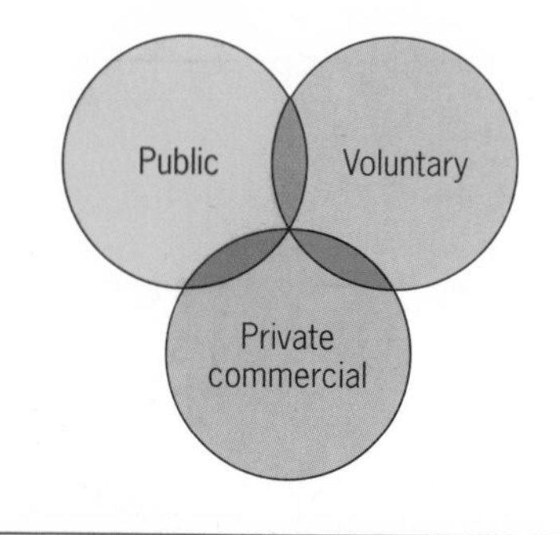

Examples

1 A local authority leisure centre may have some of the services run by a commercial company, while a number of voluntary clubs may rent the facilities as their base.

2 A voluntary club may receive a grant from central government or local authority.

3 Pitches in a public park may be rented by commercial firms and voluntary clubs for sports league matches.

Figure 4.17 Inter-relationships of the providers

4.5 Who supplies and provides leisure opportunities?

If we carry out land-use mapping of, say, an urban ward or other defined area of a city, our maps will show a wide range of spaces and facilities for leisure. One way to classify these is by *character* (e.g. open space, sports halls etc.). Another is by *activity* (e.g. tennis courts, pub etc.). Equally important, if we are to try to explain a facility's location and character, is to classify it by *provider*. As we learned in Chapter 1, there are three sectors of **supply** – **public**, **voluntary** and commercial, each with their distinctive motives and priorities. This distinctiveness influences their decisions about what they will provide and where they prefer to be located, as Chapters 5 and 6 will show. It is important to remember, however, that the three are becoming increasingly inter-connected (Fig. 4.17).

4.6 Leisure and urban regeneration

As central and inner areas of cities grow old, so they often suffer from physical, economic and social decline: buildings deteriorate, jobs are lost, communities break up or change. In some cases, whole cities and regions decline as industries change (e.g. the South Wales coalfield; Liverpool–Manchester; Glasgow and Clydeside; London's Docklands). Urban regeneration schemes aim to revitalise such areas. They vary in scale from local initiatives to national programmes – the Inner City Partnership Programme [ICPP], for instance, which began in 1978 for 10 major industrial cities. In the early 1990s we had Enterprise Zones and City Challenge programmes.

New and upgraded leisure facilities are often a component of such schemes. Some projects aim at improving the quality of life for local communities in this way. For example, leisure facilities and all-weather pitches are funded by central and local government, used by voluntary clubs and have special programmes and competitions sponsored by commercial organisations (Fig. 4.18). In contrast, some projects are much larger in scale, involving high-order facilities. These are intended to bring city-wide and regional economic, social and environmental benefits, and so raise the status and image of a city or region. A good example of this is the proposed national football stadium for Scotland, which has several cities campaigning to have it located in their territory.

22 On an Ordnance Survey (OS) map, identify a derelict or seriously deteriorated site in your local or nearby area and suggest the type of leisure facility which would be useful and appropriate for it. (Think of local and city-wide needs, the character and location of the site and who owns it.)

Figure 4.18 All-weather sports surface in the inner-city, multi-ethnic district of Highgate, Birmingham. Its nearness to the CBD can be clearly seen

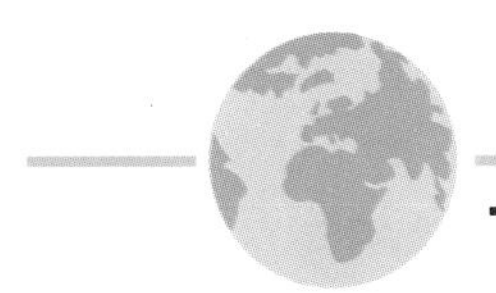

The International Convention Centre (ICC), Birmingham

The 'conference trade' combines both business and leisure and has been growing rapidly worldwide in recent years. It brings in large sums of money, creates jobs, raises a city's 'image'. It is not surprising that many cities – from **resorts** such as Brighton to industrial cities like Birmingham – have entered this competitive market by encouraging the development of conference centres.

In 1991 the ICC opened in central Birmingham. As Figure 4.19 shows, it is a massive, multi-facility complex of the highest quality, approached through an outdoor piazza (Convention Place). The complex stands on the edge of the CBD and astride a major road lined with pubs, restaurants and clubs. The ICC combines leisure (e.g. concerts, sporting events, eating out) with business (e.g. conferences, exhibitions) and so increases the usage and hence the economic benefits.

In the field of leisure, the high-order facilities of the ICC attract top-quality performers and events (e.g. the Indoor Arena hosts international sports meetings, and the concert hall is one of the finest in Europe, using high technology to produce excellent acoustics). Thus, local people as well as the regional population and international visitors enjoy improved opportunities for leisure.

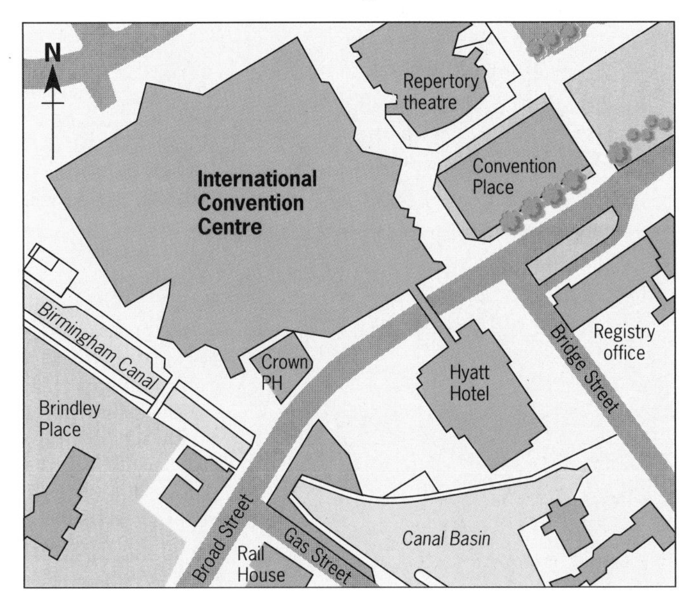

Figure 4.19 The International Convention Centre site in Birmingham, before (below) and after (above) redevelopment. The photo shows a view from the CBD. The new buildings of the complex can be seen in the middle ground, beyond the car park. On the left is the shining tower of the Hyatt Hotel, linked to the main ICC buildings by a bridge over a main road. On the right is the darker bulk of the National Indoor Arena.

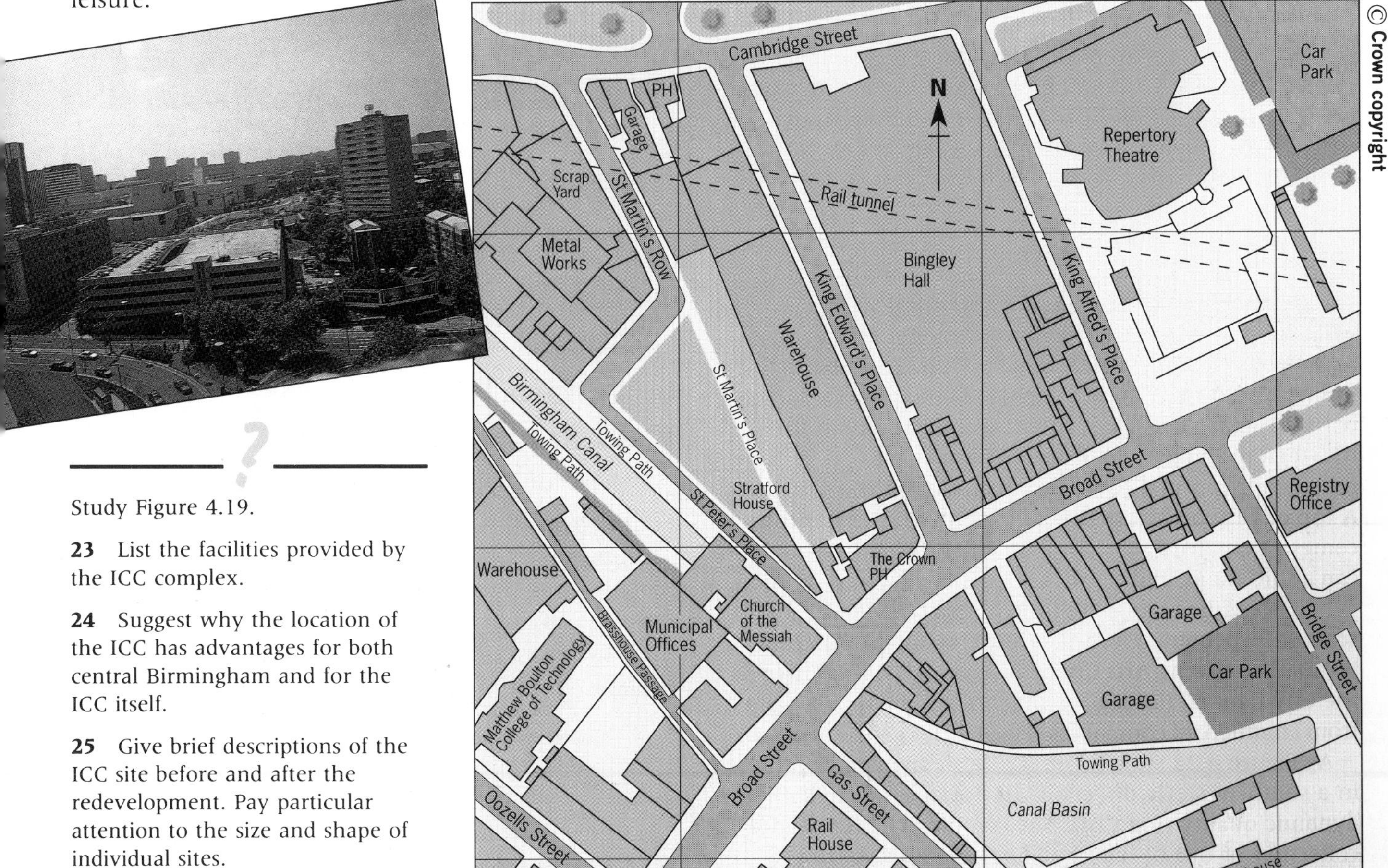

Study Figure 4.19.

23 List the facilities provided by the ICC complex.

24 Suggest why the location of the ICC has advantages for both central Birmingham and for the ICC itself.

25 Give brief descriptions of the ICC site before and after the redevelopment. Pay particular attention to the size and shape of individual sites.

ICC, Birmingham

But is it worth it?

Loftman and Nevin's findings show those projects will never be profitable and will suck funds away from basic services for decades.

In Birmingham subsidies to the ICC and NIA came to nearly £46 for every adult in the city in 1992/3 – a total of £33.6 million. It has eaten up the £11.5 million profits from the NEC and left another £22.1 million to be paid by council tax payers.

Loftman and Nevin's aim was to find out whether projects like the ICC really do enrich local populations – who after all eventually have to pay the bills.

Patrick Loftman said: 'Prestige projects like the ICC are based on the theory of Trickle-down Economics.

'The idea is that if you invest in a high-profile scheme it will create jobs and attract investment.

'The benefits will eventually trickle down to all levels of society.'

This idea, imported from the USA, has been enthusiastically adopted by British local authorities.

'But,' says Mr Loftman, 'they have adopted it so keenly that it will cause massive over-capacity.'

Birmingham's NIA, for example, faces competition from the £100 million-plus worth of facilities built by Sheffield.

Soon it will face more problems, with Manchester planning a £30 million sports arena, a £9 million velodrome and other facilities for its Olympic bid.

All will be competing for the same limited number of national and international sports events.

The ICC – already the subject of huge subsidies – will from 1995 have to compete with a new facility in Edinburgh.

A similar project is proposed for Rainham Marshes. That would be ideally placed for Continental traffic via the Channel Tunnel and would surely attract business from both the NEC and ICC.

Birmingham's world-class Symphony Hall is already rivalled by another in Glasgow and a similar one planned for Manchester.

Figure 4.20 Newspaper report questioning the benefits of high-cost prestige projects (*Source*: *Express and Star*, 14 June 1993)

Despite these apparent benefits, there is growing concern over the wisdom of such high-profile, high-cost projects (ICC = £180 million, National Indoor Arena = £46 million). Figure 4.20 summarises key points from a 1993 study by two university lecturers, Patrick Loftman and Brendan Nevin.

CBSO

The issue of how to provide the opportunity to enjoy what is often called 'high-culture' experiences at reasonable, i.e. accessible, costs, are illustrated by the example of the City of Birmingham Symphony Orchestra (CBSO). Its home base is the new concert hall in the ICC (before the ICC development it was the nineteenth-century Town Hall [Fig. 6.1] in the CBD). A top quality orchestra is very expensive, and if income comes solely from seat sales, then only wealthy people can afford them, and there may not be enough wealthy people around to support the orchestra (the concert hall seats 2200 people). Thus, the CBSO is supported partially by grants from the Arts Council (central government), the City Council (local government), and by sponsorship from commercial companies (Fig. 4.21).

As Figure 4.22 shows, the ICC has extended the CBD in a south-westerly direction, an example of the highly dynamic quality of a CBD. The complex has replaced a collection of out-of-date buildings, derelict sites (a previous, old exhibition hall had been destroyed by fire)

Sponsorship and Donations

The following organisations support the Orchestra through financial sponsorship of specific concerts and projects.

Bass Mitchells & Butlers
British Gas West Midlands
Birmingham International Airport
Coopers & Lybrand
Ernst & Young
European Arts Festival
Foundation for Sports and the Arts
Friends of the CBSO
Glynwed International
Gulf Oil
IMI plc
Lloyds Bank
Lucas Industries
Marks & Spencer
Midland Bank Artscard
National Westminster Bank
Radcliffe Trust
Shell U.K. Limited
Sounds Like Birmingham
Young & Lee

Corporate Members

Albright & Wilson
AMI Priory Hospital
Bond Foster Group
British Telecom plc
BUPA Little Aston
Central Independent Television
Hogg Insurance Brokers
ICL UK
ITNet
KPMG Peat Marwick
Marks & Spencer
The Royal Bank of Scotland
Tarmac Construction
Unisys
Wimpey Homes

Figure 4.21 Private commercial support for the arts: sponsorship of the City of Birmingham Symphony Orchestra

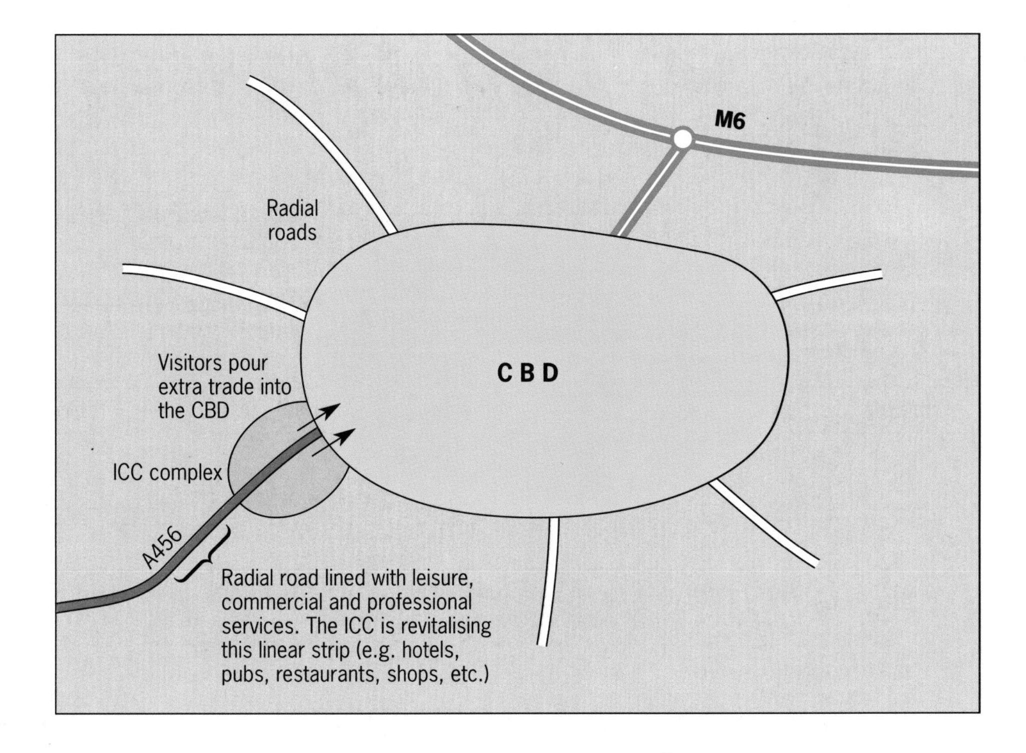

Figure 4.22 The impact of the International Convention Centre upon Birmingham's CBD: the ICC is extending the Birmingham CBD to the south-west and providing extra trade for businesses along the A456

and inadequate roads at the edge of the CBD where it meets the encircling inner city ring. The development, with its important leisure element, is a major force in urban regeneration. One significant problem that remains, however, is that the amount of traffic generated at times overloads the road and parking system.

?

26 There have been criticisms that the improvements in the road and parking infrastructure in the ICC project are not good enough. Suggest reasons for this underprovision. (Think of space requirements, costs, what makes the profits, who owns the land.)

?

27 For a suburban High Street with which you are familiar, carry out a leisure land-use survey, and build up a set of field notes based upon the features identified for Harborne High Street (Fig. 4.16). (If you wish to make this the basis of an assessment project, then you will find it useful to contact the district planning officers about the local plan.)

Summary

- Urban settlements concentrate both population and leisure facilities.
- Young people lead distinctive leisure lives and make very varied use of urban leisure facilities.
- Many types of leisure facility are spatially organised in a hierarchical structure.
- The CBD of a city is likely to contain an assembly of high-order leisure attractions, used by different age groups in distinctive ways.
- Leisure competes for urban space with other land uses.
- Leisure facilities can play an important role in urban regeneration.
- High-order facilities are expensive and are often the result of partnership between public and private sector providers.

5 Urban leisure: private sector providers

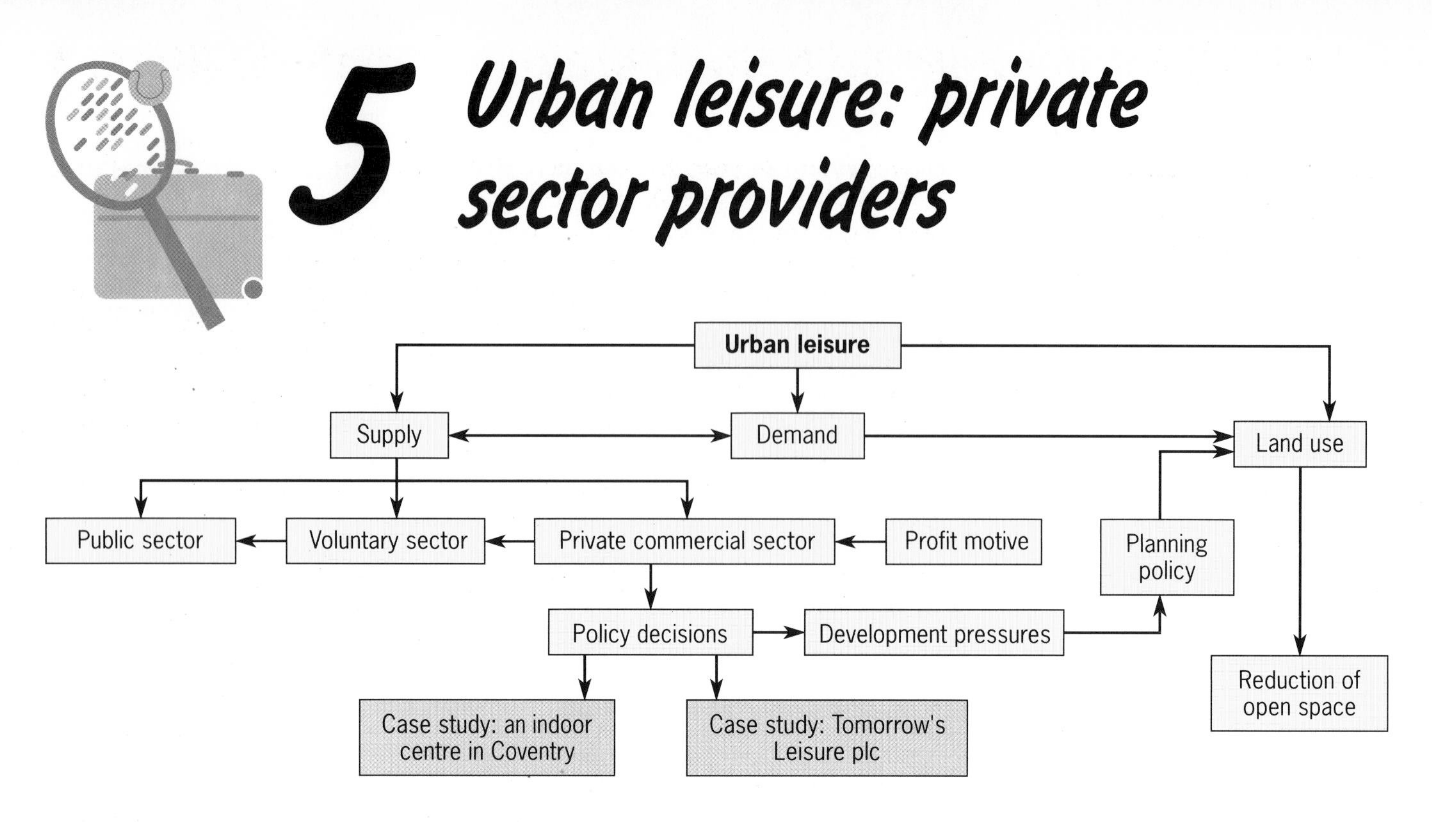

5.1 Introduction

As we shall see in Chapter 6, local authorities, supported by central government, spend huge sums of money on **leisure** and provide for a wide range of activities. Yet the diaries (Fig. 4.4) and other survey results (Figs 4.10–4.13) in Chapter 4 make it clear that a majority of people rely mainly on the **private sector**.

5.2 Commercial and voluntary providers

The **commercial sector** provides pubs, clubs, cinemas etc. while the **voluntary sector** organises a bewildering variety of activities, from badminton in church halls to youth-club discos, tennis clubs and netball leagues. It is important to remember that, while the voluntary sector plays a vital role at community level, it relies heavily upon **public sector** facilities. For instance, a swimming club will rent time in a public swimming pool; a netball league will use indoor or outdoor public courts. Table 5.1 lists the diversity of voluntary groups.

Table 5.1 Types of voluntary groups

Types of voluntary groups
Community organisations
Community Action Groups
Children's organisations
Women's organisations
Men's organisations
Old people's groups
Disabled groups
Adventure organisations
Outdoor activity organisations
Sport and physical recreation organisations
Cultural and entertainment organisations
Hobbies and interests groups
Animal and pet groups
Environmental and heritage groups
Consumer groups
Philanthropic (charity) organisations
Paramedical organisations
Uniformed groups
Religious groups
Political groups

Figure 5.1 The health and fitness craze has led to the spread of private fitness centres and clubs. The quality and expense expected of the facilities, the equipment and the staff constantly push up costs and prices. So, competition for trade becomes tougher

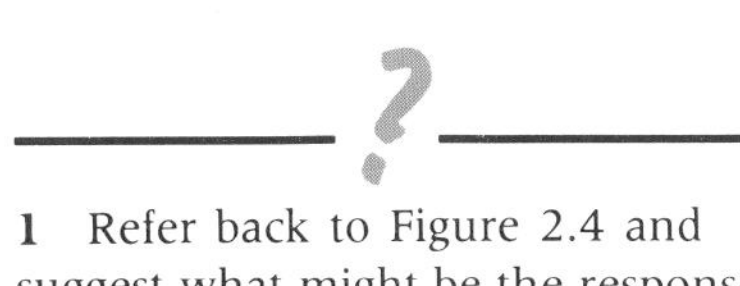

1 Refer back to Figure 2.4 and suggest what might be the response of a commercial leisure company to the demand–supply relationships shown on graphs (b) and (c).

Over the past 20 years the commercial leisure industry has changed in three significant ways: first, it has become dominated by a small number of large companies; second, it is offering an ever-widening range of leisure opportunities; and third, it is responding to customers' **demands** for higher-quality **facilities** and equipment. We demand more facilities and better conditions, and have become increasingly willing and able to pay for them (Fig. 5.1). Commercial companies see this growing demand – indeed, they use advertising and marketing to encourage it – and the opportunities for profitable **investments**. They respond by increasing the quantity and quality of **supply**, and so in turn, increase the competition.

This increase in commercial sector provision with its emphasis on quality is one reason why local authorities have been forced to raise standards of their facilities. Many voluntary groups too, with their limited funds, have felt the pressure – after all, who wants to play badminton in a church hall, with no showers, when the local public or private leisure centre offers high-quality courts, changing rooms and social facilities?

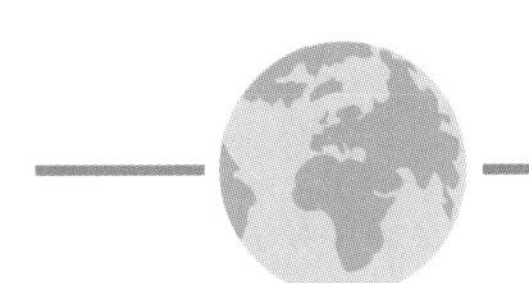

An indoor centre in Coventry

The Coventry Racquet Centre is a high-quality indoor facility for racquet games and fitness activities (Fig. 5.2). Figure 5.3 sets out extracts from their publicity material. It tells us a great deal about their marketing strategy, what opportunities they supply and for whom. The company's decision-making process will be guided by the fact that this is a private commercial enterprise which needs to make consistent profits. We can follow the company through six important elements of this process.

Location

The company seeks a *highly accessible location*. The maps in Figure 5.3 present the image of the centre at the heart of a road network, within a city of 250 000 people and a well-populated sub-regional **catchment area**.

Demand, supply and accessibility

The company selects *activities growing in popularity* – squash, badminton, keep-fit – plus a well-established activity, tennis, with a *shortage of indoor facilities*. Notice too, that the participant profile (i.e. the type of people who take part) comprises mainly car owners with some money to spend. These activities, then, are *accessible* to them via their mobility and their ability/willingness to pay.

Capacity

From the publicity material in Figure 5.3 we can see clearly that the company wants all the facilities to be used fully. Courts and activity rooms have a **physical carrying capacity**, that is, they are designed to hold a certain maximum number of people at one time. This is their **at-one-time capacity** – two people on a squash court; four on a tennis or badminton court. The centre's managers, therefore, need to decide upon (*a*) the length of the booking period, and (*b*) how many hours per day and per week they will keep the facility open. Thus, if they keep a badminton court open for 10 hours a day, and it is used for doubles play continuously in a series of one-hour bookings, then 40 people will have used the court. This is its **throughput capacity**.

Figure 5.2 Coventry Racquet Centre. A high-quality, multi-activity private facility

Pricing policy

The next step in the decision-making process then becomes: 'How much shall we charge?'. This decision is affected by (*a*) how much income the company needs to cover its invested capital, its running and maintenance costs, and to make a profit, and (*b*) how much people are willing to pay. This may be affected by the nature of the local competition. The company decides upon a *pricing policy* which takes into account that some times are more popular than others, some activities are more popular than others, and some facilities cost more to build and run than others.

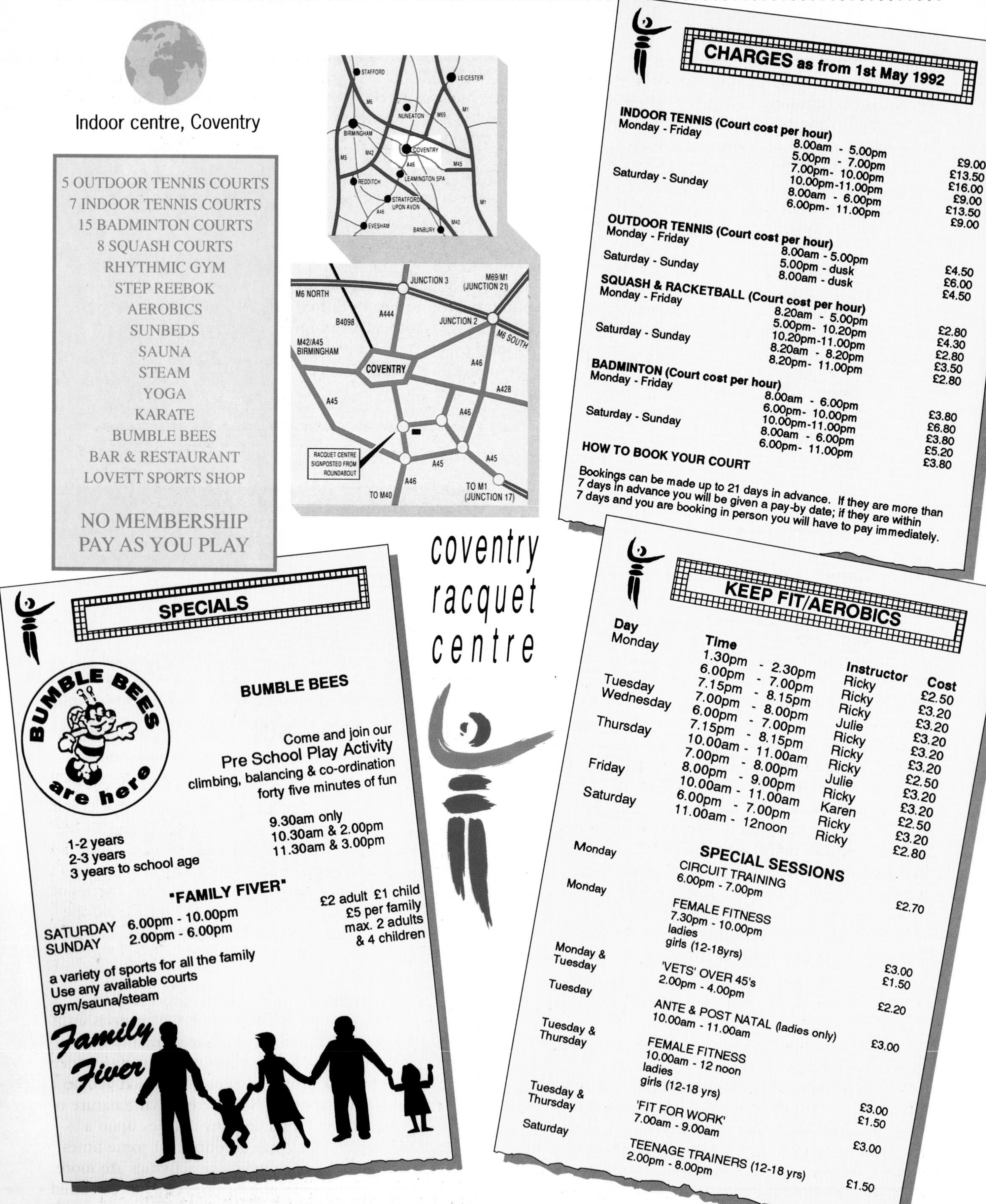

Figure 5.3 Examples of the Coventry Racquet Centre's publicity material

Target market

Now the company needs to decide upon the **market segments** it is aiming at – what demand it is hoping to satisfy, and how it can attract its targeted customers. Once it has selected the range of activities it will offer, the next step becomes the 'no membership; pay-as-you-play' decision. Thus, **access** to the centre is not restricted by membership but by ability and willingness to pay, or by qualification through a social programme (e.g. 'Access to Leisure' passes for the unemployed). It is important, too, to attract customers from as broad a market as possible in terms of age, gender and family status. Thus, the company may target certain groups and ease **accessibility** for them by pricing and timing of activities. To extend appeal still further, all skill and commitment levels are provided for. For example, the centre has received money from the Sports Council (a central government agency) to support a 'Badminton Development Programme' for young people.

Facilities

Finally, the company aims to provide a *high-quality environment*. So, the centre has saunas, sunbeds, excellent changing and shower facilities, bar and restaurant. Once more, to make best use of the expensive facilities and to increase profits, the company provides rooms for conferences, business meetings and receptions.

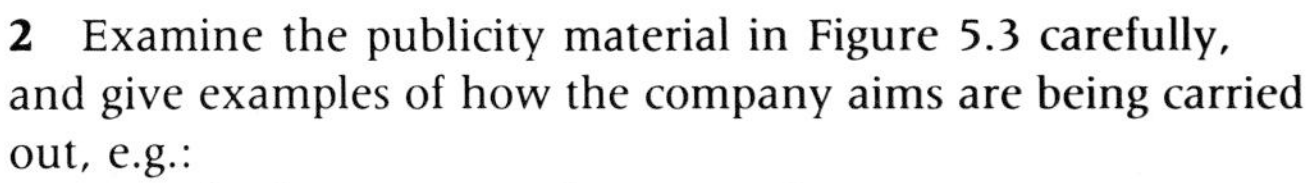

2 Examine the publicity material in Figure 5.3 carefully, and give examples of how the company aims are being carried out, e.g.:

a How do the pricing and timing policies try to raise use levels towards capacity? Why do pricing levels vary?

b Make a list of customer types being targeted.

c Why are certain groups being targeted at certain times?

d In what ways do the maps suggest that the centre is not a local 'community' facility, but a facility which aims at a broader catchment area?

3 Essay: Assess the relative importance of the main factors that influence the location and the **management** policy of private leisure clubs such as the Coventry Racquet Centre. (Use the Coventry example and if possible, an example from your local area, to illustrate your general points.)

Tomorrow's Leisure plc

This company is an excellent example of the way in which the leisure industry grew and matured during the 1980s. Tomorrow's Leisure is based in Newcastle upon Tyne and began in the early 1980s, operating a group of snooker clubs in north-east England, followed by a move into hotel development. From 1986, however, it has expanded more broadly across the leisure industry. For instance, the company has invested in two multi-leisure projects in urban areas, one on the eastern fringes of London, and the other in the heart of Liverpool. Both have involved deals with the local authorities, i.e. the public sector.

1 Fairlop Waters, Redbridge, Essex

In 1986 the company purchased a 125-year lease from Redbridge Borough Council for this 155-hectare site alongside the M25 (Fig. 5.4). Thus, it is a large site that is accessible to a huge potential urban market. The borough has permitted the company (i.e. given planning permission) to develop the Fairlop Waters site as a leisure complex with two golf courses and a driving range (built by the Borough and run by the company); a 17-hectare lake offering sailing, windsurfing and fishing; a children's attraction; restaurants and a pub. Note the choice of recreational activities – golf and watersports, both high-growth activities in recent years.

Figure 5.4 The Tomorrow's Leisure development at Fairlop Waters, Essex

Figure 5.5 'Pleasure Island', Liverpool. This development is on the site of the Liverpool Garden Festival, itself a scheme to regenerate a section of Liverpool's derelict docklands. Some remaining sections of docks can be seen at the top of the photograph. Note the size of the site, the combination of indoor and outdoor attractions and the ease of access by the improved road system

2 Liverpool Garden Festival site, redeveloped as 'Pleasure Island'

Tomorrow's Leisure has bought the 36-hectare (Fig. 5.5) Liverpool Garden Festival site (a government-backed inner-city regeneration project of the 1980s) from the Merseyside Development Corporation (i.e. the public sector). The company's managing director is very clear why he decided to invest £10 million in the project, which he calls 'Pleasure Island' (Fig. 5.6). Attractions include: 'The Works', an adventure world; 'Great Explorations', a hands-on science centre; 'Microtots', a soft play area for toddlers; a roller-skating rink; tenpin bowling. There is a membership scheme and daily entrance fees. As with the Essex project, the size of the site does allow expansion. During the 1990s the company hopes to open a 150-bed hotel, a 5000-capacity events arena, a conference centre, swimming pool, ski slope, garden centre and drive-in cinema.

?

4 List the activities/experiences offered by the two projects of Tomorrow's Leisure.

5 Suggest reasons for (*a*) the location and (*b*) the range of activities of the two projects. In what ways are they similar and what ways are they different?

There are 12 million people within an hour's travelling distance of Liverpool. There wasn't a great deal of leisure [provision] in the Liverpool area other than tenpin bowling and nightclubs, and there were no multi-leisure facilities.... Our whole concept was to build on what was there. There was a magnificent domed building, and we have converted that into multi-leisure use targeting the whole family.

Figure 5.6 Investing in 'Pleasure Island' (*Source*: John Sanderson, 1992)

5.3 Development pressures and land-use change

Space in urban areas is scarce and valuable. This is especially true of open spaces that are large, have a single owner, and are not cluttered by derelict buildings etc. It is not surprising therefore, that developers and transport planners look at recreational open spaces keenly. Both voluntary clubs and commercial companies are aware of the value of their existing sites. Recreational spaces such as parks and playing fields tend to be spacious, level, well-drained, with a full infrastructure (road access, electricity, sewerage etc.) and single ownership, making them relatively straightforward to develop. They are more attractive to developers for housing, industry and roads than derelict, awkwardly shaped sites in inner cities. Further pressure on urban open space arises when industrial companies expand on to their own playing fields or sell them for development – fewer and fewer companies are running **recreation** and sports programmes on their own grounds.

The temptation for a sports club, whether amateur or professional, to sell can be strong, especially when it has occupied the site for a long time. Today, the existing site may be poorly located for its customers, or inadequate in quality and scale by modern standards and expectations. A number of professional soccer stadiums are good examples of this kind of experience (Fig. 5.7). In the

Figure 5.7 Birmingham City Football Club, St Andrews. The stadium lies within a kilometre of the CBD. Once at the heart of a densely populated district of nineteenth-century housing, it has become increasingly isolated by redevelopment schemes and outward movement of people. Despite extensive modernisation, the facilities and the access/parking infrastructure struggle to keep up with modern needs

Figure 5.8 Stourbridge Rugby Football Club, West Midlands. Stourbridge Rugby Club used to lease land inside the town from a church organisation. In the 1960s the owners bought out of the lease and sold the ground at a high price for housing development. Fortunately, the Rugby Club received a sum large enough to be able to acquire land outside the town, but inside the West Midlands Green Belt. They gained planning permission for change of use from farming, and have been able to develop the present excellent facilities

?

6 Draw an annotated diagram to show the pressure on a sports club to relocate.

7 List the reasons why a club may not wish to relocate to a new site.

8 For your local town or city, or one you know well, give the name of at least one group, club, society etc. in as many of the categories in Table 5.1 as you can. Identify where they meet, and who provides the facilities.

voluntary sector it has become common practice for clubs to sell their sites and use the money to buy or lease bigger sites and provide better facilities. In some cases, where clubs have rented their grounds from owners, these owners have forced a move in order to sell off the land for more profitable uses (Fig. 5.8).

These shifts in land-use patterns cover a wide range of activities and sums of money. For example, in cricket, Hampshire County Cricket Club sold their Southampton ground in 1988 and began to move to a cheaper 25-hectare suburban site. In Rugby League football, in 1989, the Wigan club sold their training pitch and car park for £2.5 million to pay for modernisation of their main ground; and in 1990, Hull Kingston Rovers decided to sell their traditional Craven Park ground for £4 million and build a new stadium on the edge of town, giving high-quality facilities and room for expansion. Of course, there may be strong sentimental attachments to traditional stadiums and venues (e.g. the long battle fought by fans to keep the Charlton Athletic football ground in London) which have to be taken into account.

As sales and moves affect inner-city and older suburban districts, one result is the reduction of recreational open space in these areas. This makes it even more important that the local councils retain and, where possible, increase their provision in inner districts, despite the expense involved.

Summary

- Leisure facilities are becoming more varied and are expected to be of higher quality, and so are increasingly expensive to provide and to maintain.
- The priority for private commercial companies is to make a consistent profit.
- This influences their decisions on the location, character and pricing policies of their developments.
- Urban land values are one important reason for changes in the location of leisure facilities.
- The rising costs of leisure facilities, plus the continuing changes in demand, make investments risky.

6 Urban leisure: the role of the public sector

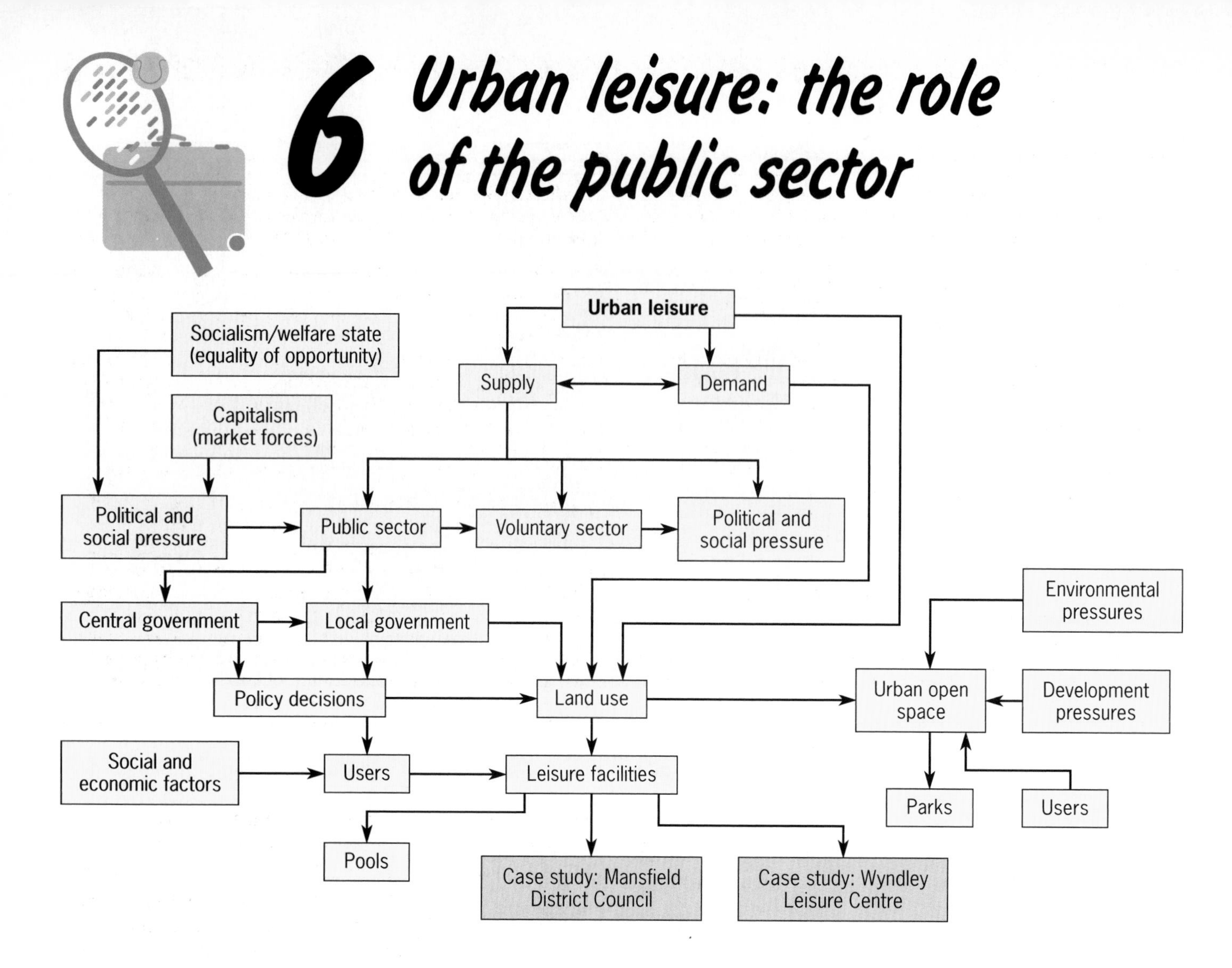

6.1 Introduction

We tend to take public parks, libraries, leisure centres and so on for granted – just places 'the council' provides. But why and when did 'the council' take on this task, and will it be able to continue to do so – indeed, should it continue?

Figure 6.1 Birmingham Town Hall, first opened as a concert hall in 1843 and extended during the 1850s. Until the opening of the new ICC complex in 1991 (see page 35), this was the city's main meeting and concert hall. Much of the surrounding area of the CBD has been redeveloped. For instance, the landscaping and open piazza was completed in 1993 to upgrade the pedestrian environment and attract people at leisure to the city centre

6.2 The historical background

The first important understanding is that local authorities have been involved in providing recreational **facilities** for more than a century. This can be illustrated effectively by a study of the CBD. Mapping the CBD of a city is a popular fieldwork project – and two of the variables that are frequently plotted are land use and building age. As field data is analysed, distinct categories can be identified. One such category you identify may be called 'cultural leisure uses in pre-1914 buildings'. This would include libraries, art galleries, museums and civic halls, as well as art and music schools, often set in fine and distinctive buildings (Fig. 6.1). However, it should be remembered that wartime damage (1939–45) and post-1945 redevelopment schemes have removed many such buildings.

By 1850, the Industrial Revolution was in full swing, and Britain was becoming an urbanised country: the 1851 population census showed, for the first time, that one in every two people were living in towns and cities. At this time, government and some of the wealthier groups in society were becoming increasingly concerned about the living and working conditions of the working population. As a result of such influential interest, laws were passed which were

Table 6.1 How public-sector leisure policies have evolved

1840s–90s: Concerns for health, moral values and quality of life lead to Parliament passing laws enabling (i.e. permitting) local authorities to provide leisure services. Town and city councils progressively set up separate Library, Museum, Baths, Parks and Garden Committees. Councils make the decisions in the belief that they have a duty 'to direct and control aspects of their citizens' lives which affect their abilities to be "good" citizens' (White, 1992).

1890s–1940s: Leisure provision continues in separate departments, with a broadening range of activities, e.g. adult education and allotments (today called 'leisure gardens'). The emergence of town planning begins the process of 'planning for leisure' (especially in the Garden City movement), with leisure-facility land use *planned* into developments such as the expanding council housing estates from the 1920s. Key motivations for the decision-makers remain the health and welfare of the working population, who themselves become better organised and more influential in improving their leisure lives (e.g. Working Men's Clubs).

1945–74: The evolution of the Welfare State brings (a) a comprehensive town-planning system; (b) a set of government policies aimed at social justice and opportunities for all. In the field of leisure, central government acts as a 'promoter', giving grants to local authorities directly, or through agencies such as the Sports Council. The local authority then becomes the 'director' by allocating this money, plus additional funds raised by local taxes, via a set of central-government guidelines.

Separate leisure departments continue and provision varies widely between cities, according to the values and priorities of key committees.

1974–88: The Local Government Act 1974, passed by Parliament sets up new local authorities and structures in England and Wales. Provision for leisure becomes organised, in most authorities, within single, integrated leisure services departments. Central-government funds continue to be channelled through the Arts and Sports Councils, and by direct grant-aid to local authorities. One result is the rapid growth in the numbers of indoor sports and leisure centres in residential areas. The primary aims of such policies are improved social justice resulting in increased participation by all sections of society (e.g. national programmes such as 'Sport for All', and 'Community Arts' schemes).

Post-1988: There is a shift away from a policy based on the motives of social justice and welfare for *communities* towards one emphasising the rights and choices of *individuals*. This is to be achieved through the policy of compulsory competitive tendering (CCT) introduced in the Local Government Act 1988. Economic motives outweigh social motives in the decision-making process. Profitability, competitiveness and tighter control by central government become more important. Local authorities must put out their services to competitive tender: they may have to bid themselves against private companies to run the leisure centres, park maintenance etc. (i.e. *commercial* criteria become stronger).

?

1 Study Table 6.1.
a For each era, list the main criteria that were applied to **leisure** policies.
b Identify the **values** and **attitudes** behind the criteria.

2 Look at Figure 6.2. Make lists of (*a*) the benefits and (*b*) the problems of joint funding and use policy to the school. (Refer to local examples known to you if possible.)

Figure 6.2 Bartley Green School and Leisure Centre, Birmingham. A typical dual-use site in a residential community

intended to improve factories, homes and the urban environment. Also, this was a period of great civic pride: councils and wealthy citizens were proud of their cities. One outcome of this combination of social concern and civic pride was the construction of many fine buildings in the emerging city centres. These buildings included what we see today as the older libraries, museums, art galleries etc. (See pp. 52–5 for the story of open spaces.) Table 6.1 outlines the 150-year story which provides the background to present-day issues.

6.3 Trends in policy since 1970

We can now focus more closely on what has been happening since 1970. During the 1970s decision-making emphasised the building of new facilities – arts centres, swimming pools, all-weather pitches, sports halls etc. These either replaced older, inadequate facilities or extended opportunities in residential neighbourhoods. In addition, national 'centres of excellence' and specialised training facilities were set up. Many of the facilities we now use date from this period, including **'dual-use'** facilities, attached to schools or colleges, to be used by both the students and the community, and funded jointly from leisure services and education budgets. For example, in 1966 there were fewer than 30 public indoor sport and leisure centres. By 1976, there were 481, with 213 of these being dual-use facilities (Fig. 6.2).

Increased participation?

The main aim of the 1970s building programme was to increase leisure opportunities for *all groups* in society. Particular attention was given to groups with special needs and those whose participation rates were low, e.g. people with disabilities, the unemployed, women and cultural minorities (Fig. 6.3). However, surveys showed that by 1980 little had changed. For example, a study of the Michael Sobell Centre in Islington (London), located intentionally in a socially mixed district, showed that very few semi- or unskilled workers used the centre. Two-thirds of the users came from car-owning households, and

Figure 6.3 Facilities are now required to provide ramp entrances as well as steps to allow accessibility for people with disabilities and encourage their participation in sport and leisure activities

Figure 6.4 Still the typical leisure-centre participant?

participation by men was much greater than by women. A speaker at a conference in 1991 said of the 1980 situation – 'With some risk of caricature one could describe the typical leisure-centre participant at the time as white, male and middle class, often using his car to drive into the intended **catchment area**.' (Lentell, 1991)(Fig. 6.4). Decision-makers had become too concerned with building and running the facilities (**supply**), paying too little attention to the potential customers (**demand**).

Figure 6.5 Cultural dance group performing the 'bhangra', a traditional Indian folk dance

Trends since 1980

So, from around 1980, policy changed in three major ways, partly forced by the Conservative policies which began to tighten the amounts of money available. First, recreation development officers were based *within the communities*, to work with local people and so encourage greater community involvement and participation. Second, groups with low participation rates (e.g. ethnic minorities and women) were 'targeted' and given special encouragement. Third, a wider range of activities was supported, often being suggested by the communities themselves, e.g. BMX, skateboarding, cultural dance and music groups (Fig. 6.5). Thus, the emphasis was on *community involvement and participation*, not simply facility provisions. For instance, central government, through the Sports and Arts Councils, funded programmes such as 'Action Sport' and 'Community Arts', while local authorities ran 'Passport to Leisure' schemes providing free or reduced price **access** to the unemployed.

Table 6.2 How much do local authorities spend in England and Wales? 1992–3

Facility	Spending (£ millions)
Urban parks and open spaces	538
Sports halls and leisure centres with pools	284
Swimming pools	132
Art galleries and museums	117
Theatres, halls, art galleries and places of public entertainment	114

Trends since 1990

By the early 1990s, many of these initiatives were struggling to survive, not necessarily because they had failed, or because the councils had lost interest. As Table 6.2 shows, local councils continue to spend very large sums of money. The problem lies with the way in which local authorities have to make their decisions: they receive less money from central government and must run their leisure services according to CCT rules. (Look again at the 'post-1988' section of Table 6.1.) Having to make hard decisions about how money is spent means that local authorities vary widely in how they see their role (Fig. 6.6).

It is not surprising, therefore, that your opportunities for leisure still depend upon where you live, as local authorities vary widely in their spending (Tables 6.3 and 6.4). Notice the strong commitment by councils in South Wales (Glamorgan) where there has been a long tradition of social welfare, which has

Figure 6.6 The spectrum of leisure policies by local authorities (*Source*: Bishop and Coalter, 1988)

SPECTRUM

Extreme ⟵⟶ Extreme

The residual approach
The public sector should fill only the gaps left by the private sector. The State acts as a 'safety net', with individuals taking responsibility for their own consumption of leisure. Public sector provision should occur only in a narrow range of traditional areas of sport, recreation and the arts.

The social justice approach
An interventionist role by the public sector. All sections of society have a right to equal opportunities for leisure in quantity and quality. It is the role of the public sector to enable this social justice by direct provision and by support of the voluntary and commercial sectors.

I believe that there is a greater potential increasing pricing rather than in provision at the expense of the ratepayers at large.

Borough Treasurer

We can't leave the profitable elements to the private sector ... you can't just take the loss leaders, otherwise you will inhibit the potential, and therefore not give the public, whom we serve, all the options.

Director of Leisure Services

I like the extent to which local clubs have taken a financial part in their activity and provided their own club premises and so on.... It saves the Council money because if they were not provided in that way the Council would have to.

Borough Treasurer

There are limits to the support we can give ... driving the voluntary sector needs effort and time because of their limited organisation, and funds.

Chief Leisure Services Officer

?

3 Study Figure 6.6. Write a brief statement in the form of a letter to the chairperson of your local Leisure Services Committee. Set out and justify your opinion on the role the local authority should take in leisure provision.

Table 6.3 Who spends most? Who spends least?

(£ per head of population)

A ENGLAND AND WALES

Authority	Amount
Most	
West Glamorgan	67
Mid Glamorgan	60
Northumberland	50
South Glamorgan	47
Tyne and Wear	46
Least	
Hereford and Worcester	22
Gloucestershire	22
Cornwall	21
Buckinghamshire	21
Somerset	18

B SCOTLAND

Authority	Amount
Most	
Shetland	48.3
Glasgow	46.5
Renfrew	44.4
Midlothian	43.9
Kyle and Carrick	43.6
Least	
Gordon	16.0
Sutherland	15.0
Stewartry	14.0
Badenoch and Strathspey	12.5
Skye and Lochalsh	11.4

continued through the decline of the coal and steel industries, accompanied by severe social, economic and environmental problems. In such areas, high spending in leisure services is part of a social policy to improve the **quality of life** of local people.

This is apparent too, in Scotland, where two very contrasting local authorities top the ranking lists. The rural Shetland Islands benefit from the wealth generated by the oil industry, while Glasgow has a strong commitment to the quality of life of the urban population.

Table 6.4 Leisure spending – variations in urban districts: South Yorkshire (*Source*: CIPFA, *Leisure and Recreation Statistics, 1992–93, Estimates*, 1992)

District	Population (thousands)	Area (thousand hectares)	Spending per head of population (£) Indoor	Outdoor	Arts	Other	Total
Barnsley	222	33	17.7	10.5	3.3	3.5	**35.0**
Doncaster	294	58	5.5	9.3	3.5	3.9	**22.2**
Rotherham	255	28	12.0	10.7	3.4	4.5	**30.6**
Sheffield	523	37	11.6	11.7	9.8	4.1	**37.2**

?

4a We must be careful about making generalisations. Table 6.4 lists four apparently similar towns: all traditional industrial districts in Yorkshire. Yet their spending policies are quite different. List the factors that might influence these differences. For instance, parks are expensive to run, and Doncaster has relatively few. Might their population structures be different, and how might this affect needs and spending?

b Write a hypothesis about the role of your local authority in leisure provision that you could test by library research.

5a List the factors that may have influenced the decisions of the five lowest spending councils of Tables 6.3 A and B to allocate such relatively low funding to leisure?

b Write a hypothesis that summarises your findings.

Mansfield District Council

Because people are no longer satisfied by a narrow range of activities, outdated buildings, and poor quality courts and pitches, the costs of providing and running facilities are rising. Further, government policy and increasing competition from private leisure companies (see pp. 45–6) are forcing local authorities to make hard decisions. One council that is strongly committed to providing a wide range of high-quality leisure opportunities for all sections of its population is Mansfield.

Mansfield is a Nottinghamshire town with a population of approximately 104 000, at the centre of a County District on the Nottinghamshire coalfield (Fig. 6.7). Under the rule of CCT, the Leisure Department put in a bid to its own District Council to run the town and district public-sector leisure services. It succeeded, and since January 1992 it has had the contract to manage all leisure facilities, including the parks, 16 community centres, a lottery, the Civic Theatre and Museum. The materials in Table 6.5 illustrate the range and quality of the opportunities for **recreation**. Notice too, how expensive it is to provide the top-quality experiences necessary to attract people and compete with the **private sector**.

Meden Sports Centre

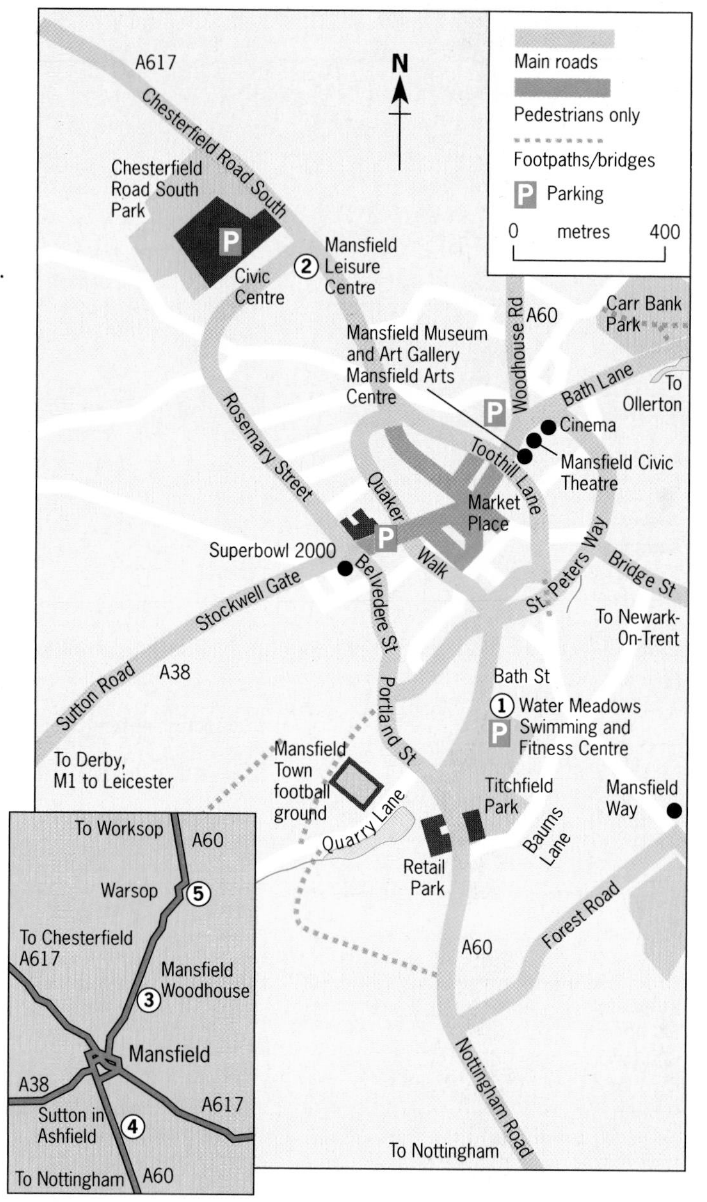

Table 6.5 Examples of leisure provision by Mansfield District Council

1 The Water Meadows at Titchfield Park: An investment of £6.5 million has produced a 500sq.m. leisure pool with wave machine, water channel, weir and beach-effect area; a 6-lane competition pool with seating for 250 spectators; a 10-metre teaching pool; a health-fitness centre; a bar and restaurant overlooking the pool.

2 The Mansfield Leisure Centre: Facilities include a 9000sq.ft. multi-purpose hall for sports, theatre and concerts, seating up to 1500 people (e.g. for plays, cabarets, fashion shows, volleyball and badminton tournaments); a social hall for table tennis, martial arts, yoga and keep-fit; solarium; squash courts.

3 Manor Park: The council has invested £3 million to turn a disused sewage works into a sports complex. Some of the money comes from the Sports Council and government 'derelict land support grants'. There is a new sports pavilion and tennis courts, cricket nets and an artificial playing surface with floodlights used for a wide range of competitive, recreational sports and coaching. There are also two outdoor bowling greens and ten grass pitches. The site has been landscaped and provides trails for walking and jogging, with car parking and facilities for the disabled.

4 Berry Hill Park: £9 million has been invested to build a pavilion and international standard athletics track: a synthetic, all-weather surface with eight lanes and a ten-lane straight. The park is run as a Social Welfare Centre, managed by a joint committee of British Coal, the Mining Unions and Mansfield District Council.

5 Meden Sports Centre: A *dual-use* facility at Warsop Meden Comprehensive School, funded jointly by the District and County Councils to allow educational use during school hours and community use at other times. There is a 20-metre swimming pool; a 27m. × 16m. sports hall (badminton, football, basketball, volleyball, hockey, netball); a gym; squash courts; multi-purpose childrens' play room; tennis courts.

Water Meadows

WATER MEADOWS
Tel: 22507
Tuesday 8.00am-8.45am
Wednesday 12 noon-3.00pm
Thursday 8.00am-8.45am

SHERWOOD BATHS
Tel: 663082
Monday and Friday
8.00am-8.45am – 12 noon-1.15pm
School Holidays 8.00am-3.00pm
Wednesday 12 noon-1.15pm
Summer Holidays only
Tuesdays and Thursdays
8.00am-3.00pm
Wednesdays 8.00am-12 noon

MEDEN SPORTS CENTRE
Tel: 842865
Monday and Friday
12.30pm-3.00pm
Squash and Weight Training
Swimming *(School Holidays only)*

OAK TREE LANE CENTRE
Tel: 23926
Monday and Friday
9.00am-3.00pm
Badminton, Table Tennis
Weight Training only

CONDITIONS OF SCHEME

1. All facilities SUBJECT TO AVAILABILITY
2. Concessions only available at the stated facilities and at the stated times
3. These concessions are only open to the following people:

***UNEMPLOYED AND ACCOMPANYING CHILDREN**
(to include those engaged on EMPLOYMENT TRAINING SCHEMES – on production of Form B83)

***SENIOR CITIZENS**
Aged 60 and over

***REGISTERED DISABLED PERSONS**
(on production of a Green Card)

***EARLY RETIRED/JOB RELEASE**
(on production of an Income Support Order Book or a Family Credit Order Book)

***SINGLE PARENTS AND ACCOMPANYING CHILDREN**
(on production of an Income Support Order Book or a Family Credit Order Book)*

Please Note:
- Concessions only available to recipients of Family Credit or Income Support.
- Applies only to residents living within the boundaries of Mansfield District Council.
- Please ring and confirm your attendance.
- Please contact facility before intended use.

WILLIAM KAYE HALL
COMMUNITY CENTRE

MONDAY	Bingo	7.15pm-8.45pm
TUESDAY	Wine Making (every 3rd Tuesday)	7.00pm-10.00pm
	Dance School	5.00pm-10.00pm
THURSDAY	Fellowship Group	1.30pm-4.00pm
	RSPB (Juniors)	6.00pm-7.00pm
	RSPB (Seniors) (every 1st Thursday)	7.30pm-9.30pm
	Aerobics/Step Aerobics	6.00pm-9.00pm
FRIDAY	Bingo	7.15pm-8.45pm

One of the largest Community Centres in Mansfield, the William Kaye Hall has a main hall which seats 200 and staging suitable for concerts and shows.
The smaller room is ideal for children's parties, family get-togethers, meetings or classes.
Close to the Town Centre, the building is easily reached on foot or by bus and there is ample parking space to the rear of the building.

For further information/bookings contact Mr P Norman on 658471

MANSFIELD · LEISURE · SERVICES

As of April 1992

Figure 6.7 The Mansfield district – leisure provision. The photos show the interiors of the Meden Sports Centre and Water Meadows

?

Use the materials in Figure 6.7 and Table 6.5 to answer the following questions:

6 List the range of activities provided.

7 Why do you think that many of the facilities are located some distance from the town centre?

8 In what ways do the examples given illustrate the increasing emphasis upon high quality and standards of opportunities?

9 What evidence is there of policies to attract from all sections of the community, especially those who might be described as 'disadvantaged'?

10 Which of the council facilities involve partnerships with or are supported by other organisations? Suggest reasons for these partnerships.

11 Which types of leisure activities appear *not* to be provided by the District Council? Can you suggest reasons why this is so?

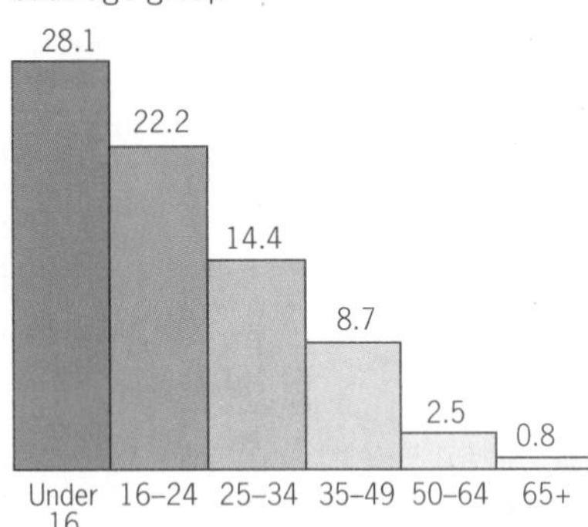

Figure 6.8 Age of users of the Kelmscott Leisure Centre, Waltham Forest (*Source*: Waltham Forest Recreation Services)

Table 6.6 Most popular activities: Kelmscott Leisure Centre (% of total participants)

Activity	%
Keep-fit	24
Badminton	9
Squash	9
Football	9
Fitness room	7
Table tennis	6
Toddlers' activities	6
Kids' Clubs	4

6.4 Who uses the facilities?

As it is so expensive to provide and run modern leisure facilities, we need to ask questions such as – 'Is it worth it?' and 'Are the people that are targeted actually taking part?'. The answers are not simple. As an example, let us analyse the results of a survey of Kelmscott Leisure Centre, a Waltham Forest Recreation Services centre opened in 1983. During 1985 and 1986 attendances averaged almost 400 a week, excluding club bookings and spectators. With an estimated population of 24 000 living within a radius of one mile, a 1986 survey showed that 12 per cent of this population had used the centre in the past 12 months. Looked at from another angle, 88 per cent had *not* used the centre. Just over 40 per cent of these users visited the centre at least once a week. Figure 6.8 shows that it was younger age groups that dominated the usage. The lowest rates of participation were among the elderly, the unemployed and housewives. As these were the groups that the centre especially wished to attract, the results were disappointing. Yet the results for two other 'target' groups were encouraging: the participation rate for the Afro-Caribbean community was 20 per cent, while sessions for women were very popular – Keep Fit 96 per cent full; recreation activities 73 per cent full.

One measure of success is how fully the facilities are used. At Kelmscott, the main sports hall was being used to 88 per cent of its capacity, and other rooms, courts etc. were achieving a usage level of 60 per cent or more. Table 6.6 lists the most popular activities, and, with the exception of Keep Fit, there are a wide variety of activities each with low participation percentages. Providing such a great range of activities for relatively small numbers of customers makes it difficult for managers to make the best use of their facilities. One solution is to encourage people to take part in several activities, but the survey showed that only one in four users took part in more than one activity.

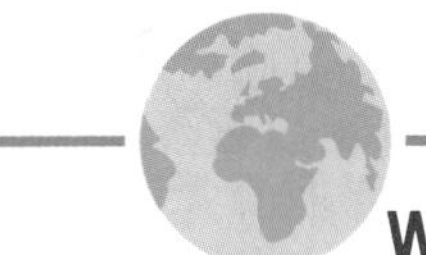

Wyndley Leisure Centre, Sutton Coldfield, West Midlands

This multi-purpose centre is centrally located in Sutton Coldfield, a district of around 100 000 people on the north side of Birmingham (Fig. 6.9). It is open from 0900 to 2300 hours each day, for members, 'pay-and-play' users, clubs and school bookings, with charges varying from peak to off-peak times. The information in Figure 6.10 tells us how the centre was being used in 1990.

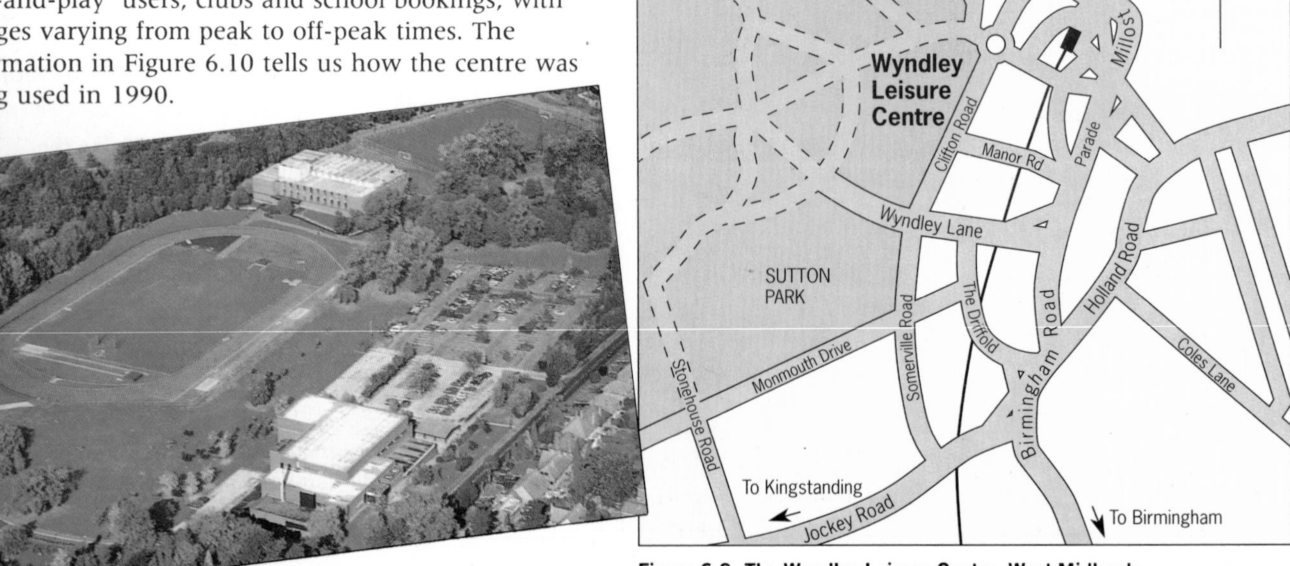

Figure 6.9 The Wyndley Leisure Centre, West Midlands

Figure 6.10 **Results from the Wyndley Leisure Centre participation survey, Jan–Feb 1990**

Wyndley Leisure Centre: Participation survey January–February 1990

Facilities

- Swimming pool complex with diving bay; learner pool
- Floodlit all-weather pitch
- 400 m 8-lane running track
- Fitness studio; keep-fit studio with sauna, sun-beds
- 5 badminton courts
- 6 squash courts
- Indoor bowls
- Trampolining
- Disabled and crèche facilities
- Restaurant and sports shop

'Target group' schemes

- Crèche, 'tumble tot' and 'water play' sessions for parents and pre-school children, weekday mornings and afternoons
- Late afternoon, Saturday and holiday recreation, swimming coaching sessions for school-age juniors
- Women-only weekday keep-fit, aerobics, jogging, swimming and beauty treatment sessions (use of crèche if needed)
- 'Passport to Leisure' scheme giving reduced rates to unemployed and students during off-peak periods

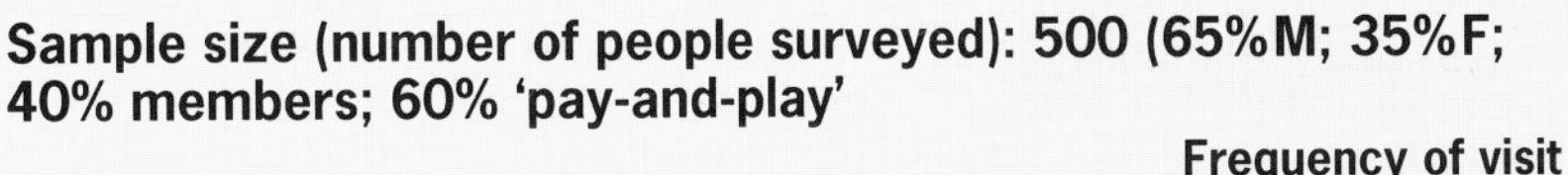

Sample size (number of people surveyed): 500 (65%M; 35%F; 40% members; 60% 'pay-and-play'

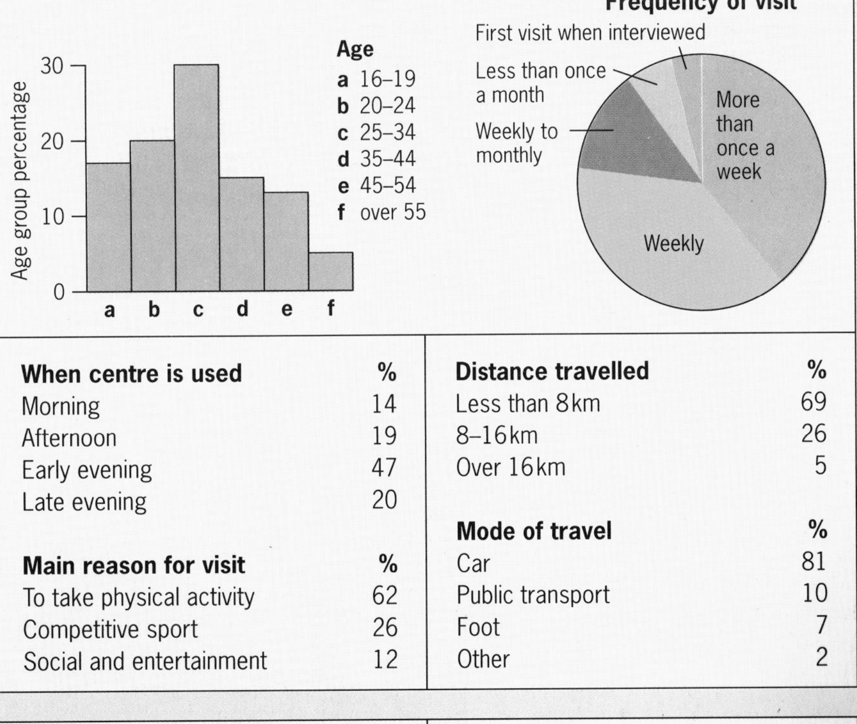

When centre is used	%
Morning	14
Afternoon	19
Early evening	47
Late evening	20

Main reason for visit	%
To take physical activity	62
Competitive sport	26
Social and entertainment	12

Distance travelled	%
Less than 8 km	69
8–16 km	26
Over 16 km	5

Mode of travel	%
Car	81
Public transport	10
Foot	7
Other	2

1990 full-year usage figures (52 weeks)

Facility	No. ('000)
Swimming baths	501
Main sports hall	251
Social use	175
All-weather pitch	34
Athletics track	15
Total	**976**

Most popular activity types in sports hall

Rank	Activity	No. ('000)
1	Badminton	62
2	Club bookings	45
3	Squash	45
4	Classes (fencing, keep-fit, yoga, trampolining	30
5	Fitness studio	24

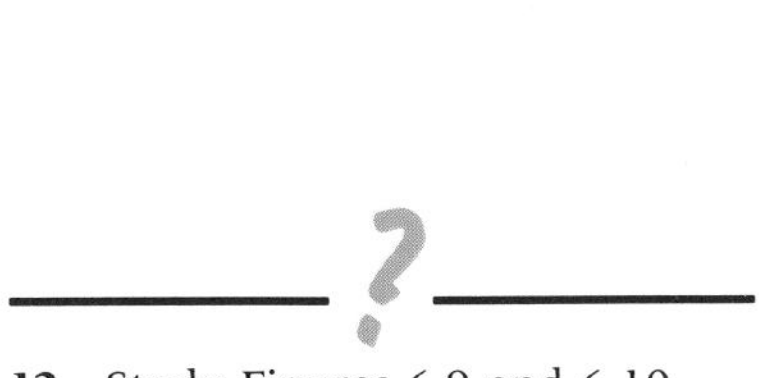

12 Study Figures 6.9 and 6.10. Describe the character of the centre briefly, and how the managers try to attract a wide variety of users.

13a Who uses the centre?
b How often and when do most people use the centre?
c How far do most people travel to use the centre, and how do they travel?
d Why do people use the centre and what are their favourite activities?

14 The survey results do not separate weekdays from weekends. What differences would you expect to find in participation and in **management** policies (e.g. pricing, target groups) between these two parts of the week?

15 The all-weather pitch and athletics track are expensive facilities, yet seem to have relatively low levels of usage. Can you give reasons why this is so? (Remember – the facilities *might* be fully used but because of the type of activities involved [e.g. lengthy team games] the total numbers are restricted. In this case, the facility would have a low **throughput capacity**.) If they are not fully used, suggest ways in which the managers could increase their level of usage.

16 What information, which would be useful in assessing the success of the centre, do the figures *not* give us?

17 Compare and contrast the provision and participation patterns of the Kelmscott and Wyndley Centres.

6.5 Urban open space

Because there is much competition for land in urban areas, it tends to be expensive. So, any sizeable open spaces are under constant development pressures. For instance, during the 1980s, the UK Government required Local Education Authorities to see if there were any school and college playing fields 'surplus to requirements', so that they could be sold off to raise money. Yet all towns and cities have a wide range of public open spaces, from small grassy areas on housing estates to large parks and playing fields. Often called a city's 'green lungs', they are, for the most part, lovingly maintained despite the expense, and are widely used (Fig. 6.11).

Figure 6.11 Valentines Park, a popular urban park in London

Historic urban parks

As Figure 4.14 and page 32 tell us, land values tend to decrease as distance from a city centre increases. Therefore, we might expect the amount of open space to increase towards the outer suburbs, i.e. where land is cheaper. (Land sold for housing, offices etc. fetches a much higher price than land for open space because of the value of the development to be put on the land.) Also, the outer districts are generally newer developments, where open space is part of the planned environment.

For most cities, these ideas or hypotheses seem to be true. However, central areas do contain high-order, often famous open spaces, with a long history and which are now part of a city's heritage, e.g. Hyde Park, London; Central Park, New York. Some of these parks originally lay outside a city and have been absorbed into the urban landscape as the built-up area expanded. (The Moor in Newcastle-upon-Tyne is an outstanding example.)

To explain the location and continued existence of these historic open spaces, we need to identify their origins. The examples given above illustrate three of the main ways such parks were created: first, as gifts or bequests by royalty or aristocracy (e.g. Hyde Park); second, as elements in town plans (e.g. Central Park, in the formal plan for Manhattan Island); third, as common lands, with traditional rights of communal use (e.g. The Moor). Many of the more elaborate and specialised parks relate back to two important eighteenth- and nineteenth-century traditions. First, there were large parks, known as 'Pleasure Gardens' – fashionable places of entertainment with lakes, broad paths, formal flower gardens, entertainment halls for shows and concerts, restaurants etc. Tivoli Gardens in

Figure 6.12 Balboa Park, San Diego, California

Figure 6.13 **Adderley Park: Birmingham's first public park (1867). Now modernised and within a multi-ethnic inner-city community only 1km from the CBD**

Copenhagen, Denmark, remains today as a fine example of a Pleasure Garden. Second, there were the 'Botanical Gardens', where the primary objectives were scientific, with displays of exotic plants from around the world (e.g. Kew Gardens in London and the Royal Botanical Gardens in Edinburgh). Some, more modern parks combine features of both, e.g. Balboa Park in San Diego, California (Fig. 6.12).

Local parks

Far more numerous are district and neighbourhood public parks (i.e. middle- and low-order facilities) scattered throughout a built-up area. They vary widely in size, character and age. As we saw earlier in this chapter, parks are one of the oldest of a local council's leisure responsibilities, dating back to the social changes of the mid-nineteenth century. For instance, the first public park in Birmingham dates from 1867. This is Adderley Park which, today, is in the inner-city district of Saltley (Fig. 6.13) but which in the 1860s was part of Lord Cobham's estate, outside the city. The land was being sold off for the rapid expansion of a suburb of workers' terrace housing and industry. To provide open space for this new community, Lord Cobham donated land to the city for setting up a park. Many industrial cities have similar examples – the parks may look ordinary and even shabby today, but they have been a vital part of the leisure lives of the local communities. Those which survive in inner-city areas have benefited from recent inner-city improvement schemes, with funding from central and local government providing new fencing, all-weather play surfaces, landscaping etc.

18a Describe the pattern of use of an urban park shown in Figure 6.14, and detail the ways in which the various groups use the park.

b Which groups might come into conflict with each other over their use of the park? Draw and complete a compatibility matrix like the one below, using a cross to indicate where conflict might arise.

	Joggers	Dog walkers	Parents and babies	Retired people	Workers	Unemployed people	Teenagers	Cricketers
Joggers								
Dog walkers								
Parents and babies								
Retired people								
Workers								
Unemployed people								
Teenagers								
Cricketers								

19 For a selected urban park, analyse its character in terms of safety, especially for women and children. Suggest ways in which safety could be improved.

How are local parks used?

The use made of parks depends upon their location, size and facilities, but most parks serve a local catchment area of a 1- or at most 2-kilometre radius. Except when taking part in formal sports on greens, courts and pitches, most users walk to the parks.

Figure 6.14 summarises the use of a typical urban park for informal recreation during a summer weekday in fine weather. Use-profiles like this make it clear that it is difficult for a local council to run parks for profit – especially where a park has open entry, i.e. having no fences and gates, so entry is free.

Parks are among the most costly facilities a council provides but they are used by a wider range of the community than any other facility. Furthermore, the way people want to use parks is constantly changing, and many councils have adapted their parks accordingly. For instance, for safety and health reasons as well as shifts in demand, children's paddling pools, which were once so common, are now rare, and are being replaced by equipped play areas. Again, fashions such as BMX have been accommodated, as has the health trend by the laying out of jogging tracks and 'Trim Trails'. To allow more intense use and to reduce erosion, all-weather pitches and courts are replacing grass surfaces – they are more expensive to install but cheaper to maintain than grass, and can raise more money because of their high **carrying capacity**.

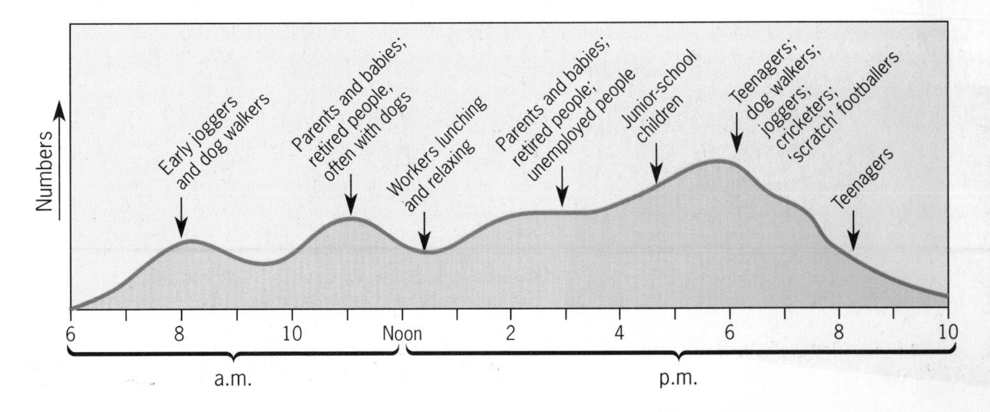

Note: This shows 'informal' use, and excludes bookings of tennis courts, bowls greens, 'pitch-and-putt' golf and all-weather playing surface.

Figure 6.14 **The use of an urban park**

Open space and the environment

One trend in the management of open spaces brings together leisure provision and concern for the environment. Many councils have carried out major tree planting and landscaping schemes, including the development of 'wild' or 'natural' areas, often in co-operation with local conservation groups. Their aim is to enhance the landscape's beauty and to broaden the range of habitats for wildlife. For example, Dudley Metropolitan Borough manages four such 'greenspaces' as nature reserves, totalling 250 hectares. The first of these, Saltwells, was declared a local nature reserve in 1981, under the Council of Europe's 'Campaign for Urban Renaissance' (Fig. 6.15). The project is overseen by the Blackbrook Valley Group, which consists of local people, interest groups, local council officers, and is chaired by the Borough's Leisure Services Department.

A second aspect of some recent schemes is the linking together of open spaces by creating 'green ways' or 'green trails', allowing both people and wildlife to move more freely through the urban environment (Figs 6.16 and 6.17). The Nuneaton and Bedworth Borough Council (Warwickshire) has established a 'Your Green Track' project which is creating continuous green corridors as recreational and wildlife habitats. A key to its success has been a grant of money from central government (Department of the Environment) after the Borough was made a Derelict Land Clearance Area in 1982 (a designation given because of the extent of derelict land, which qualifies the area for special government funds, e.g. Derelict Land Grant). This has allowed the reclamation of disused quarries and railway lines.

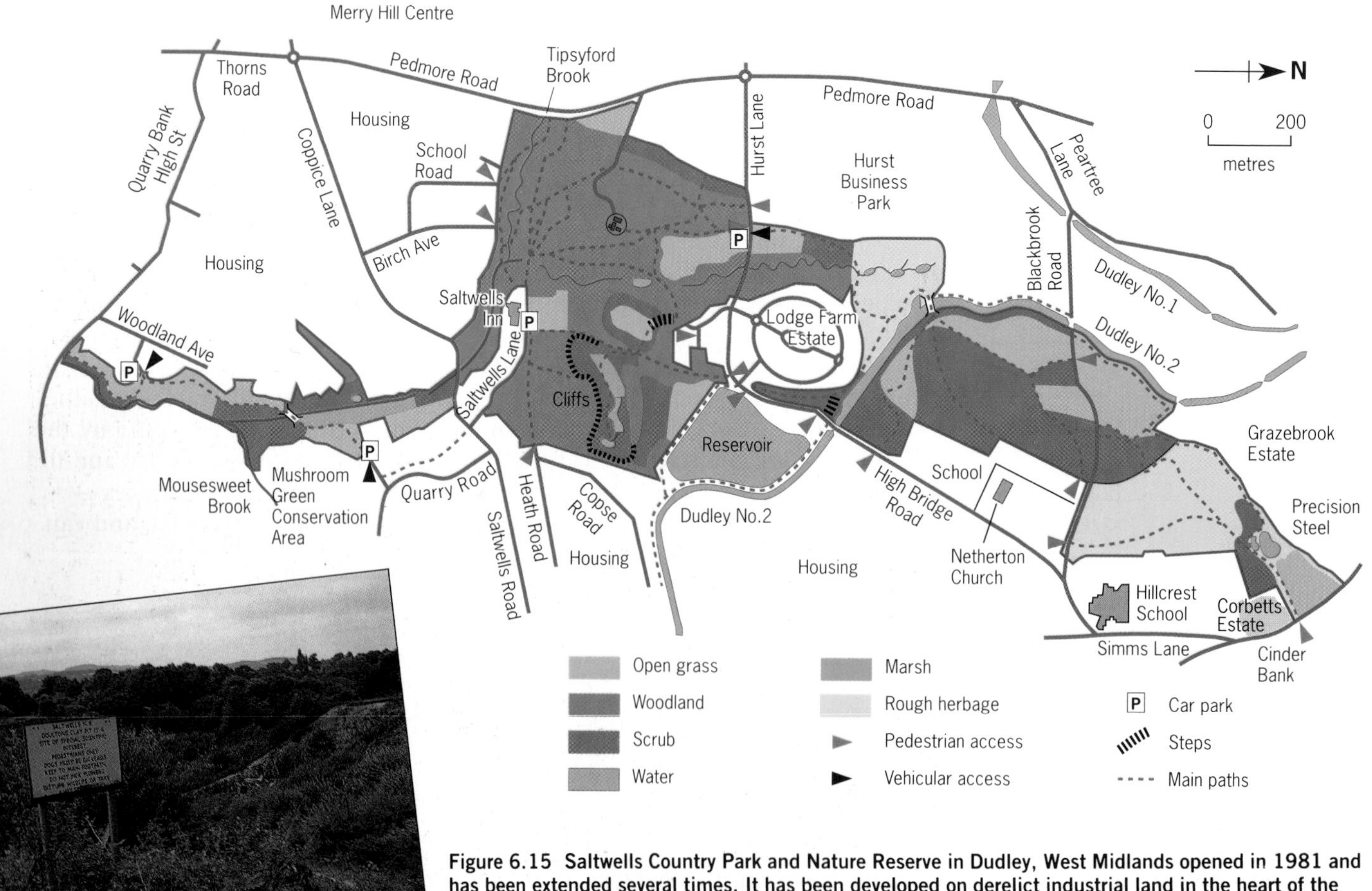

Figure 6.15 Saltwells Country Park and Nature Reserve in Dudley, West Midlands opened in 1981 and has been extended several times. It has been developed on derelict industrial land in the heart of the Black Country. Part of the site is on old clay pits, which can be seen in this photo. Notice the balance between conservation and recreation values – the vegetation is being encouraged to allow the recovery to a woodland ecosystem while still permitting recreational access

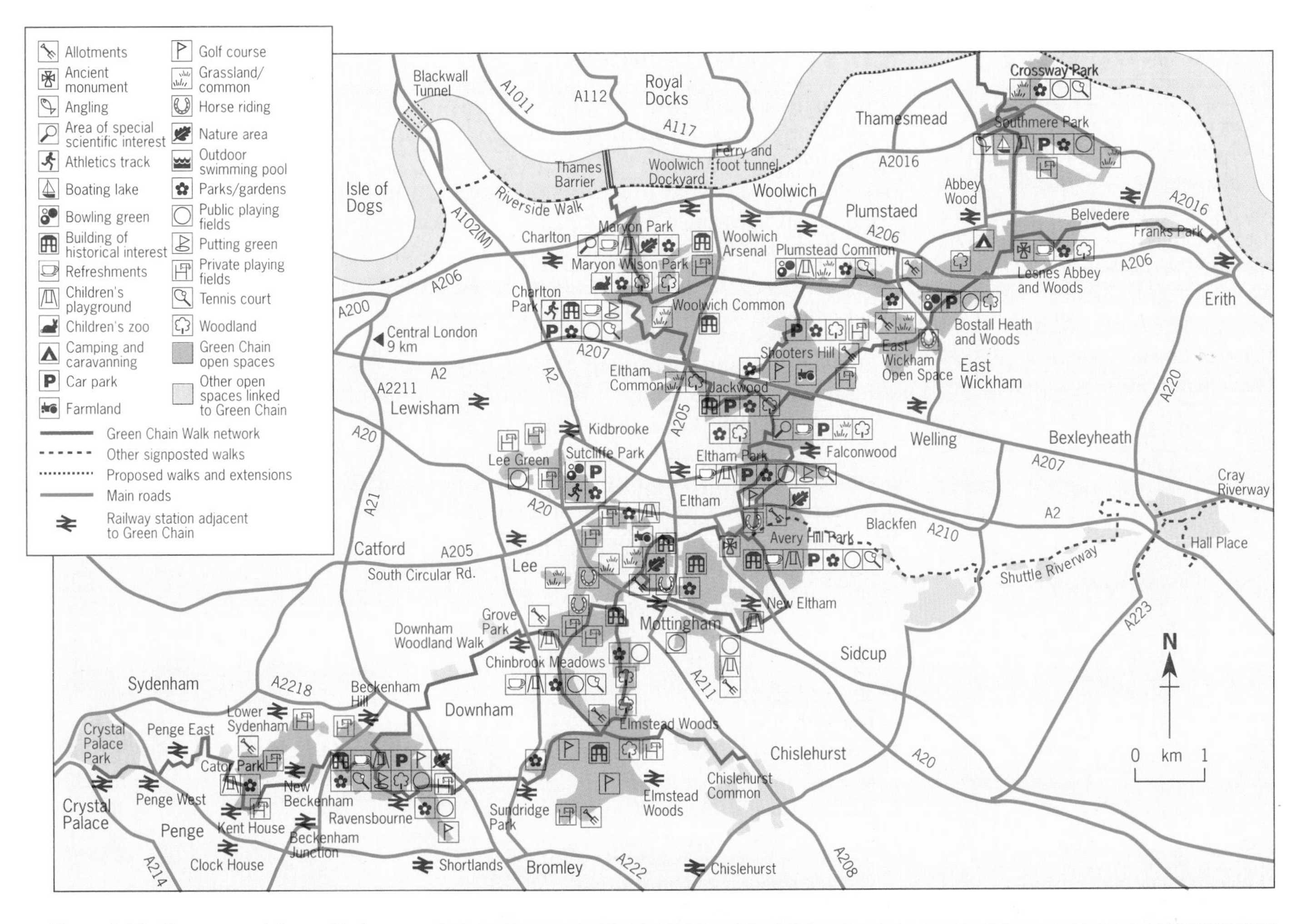

Figure 6.16 The proposed Green Chain for south-east London. This is a large-scale example of linking open spaces. It involves co-operation between several councils. Note the range of activities included

Figure 6.17 Aerial view of the Eltham area

?

20 Study Figure 6.17 and locate it on Figure 6.16. (Use a road atlas to help you pinpoint the major roads.)

Table 6.7 **Why we go swimming (*Source*: Sports Council, 1991)**

For enjoyment	43.5%
To keep fit and healthy	42%
For relaxation	16.5%
Just for something to do	7.5%
Because it is familiar	7%
For a physical challenge	6%
Because I'm good at it	4%
To escape from family pressures	4%
To escape from work pressures	3.5%
To develop a skill	3%
Other reason	11%

6.6 Swimming pools or leisure pools?

Look again at Table 3.4: the figures tell us that swimming is one of the most popular physical recreation activities for both males and females across the age range. A 1990 survey of leisure centres by the Sports Council found that over 50 per cent went to swim, and that six out of ten swimmers participated regularly at least once a week (Table 6.7). Many doctors recommend it as the best all-round health and fitness exercise. Local authorities have a long tradition of providing pools, which are found embedded in neighbourhoods in just about every town, and most people in the UK learn to swim during school swimming lessons in these local pools (Table 6.8).

However, 'going swimming' is changing. Participation has always ranged from serious training and competitive swimming to simply having fun in the water, and from beginners to experts. In the past, all types of swimming took place in traditional rectangular pools in often barn-like buildings, with perhaps a 'kiddies' pool'. Today we demand more from our pools: while serious swimmers, divers and learners under instruction still require traditional straight-sided pools, the fun-swimmers (the 'splashers') are attracted to 'leisure pools'. Older pools are losing their appeal and are expensive to maintain. Yet so often, they are easily accessible. Modern leisure pools are expensive and so are fewer in number (Fig.

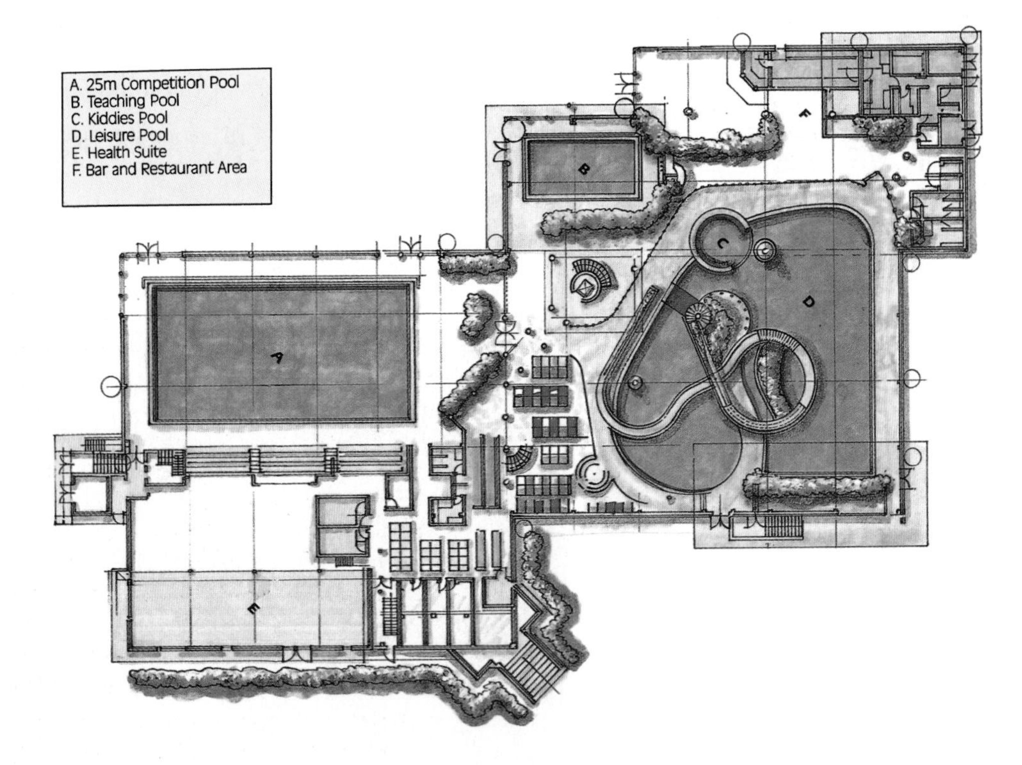

Figure 6.18 Mansfied Water Meadows Leisure Pool complex

Table 6.8 How much are facilities used? – swimming pools (*Source*: CIPFA, *Leisure Usage Statistics, 1990–91*, 1991)

Area	Conventional indoor pools				Indoor leisure pools			
	Average no. of pools	Ticket admissions ('000)	School admissions ('000)	Coaching lessons ('000)	Average no. of pools	Ticket admissions ('000)	School admissions ('000)	Coaching lessons ('000)
London Borough	3	350	92	50	1	222	41	23
Metropolitan District	6	514	163	88	1	298	4	40
Non-metropolitan District	8	168	36	18	1	183	20	11

Note: Figures are based on those authorities for which information is available. Not all local authorities returned statistics.

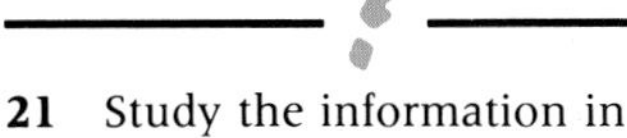

21 Study the information in Figure 6.19.

a Describe the trends in demand.
b Why are local authorities finding it difficult to meet the variety of demands?
c Why is the Amateur Swimming Association concerned about the growth of leisure pools, and what policy does this organisation favour?
d List the advantages and limitations of conventional pools and the leisure pool complexes.
e Write two brief reports:
- In support of giving priority to building and maintaining conventional pools;
- In support of spending on leisure pool complexes.

22 Essay: Outline the factors influencing the location of swimming pools and discuss why conventional pools and leisure pool complexes may have different locational patterns. (You will find it helpful to examine the provision of pools in your local town or city.)

6.18). This means that they may be widely spaced and less easily accessible. For conventional pools, 70 per cent of users travel less than 5km, but for leisure pools the figure is less than 60 per cent. People may have to travel farther to leisure pools, but seem willing to do so. The extracts in Figure 6.19 illustrate the key trends, but also highlight some of the problems and issues.

In some cases, leisure pools have directly replaced conventional pools and their development has been associated with the closure of other pools. On the other hand a leisure pool can exist alongside existing conventional pools, providing extra water space for conventional swimmers and club use. Such an approach may increase overall participation levels.

Issues

With the heavy emphasis on leisure pools, facilities for the competitive swimmer and the teaching of swimming could be falling by the wayside. The Amateur Swimming Association (ASA) is aware of free-form leisure pools, where the accent is upon enjoyment and thrills, but questions their capability to cope with the demand from the serious swimmer. . . . They believe that the teaching of swimming is better conducted in traditionally shaped pools. In some free-form leisure pools there are no straight edges where a class and teacher can assemble for a lesson. . . . The addition of leisure equipment into traditional pools means that fewer and fewer pools are suitable for the teaching of swimming.

Trends

For swimming, flexibility, fun and fitness characterise the spirit of the new decade. An increasing trend over the past few years has been to design pools for more flexible use. The Suncentre at Rhyl, which opened in 1980 with all pools dedicated to fun, summed up a decade of relatively affluent lifestyles. Leisure pools boomed in the 1980s, and have undoubtedly been partly responsible for the increase in swimming amongst women.

Changing provision is illustrated by the recently opened Ponds Forge complex in Sheffield. The three pools in this international facility – a diving pool, warm-up pool, and what is claimed to be the most versatile 50m pool in the world – allow maximum flexibility. Although the complex has been designed for world class competition, the warm-up pool is located within a 650sq.m water area which has a wave machine, a river ride and twin 90m long flumes. The facility combines a high level performance pool with fun-based leisure pools within the same complex.

Water play does not appeal to all, and providers have become increasingly aware of the need to provide separately for more 'athletic' swimming. Ponds Forge is one way to achieve this flexibility. . . . Flexibility can also be achieved by a mix of facilities within a district. 'Playing' in the water will maintain its appeal, but facilities that provide only for play may find it increasingly difficult to be cost effective.

Social welfare objectives are high among councils' reasons for providing swimming facilities, but they are increasingly attempting to balance such objectives against the need to improve their income–expenditure balance.

Profitability seems to depend not so much on type of pool as on pricing structures and programming of sessions. The need to control costs, and the deterioration of ageing swimming pools, indicate that modernisation and refurbishment programmes will predominate over replacement in the next decade.

Figure 6.19 Issues and trends in swimming pool provision (*Source*: Standeven, 1991)

The Amateur Swimming Association have published some guidelines on leisure pools:

1 Where a real need exists, a leisure pool can be a great asset to an area.

2 Leisure pools must supplement conventional pools and not substitute or replace them.

3 Key questions to be asked about leisure pools:
True running costs?
Can they meet the needs of the teaching of swimming?
What effect will they have on conventional pools in the area?

4 When a leisure pool is to replace an existing conventional pool, alternatives should be considered:
Retain the existing pool and run it through a local club;
Provide a leisurised conventional pool, e.g. add flumes, fountains etc.;
Provide a traditional rectangular pool in addition to the free form pool, preferably in a separate room.

6.7 Review: public and private provision

Figure 6.20 identifies leisure trends and a growing market segment. The information raises questions for leisure providers in the private and **public sectors**. The questions (23, 24) ask you to evaluate this review from the viewpoint of each sector. You should use your understandings gained from Chapters 4, 5 and 6 when making your decisions and writing the reports.

?

23 You are a research officer in an urban local authority Leisure Services department. Your Director has asked you for a brief report on what this review might mean for her department. She wants your report to include answers to these questions:
a What are the main characteristics and trends in the leisure market and in the behaviour identified?
b What type of leisure facilities should we be providing for this market?
c Why should we be providing for this market segment?
d Where should such facilities be located (e.g. dispersed, small-scale facilities, or single, high-grade facilities)?
e What should our pricing policy be? What *other* groups of our community should we hope to attract, and how would location and pricing affect their participation?

24 You are the market research officer for a large **commercial** leisure development company. The company is interested in a major **investment** in a coastal city with a population of 100 000, where it wants to build a 50-hectare marina-based development with associated retail and service facilities. Your Marketing Director wants a brief report to answer three key questions:
a Is the market segment outlined in the review likely to be a profitable one, and why?
b What type of facilities/activities/experiences/services should we be providing for this type of consumer?
c Why might the local authority be interested in supporting us?

25a Design a fieldwork exercise for a local park to test one of the following hypotheses:
- Urban park use varies in volume and character during the day.
- Weekday use of urban parks is different from weekend use.
- Groups vary in the parts of an urban park they use, according to their interests and activities.

b Carry out your survey for a selected urban park. (If time permits, or it is a group project, select two parks in contrasting locations.)

The impact of demographic change and emphasis on HEALTH

AS IT AGES, so the population structure is shifting. More attention is being paid to those in middle years and early old age who are also affluent. These groups have become used to ever rising standards and increased apparent choice, even if this is a choice between similar products. They are more concerned with finding an opportunity or product which meets their needs than with worrying about who the provider might be. These consumers are sophisticated in their understanding of differences between what is available, and have become more adept at weighing up value for money between different provision. They are able to influence provision through market choice and as they represent a large proportion of the spending population, their potential impact on provision is considerable.

The diversity and variety of experience they seek reflects the range of opportunities of which they are made aware. The increasing segmentation of the markets seeks to ensure that the affluent fast-moving leisure seeker is never bored, understimulated or guilty. The increasing emphasis on healthy living habits and new activities has encouraged the development of new and different supporting industries such as new foods, new drinks, equipment and clothing, which have used the benefits of new technology to improve quality and value for money. Undoubtedly, the development of hundreds of new indoor sports facilities by local authorities during the 1970s and early 1980s stimulated economic development in commercial sector leisure-goods retailing. Research has underlined the gains made in health from even limited amounts of regular exercise, and all providers have been keen to emphasise the increased sense of well-being their clients will enjoy from using their facilities. Linking health and exercise to 'looking good and feeling great' has become a potent marketing slogan.

Figure 6.20 Identifying a growing market segment (*Source*: White, 1992)

Summary

- Local authorities (public sector) have been involved in leisure provision for over 100 years.
- Between 1945 and 1989 the public sector steadily broadened its provision for leisure, but since then the policy of CCT has begun to reduce this role.
- Public sector provision aims to improve the quality of life for *all* sections of society, i.e. social motives take priority over economic profit. This affects where facilities are located, what is provided, and who is encouraged to use them.
- Local authorities vary widely in their policies and spending on leisure, but all are finding it difficult to serve all sections of the community.
- An increasing number of facilities we use are provided by partnerships between the private and public sectors.

7 The great outdoors: countryside recreation

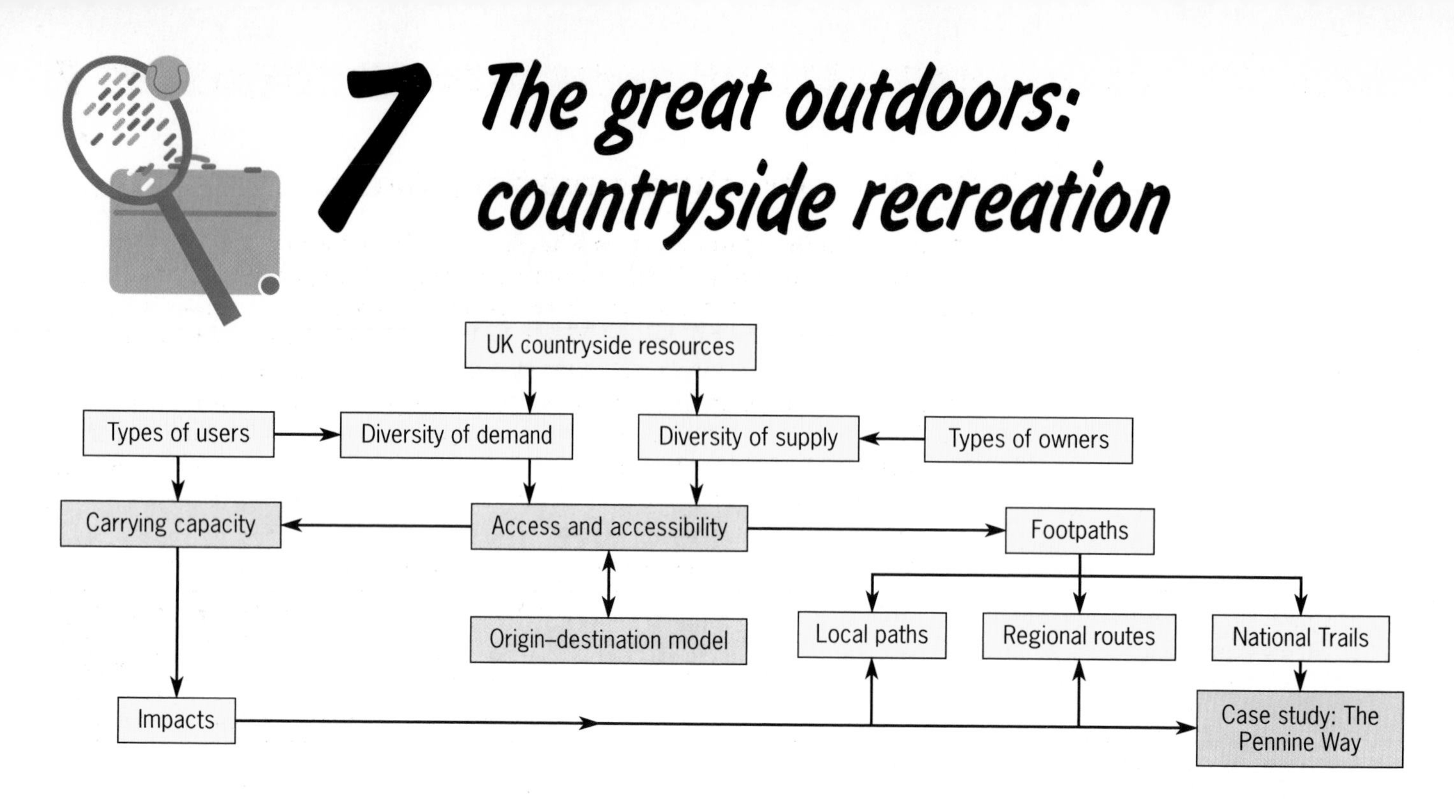

7.1 Introduction

'There were more than 1600 million trips to the countryside in 1990, an equivalent of more than 3.3 trips per person each four-week period throughout the year' (*Countryside*, May/June 1992). This makes countryside **recreation** the third most popular out-of-home **leisure** activity, after 'going out for a drink' and 'visiting friends and relatives'. The Countryside Commission estimate that on a typical summer weekend there are at least 18 million countryside recreational visits in England and Wales alone. These impressive figures signal to us that recreation and sport are putting the countryside under great pressure, but they also bring jobs and income to rural communities. (There is too, the growing market for **rural tourism** [Chapter 8]).

Outdoor recreation is a global phenomenon. The demands it makes on resources and the impacts it has give rise to growing environmental concerns. For instance, footpath erosion is as severe in parts of New Zealand or Alaska as it is in the Pennines (Fig. 7.1); off-road vehicles can penetrate fragile wilderness areas as easily in Malawi as in Scotland. In the USA, Yosemite National Park in California has been closed on several occasions because of air pollution, caused by motor vehicle emissions. At the Grand Canyon National Park in Arizona, to obtain a permit for back-country camping or hiking, you need to book at least a year in advance.

As you follow the various aspects of countryside recreation covered in this chapter and in Chapter 8, you will find it useful to keep in mind the 'concepts cascade' (Fig. 2.3). The materials will help you develop understandings of the following:

Figure 7.1 Footpath erosion and management in Tongariro National Park, New Zealand

1 The range of attractive resources, and the close relationship between **conservation** and the quality of outdoor leisure experiences.

2 The issues created by the diversity of **demands** for the outdoors.

3 The main decision-makers and the organisers of the **supply** of opportunities.

4 The complexity of decision-making in outdoor recreation issues.

5 The main economic, social and environmental benefits and costs of outdoor recreation.

6 Alternative strategies for sustaining high-quality outdoor experiences.

7.2 Who uses the United Kingdom countryside?

The participation figures given in Chapter 3 (Tables 3.3 and 3.4, p. 22) show that (*a*) the variety of activities is enormous, and (*b*) the percentage of people who take part in any one activity is relatively low. As over eight in every ten people in the UK use the countryside at some time, their needs vary widely: different activities require **access** to different resources and **facilities**. Even the same activity can be enjoyed at many different levels of skill, commitment and frequency (Fig. 7.2). This diversity is illustrated by the participation profiles (i.e. data about the people who take part) of the six activities in Table 7.1. Notice that the figures are percentages of those who took part, not of the total population. Remember too, that the behaviour patterns shown in these and other survey figures may reflect what opportunities were available rather than the ideal, preferred patterns of the people surveyed.

Table 7.1 Results from a survey of outdoor recreation in Scotland (*Source*: TRRU, 1987)

Activity type	a How often? (% of participants taking part within the past 4 weeks)	b Who with?* (% of participants) Alone	Family	Friends	Team/party	c How far? (Average distance travelled – miles)	d How long? (Average time spent away from home – hours)
Countryside and hill walking	55	18	56	26	7	28	6
Golf	62	14	23	64	2	13	5
Sailing	43	4	36	60	8	40	9
Mountaineering	25	10	24	34	35	104	17

*The % add up to more than 100% because some people responded in more than one category.

?

Study Table 7.1.

1 For each activity type in turn, write a brief descriptive participation profile. For example: '55 per cent of people taking part in "countryside and hill walking" have done so within the past month. This is mainly a family activity (56 per cent), although walking with friends is quite popular (26 per cent). People travel 28 miles on average, and typically spend 6 hours on the journey and activity.'

2a For each activity, list the necessary or desirable resources, facilities and equipment. Think about those resources etc. which are commonly available and **accessible**, and those which are widely spaced, might be far from population centres, or have special qualities. Remember too, that golf is a very popular and readily available sport in Scotland.
b Rank each activity, from the most expensive to the cheapest.

3 For each of the four variables (a–d), describe the differences between the activities, and suggest possible reasons for them. (Your answers to Question 2 may help you.) For example – why do some activities involve longer travel and time commitments?

4 What do the figures *not* tell us about the participants?

5 Choose any one activity type from Table 7.1. What factors might cause the participation profile to change in one or more of the four variables (a–d)?

Figure 7.2 Experts praise outdoor recreation as promoting mental and physical health, a sense of well-being, self-reliance, relaxation, companionship, challenge and heightened awareness of environmental values and issues

A Activity type

1 Walkers
About 40 per cent of the survey sample; most commonly middle-aged, employed, with above-average income and in social grade B; predominantly car owners and likely to be members of conservation and sporting organisations, e.g. National Trust and Ramblers Association; likely to have lived in or near the countryside for at least part of their lives.

2 Sports participants
Those who fish, ride, hunt, shoot, climb or take part in organised sports in the countryside, and who make up 10 per cent of the sample; have higher than average incomes, employment levels, and access to a car; more likely to be youngish, male and members of sports organisations. A distinct sub-group are the anglers, who are less likely to be affluent or to live in the countryside.

3 Informal recreationists
Approximately 50 per cent of the sample, whose use of the countryside is generally less strenuous than the other groups. Most popular activities are drives, picnics, strolls in the country and visits to historic buildings. Often known as the 'car-and-stroller' group, they are likely to live in larger cities, have lower incomes, be in social grades D–E, be relatively old and less likely to belong to conservation or sports organisations.

B Frequency of use

1 Frequent users
Visit the countryside at least once a week during the summer, are generally well informed about the countryside and tend to use familiar local territory; more likely to be in social grades A–C, be relatively affluent, employed, own a car and live in or near the countryside. Although they make up only 18 per cent of the population, they generate 68 per cent of all countryside recreation trips. Many walkers and sports participants fall into this category.

2 Occasional users
Use the countryside rarely in winter and perhaps twice a month during the summer; make up about 65 per cent of the population across a broad socio-economic spectrum and a wide range of interests.

3 Non-users
About 17 per cent of the population, and include those without interest as well as those for whom the countryside is inaccessible; more likely to be in social grades C–E, be unemployed, retired or housewives, live in larger cities and have low levels of car ownership.

C Values and attitudes

1 Aesthetic values
Place a high value on the countryside for its scenic beauty, tranquillity and unspoilt character. Such valued characteristics can be maintained only if access is in some way restricted, i.e. this category is essentially élitist and exclusionary, and includes some amenity and conservation groups.

2 Instrumental values
Those who see the countryside as resources to be used for their particular activities, and hence attempt to 'claim' resources for their own use, preferably exclusively. This exclusionary approach contains much potential for conflict through competition for the same resources.

3 Social values
Those who see the countryside as a place to be with their family and friends, or as an escape from urban environments. They tend to be more content with the more 'managed' sites such as country parks, and include the 'car-and-stroller' groups; they are not exclusionary and are generally tolerant of relatively high user densities.

Note: A guide to 'social grade':
- A = Top management, executives, senior professionals
- B = Middle management and professionals
- C = Skilled industrial and clerical workers
- D = Semi-skilled workers
- E = Unskilled workers

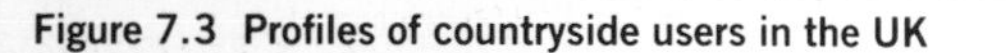

Figure 7.3 Profiles of countryside users in the UK

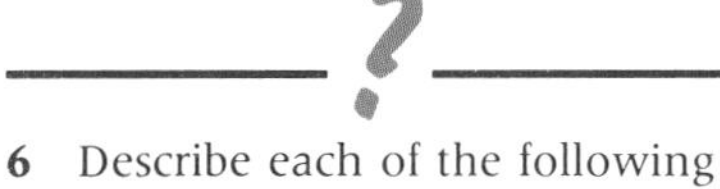

6 Describe each of the following in terms of the three categories in Figure 7.3:

a A family who drive out occasionally for picnics.

b A competitive orienteer.

c An angling club.

d Two friends who walk seriously most weekends.

7 Essay: With reference to Figure 7.3, outline how different values and attitudes towards the countryside can lead to conflicts between different users. Illustrate your answer by discussion of examples and suggest ways of reducing the conflicts.

Classifying countryside users

It may seem impossible to make sense of the chaotic diversity of use. However, the Countryside Commission has used the results of their 1984 National Countryside Recreation Survey to produce a classification of users, based on (*a*) activity types, (*b*) frequency of participation, (*c*) **values** and **attitudes** (Fig. 7.3). This classification is useful as a basis for making decisions about the provision of recreational and sporting opportunities, but it also illustrates how difficult making such decisions can be. For instance, not only do the user groups demand different resources, they also have differing attitudes and understandings about how the countryside should look and be used. As the old saying goes, 'You can't please all of the people, all of the time'! Notice in particular that many interests are 'exclusionary' or even elitist: users try to claim preference and priority over desired resources. Anglers try to exclude canoeists from stretches of river, walkers object to mountain-bikers on footpaths, etc.

7.3 Ownership and access

A variety of institutions and individuals in the UK own the resources and control access to leisure experiences. They have a powerful impact on our use of these resources.

Access and accessibility

Whether you can enjoy a relaxing picnic in a field, exhaust yourself orienteering through woods, pit your wits against a fish in a stream, or test your stamina at an open-air rock concert, depends above all upon who owns the resources to which you need access – field, forest, water, parkland. Of course, there are other factors such as your own interests, what money you have, how mobile you are, where you live, and so on, but essentially you rely on land and water space being made available to you. That is, you need *access*, and the resources need to be *accessible* to you. It is important to distinguish between these two concepts (Fig. 7.4).

Figure 7.4 The access and accessibility spectrum

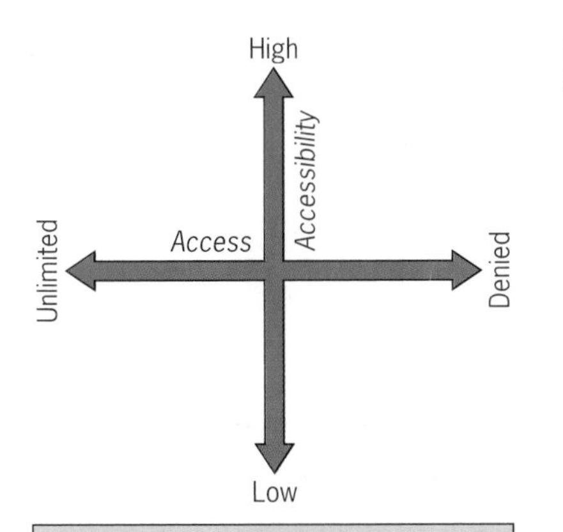

Access refers to certain rights of approach or entry and use. These rights may be defined by law (*de jure*) or by convention and common usage (*de facto*), i.e. are you allowed in and on what terms?

Accessibility refers to the extent to which these rights can be exercised at a particular time by an individual or group, i.e. whether you are aware of access rights and whether you can afford to enter or can get there.

Figure 7.5 Newspaper report on the army acquiring more and more land in the countryside (*Source*: *Guardian*, 2 February 1993)

Smaller army needs more firing ranges

THE MINISTRY of Defence is poised to acquire more countryside and fire additional weapons in national parks, despite a 45,000 reduction in the strength of the armed forces.

The MoD owns more than 226,000 hectares of countryside but its need is increasing because of the loss of German training grounds and the return of 32,000 troops from Germany.

Another 450 hectares – a hectare equals 2.47 acres – was acquired last year for £3.8 million to extend the army's 37,000 hectares on Salisbury Plain in Wiltshire.

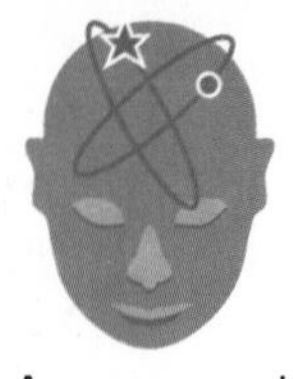

Access and accessibility

Over 80 per cent of the UK is still privately owned. At least 35 per cent is under the control of owner-occupier farmers, with 300 titled families owning another 30 per cent. Nine major institutions control a further 10 per cent (Table 7.2). These are the key 'gatekeepers' and decision-makers in the access game. In turn they have a crucial influence upon how conservation works in the British countryside. Owners vary in their policy towards access across the spectrum of Figure 7.4: from permitting maximum access and thereby reducing tensions, to permitting minimal access and so heightening the potential for tension and conflict (Fig. 7.5). Imagine the diagram in Figure 7.6 as an elastic sheet, with the four major 'actors' pulling at the corners: whoever has the most powerful pull dominates the character of access to countryside resources. The relative pulling powers vary over time (Fig. 7.7).

Table 7.2 Major institutional owners of the countryside

Forestry Commission	1.2 million ha
Ministry of Defence	230 000ha
National Trust (England and Wales)	216 000ha
Crown Estates	109 000ha
British Coal	72 000ha
Church of England Commissioners	70 000ha
Duchy of Cornwall (Prince of Wales)	52 000ha
National Trust for Scotland	40 000ha

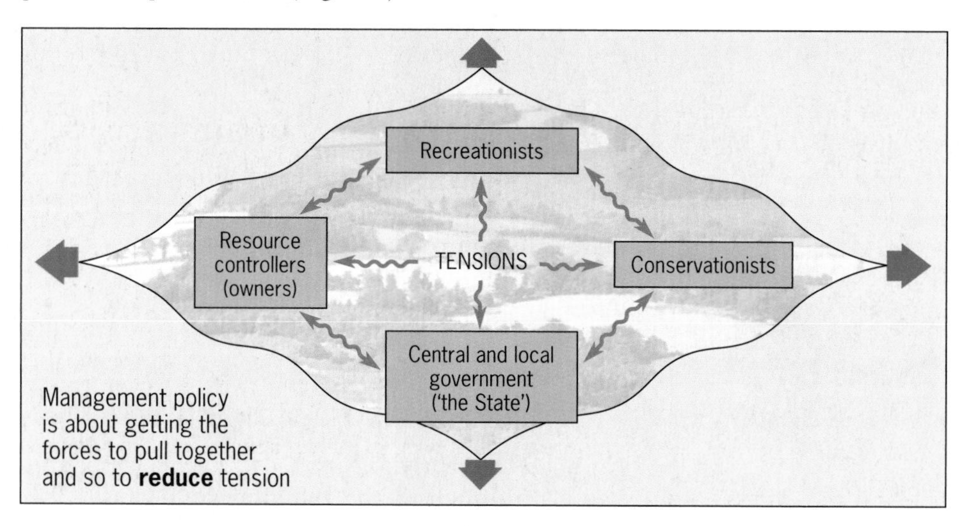

Figure 7.6 The tensions of access – 'Conflicts surrounding access frequently concern conflicting perceptions of the countryside and of what constitutes legitimate recreational and sporting activity' (Countryside Commission, 1986)

Figure 7.7 Ramblers Association access protest walk (*Source*: *Guardian*, 18 September 1989)

?

8 Illustrate the concepts of access and accessibility through an analysis of the use of a Country Park by the following people. (They all live in the same road, about 6km away from the park.)

a a young, healthy couple with a car

b a group of teenage friends who have bikes

c a wheelchair-bound elderly woman who does not have the regular use of a car

Moving through the countryside

The type of access you need depends upon what you want to do. Look again at the user types in Figure 7.3, this time in terms of access requirements: some demand access to a single location and a specific resource (e.g. climbing a certain rockface); others need access to a variety of sites and resources (e.g. walking trips).

The origin–destination model

The simplest spatial pattern of countryside use is shown in Figure 7.8a. We leave home and travel directly to a resource or facility – picnic site, country pub, beach, lake – enjoy the opportunities the attraction has to offer, then return home by the same route. In this model the travel component of the trip may not be seen as part of the leisure experience, but as a necessity to overcome the distance. Time, distance, and perhaps travel cost become factors affecting accessibility. For instance, driving for an hour with your sailboard to get to a lake may be a tedious chore and may influence your motivation to participate: 'Oh heck, it's too far, I don't think I'll bother.' In turn, reducing this travel element, and so increasing accessibility, may influence decisions about where to locate opportunities and facilities (i.e. to bring supply nearer to the demand). For instance, the building of climbing walls and dry ski-slopes in urban areas allows you to practise for 'the real thing' without having to travel far. In formal terms, the facility becomes **demand-based** rather than **supply-** or **resource-based**.

However, over one-half of all informal recreational trips to the countryside include the element of 'driving for pleasure'. As Figure 7.8b shows, with such trips there may or may not be a primary destination, and the outward and return legs may take different routes. Indeed for some trips and experiences the travel may be the primary pleasure (e.g. 'going out for a drive', cycling). County councils and the Countryside Commission have responded to this demand by signposting scenic routes and attractive sites (e.g. 'leisure drive', 'picnic site').

Figure 7.8 Two countryside-trip models

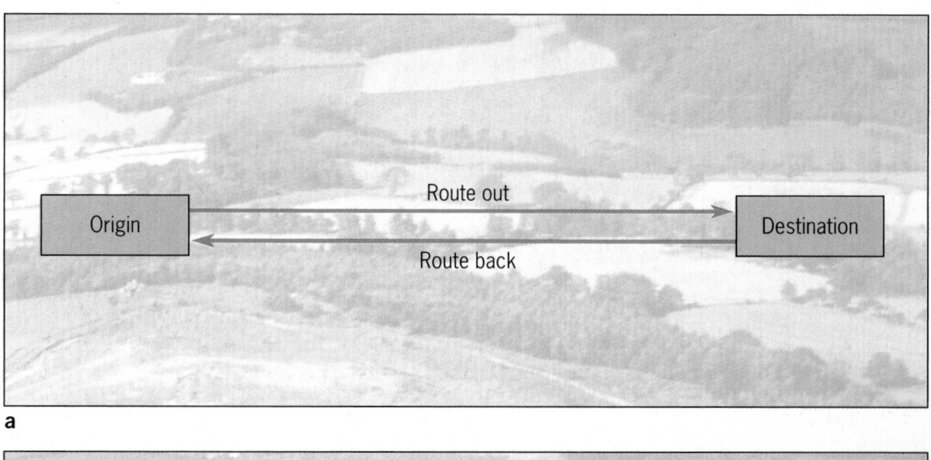

a

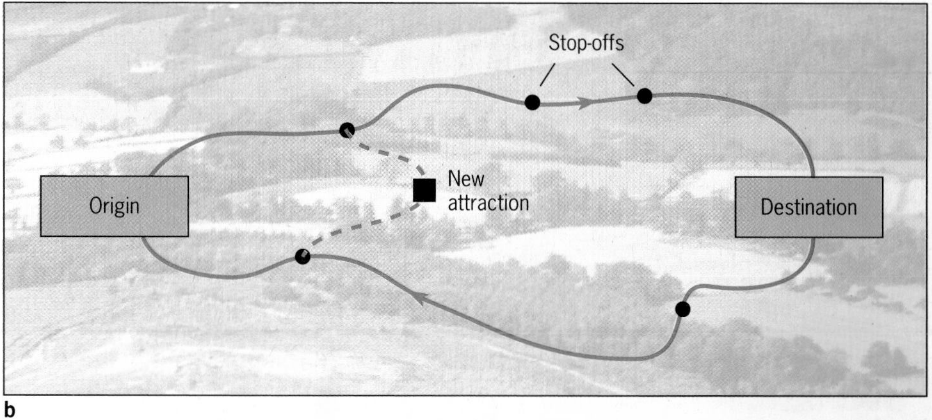

b

?

9 Use the models in Figure 7.8 as a basis to draw the route and stops of a countryside trip you plan to take. Use an OS map of the area. Describe briefly the resources/ facilities you want to use and the activities you want to do at each stop. Who will provide them and on what terms will you be permitted access (e.g. free, entrance fee etc.)? Approximately how far will you travel, how long will the trip take and what proportion will be the 'travel' element?

7.4 Footpaths and access

Figure 7.9 Kimbolton, Cambridgeshire. This gate obstructs a footpath right-of-way. The gate is bolted shut and fringed with barbed wire.

Footpaths form the main part of the 240 000km of public rights of way in the UK, and have been called 'the linchpin of rural recreation' (Shoard, 1987). We take them for granted, yet no other country has such a network, and their value lies in how they enable us to penetrate the privately owned countryside. They are a unique and precious resource, but are under threat from development pressures, changing farming techniques and private landowners reacting to the increased numbers of people using those paths that still exist. A 1990 survey showed that 40 000km of paths are out of use, and the Ramblers Association claim that five more paths are being removed each day (Fig. 7.9). Footpath access has, therefore, become a major issue in the countryside (Fig. 7.10).

Evolution of footpaths

The first thing to understand is that the footpath network developed to serve a quite different purpose from the way it is used today. Over hundreds of years, footpaths have evolved to fit the *economic* activities of rural communities. It was part of everyday life for people to walk from their homes in villages or on farms, to the fields, woods, ponds, streams, commons and moors. Thus footpaths became threaded through the rural landscape as part of a traditional economic and social system (Fig. 7.11).

The battlefield and weapons: guns, barbed wire, bulls and dogs

There are 134,00 miles of footpaths and bridleways in Britain. Few people realise, though, that every footpath, however humble, is legally regarded as the Queen's Highway and that any farmer obstructing a path with barbed wire is as guilty of an offence as if he dug up a motorway to grow potatoes.

These facts I learn from Ken Ward, a passionate believer in the pleasures of exploring the country on foot, as we plod across a field of beans somewhere in Oxfordshire.

'The only way you'd know this is a footpath is from my map,' shouts Ken, up to the knees in beans and jabbing them with his walking stick. 'These are illegally-grown beans. It wouldn't take the farmer ten minutes to plough the path back through them. The 1990 Rights Of Way Act states that the path should be one metre wide and clearly marked. It will be impossible to walk across this field when the beans are up, and faint-hearted walkers won't dare because they'll mistakenly think they're trespassing.'

He consults his map, fiddles with his compass and we trudge on until we reach thick brambles, nettles and a fence topped with barbed wire.

'This is an obstruction,' roars Ken, whipping out some secateurs from a trouser-leg pocket and snipping at the brambles. 'By law there should be a stile here. But no. We'll have to risk permanent injury in order to follow the path.'

THE BATTLE to preserve the rights of walkers and ramblers is forever becoming more ferocious and vicious.

It can involve shotguns, barriers of barbed wire, fierce dogs and bulls and tractors used in fields to harass people.

In Ken Ward's years of wandering the countryside he has frequently met the wrath of landowners and farmers obstructing the public footpaths through their property although, by right, every pathway is the Queen's Highway.

'A few years ago I was on a footpath tour of the Cotswolds. We were following the footpath through a wood, but it vanished under bracken. There were no signposts, so we made our way the best we could. We came into a field and set out in the direction marked by our map.

'Suddenly, we heard a tractor tearing towards us, with the farmer at the wheel shouting and waving. We asked him to show us the footpath and public stile so that we could continue our walk; he did so by nudging us along with his roaring and revving tractor.

'I've even been threatened by a gun, though guns can sometimes be less intimidating than a ferocious-looking dog.

The Open Spaces Society is Britain's oldest national conservation body, and one of the most active campaigners for protecting the environment. One of its long-running battles is with the National Trust at its Hidcote Manor Gardens in Gloucestershire.

According to Kate Ashbrook, secretary of the Society, a footpath through the gardens is blocked by tall hedges and flower beds. The NT made an unofficial diversion taking walkers outside the gardens, but after further objections from the Society, the NT has been pushed to apply for official permission to the Cotswold District Council and is currently awaiting a public inquiry.

'You would expect the National Trust to be exemplary in their behaviour, but they only want people who pay to go through their gardens,' says Kate.

Multi-millionaire Peter Gabriel, former Genesis singer, has a 240ft stretch of footpath through his recording studios estate in Box, Wiltshire. But hordes of fans have been treading the public path hoping to catch a glimpse of the star. Now Gabriel, with the backing of the county council, is applying to the Environment Department for permission to re-route the footpath and regain his privacy.

Figure 7.10 Newspaper report on the fight for footpaths (*Source*: *Daily Mail*, 22 June 1991) © *Daily Mail*/Solo

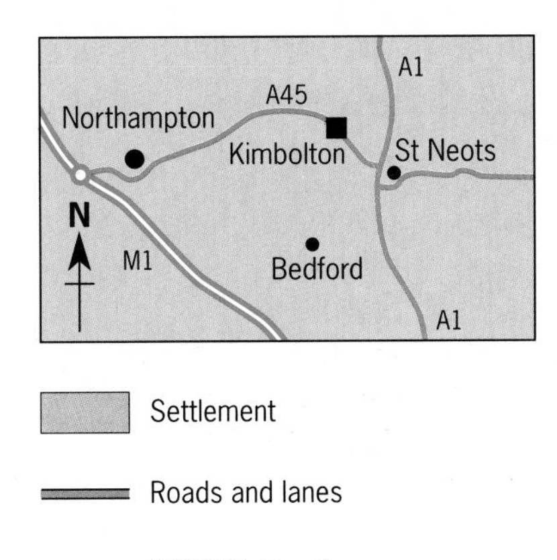

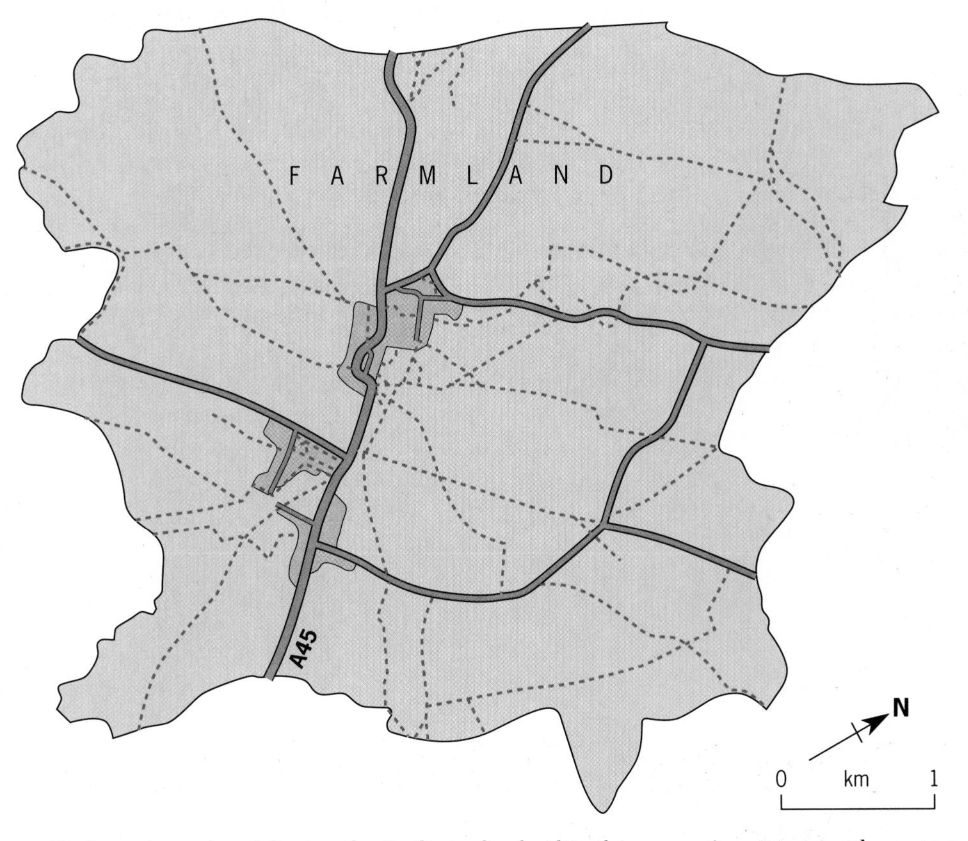

Settlement

Roads and lanes

1986 Rights of way

Figure 7.11 The footpath network of Kimbolton parish, Cambridgeshire. Notice how the footpaths radiate outwards from the nucleated settlement. A few link up with paths in neighbouring parishes (*Source*: definitive parish map)

?

10 Two important requirements of local paths are: first, that they should be continuous and, second, that there are opportunities for people to follow a loop, i.e. not out and back along the same stretch. Examine the footpaths of Kimbolton parish (Fig. 7.11) and on an overlay suggest ways of improving the network.

Today, the role of footpaths is that of a facility for *recreation*. We use them to exercise the dog, to relax, to enjoy peace and quiet etc. Keeping them accessible and usable is the responsibility of a county council highways department, working through local parish councils (Fig. 7.12). The central issue in path **management** arises from the fact that footpaths cross private land, and even run through farmyards and kitchen gardens. So, we need to clarify what is meant by a 'public right of way'(Table 7.3).

As footpath history goes back for centuries, there may be a lack of formal documentation, and 'rights' are uncertain. The present-day legal basis for the categories in Table 7.3 lies in the National Parks and Access to the Countryside Act 1949, the Countryside Act 1968, the Wildlife and Countryside Act 1981, and the Footpaths Act 1990. These Acts of Parliament allow formal status to be given, funding to be made available for management, and a system in which this management can happen.

Figure 7.12 Footpaths – who cares?

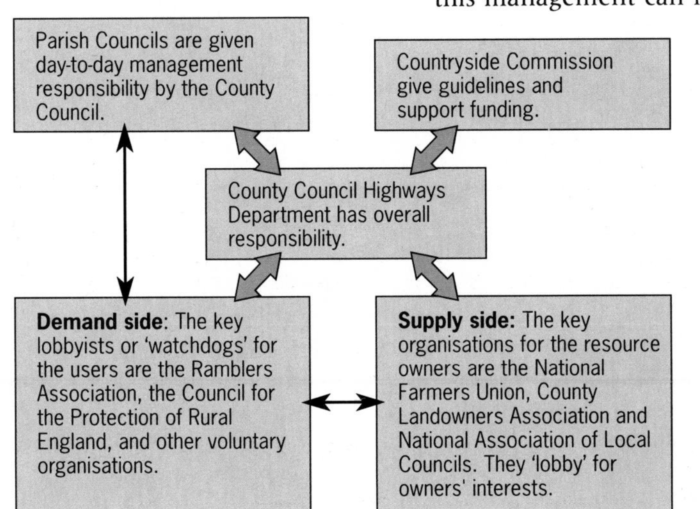

Table 7.3 Rights of way and access

Categories

Footpaths – use on foot only

Bridleways – usable on foot, horseback or bicycle

Byways – open to all traffic

Roads used as public paths (RUPP) – essentially lanes, but where pedestrians have certain rights

Access categories (look again at the definitions on page 63):

1 As of legal right (*de jure*): Use is safeguarded by a legal document

2 As of established right (*de facto*): No legal documentation, but 'customary' use is established

3 Permissive use: Agreement is reached with the landowner for use under certain conditions. These may be *de jure* or *de facto* agreements

4 Use without permission, ie. trespass

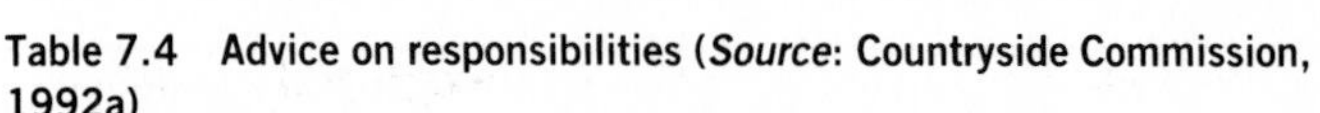

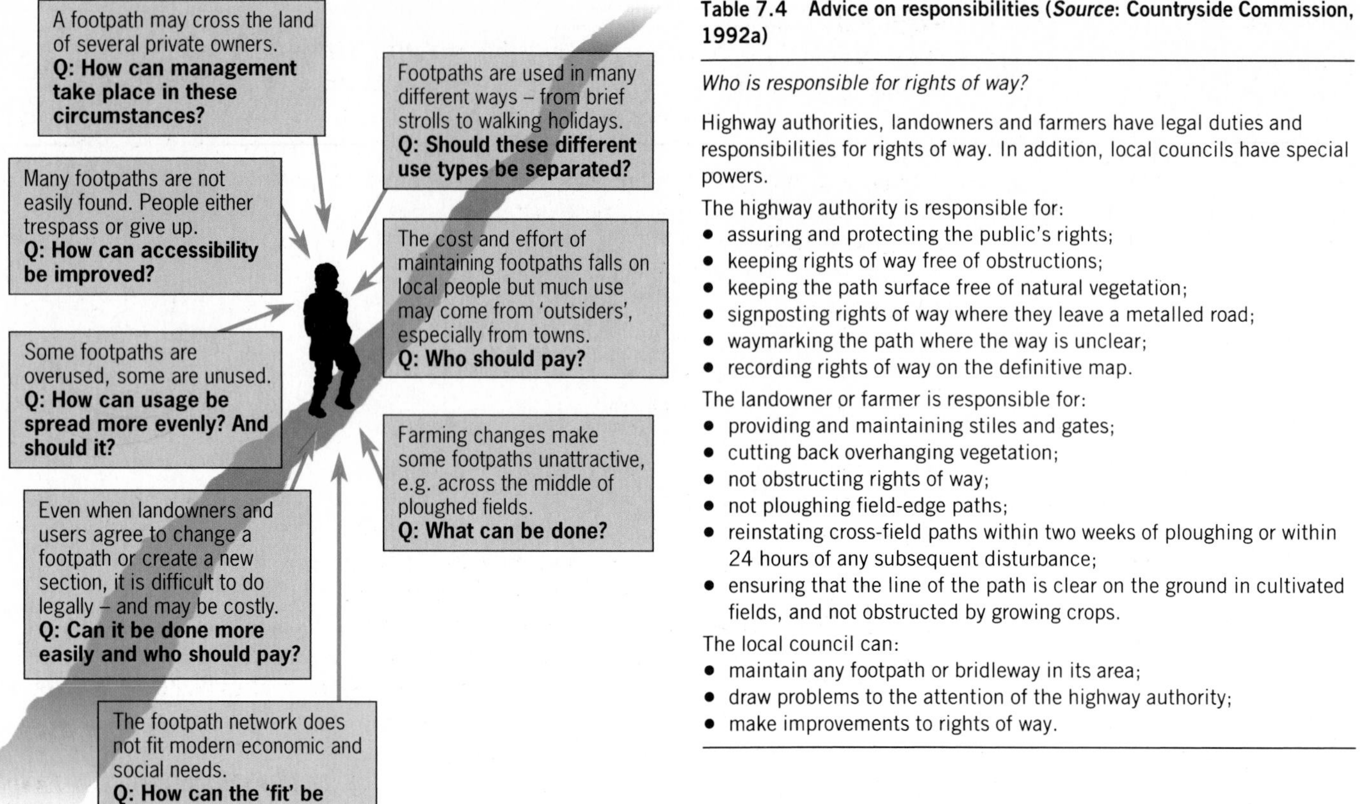

Figure 7.13 Issues in footpath management

Table 7.4 Advice on responsibilities (*Source*: Countryside Commission, 1992a)

Who is responsible for rights of way?

Highway authorities, landowners and farmers have legal duties and responsibilities for rights of way. In addition, local councils have special powers.

The highway authority is responsible for:
- assuring and protecting the public's rights;
- keeping rights of way free of obstructions;
- keeping the path surface free of natural vegetation;
- signposting rights of way where they leave a metalled road;
- waymarking the path where the way is unclear;
- recording rights of way on the definitive map.

The landowner or farmer is responsible for:
- providing and maintaining stiles and gates;
- cutting back overhanging vegetation;
- not obstructing rights of way;
- not ploughing field-edge paths;
- reinstating cross-field paths within two weeks of ploughing or within 24 hours of any subsequent disturbance;
- ensuring that the line of the path is clear on the ground in cultivated fields, and not obstructed by growing crops.

The local council can:
- maintain any footpath or bridleway in its area;
- draw problems to the attention of the highway authority;
- make improvements to rights of way.

Although footpaths etc. are marked on OS maps, if you wish to find out about public rights of way at parish level, you need to refer to what is called the 'definitive map'. This may be kept by the district council or by the parish council (in many parishes, one council member is designated as 'footpaths officer'). The definitive map is the basic document around which issues between interest groups can be discussed and management plans developed (e.g. signposting, stiles, change of route etc.). Thus the Kimbolton paths in Figure 7.11 were plotted from the definitive map for the parish.

Management policies for footpaths

The difficulties of maintaining, modifying and managing the footpath network are made clear in Figure 7.13. In an effort to deal with all these variables, the Countryside Commission bases its management strategy upon a three-tier hierarchy: 'local paths' at parish level, 'regional routes' and 'National Trails'.

Local paths

In 1992 the government announced its 'Action for the Countryside' policy, which will channel £13 million through the Countryside Commission for paths, hedges and landscape improvement schemes, largely at local level. A central element of the policy is the 'Parish Paths Partnership Scheme', which is to receive £3.75 million over the 1992–5 period. The scheme offers grants to parish councils or local groups for surveying and improving paths. The parishes can get advice from Parish Path Liaison Officers appointed by county highways departments (Table 7.4). The aim is that by 1995 there will be 1350 parishes involved, managing 24 000km of rights of way. Notice that the emphasis is placed upon giving local people the opportunity and responsibility for managing their leisure environment. In the first year, 1992–3, both urban and rural councils became involved. The scheme builds upon initiatives already begun by a number of counties and sponsorship schemes by private companies (e.g. the ESSO Community Footpath Scheme).

Regional routes

These are medium-length routes which wind through scenically attractive areas. Generally 15–150km long, they have been assembled from existing stretches of rights of way, and may link up **Country Parks** and forest walks. One of the longer routes is the Cotswold Way, which crosses the attractive Cotswold Hills between Bath and Chipping Campden. Equally important are routes near to large urban centres, such as the North Worcestershire Path which runs along the south-west fringes of the West Midlands conurbation, passing through several Country Parks on its way. Two new regional routes opened in 1992 are the 160km Icknield Way which links the Peddars Way in Norfolk with the Ridgeway in the Chilterns, and the 16km Colne Valley Way in Middlesex which links the Thames Path with the Grand Union Canal, making possible a long-distance walk from London to Birmingham.

National Trails

Footpaths are a valuable part of 'a day out in the country'. But what if we want to take a walking holiday, or challenge ourselves with some serious walking? For such activities longer, continuous routes are important. The origins of the long-distance footpath lie in the National Parks and Access to the Countryside Act 1949, and were developed further in the Countryside Act 1968. Finally, in 1988, their official title became 'National Trails'. By 1992 there were 10 designated National Trails in England and Wales, with a total length of over 2800km (Fig. 7.14). More are in the planning and development stages , such as the Thames Path, to open in 1994, which will follow the entire length of the River Thames, over 300km. (Scotland's paths retain the title 'Long Distance Path', e.g. the West Highland Path.)

The Countryside Act 1968 provides a clear definition of a National Trail, which can be used as a basis for decision-making, funding and management policy: a route where 'the public should be enabled to make extensive journeys on foot or on horseback or on a bicycle, not being a motor vehicle, and for which the whole or greater part of its length does not pass along roads mainly used by vehicles'. The first of these was the Pennine Way (Fig. 7.15).

Figure 7.14 The National Trails of England and Wales

Figure 7.15 'The Pennine Way was originally conceived as a challenging walk through fine upland scenery for all those suitably equipped to tackle it. The nature of the route has always demanded a reasonable degree of fitness, stamina and strong footwear' (Countryside Commission, 1992b)

These routes are generally over 100km long and so pass through land owned by all sorts of people, institutions and local councils. Thus, the Countryside Commission, which is responsible for establishing the routes, must negotiate separately with all these individuals and bodies. Attitudes vary widely – those who benefit economically (e.g. shopkeepers, publicans, bed-and-breakfast owners etc.) are likely to support it, while farmers, villagers etc. often oppose it strongly. It is hardly surprising therefore that, although National Trails largely follow existing rights of way, it can take up to 20 years to complete a continuous string of footpath.

Carrying capacity

Long-distance walkers tend to prefer to meet few other people, i.e. they enjoy low visitor densities. Along intensely used **honeypot** sections of a long-distance trail they meet all the other types of walker and quickly begin to feel 'crowded', and consequently less satisfied: such people are said to be 'crowding-sensitive'. For them, the social or **perceptual carrying capacity** of that section may be quickly exceeded. Family groups and friends enjoying a casual walk tend to be less sensitive to the presence of others, and are said to be 'crowding-tolerant' (Fig. 7.16).

Second, heavy visitor usage results in environmental damage such as erosion, litter, as well as noise pollution. In such instances, the **environmental carrying capacity** is being exceeded.

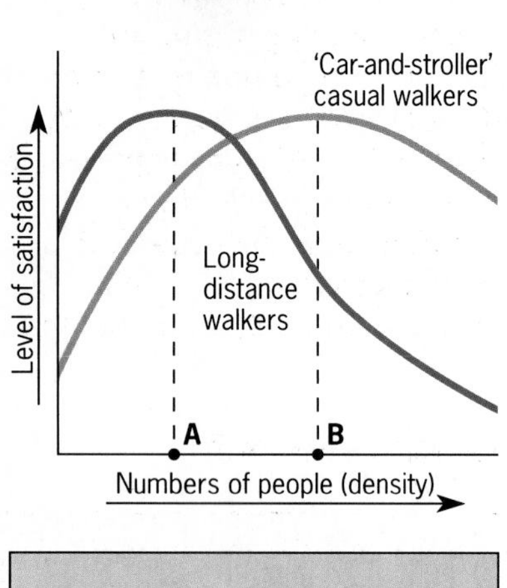

A = Density at which long-distance walkers begin to feel 'crowded'

B = Density at which casual walkers begin to feel 'crowded'

Figure 7.16 When do you begin to feel crowded?

Figure 7.17 Visitors to the Peak District National Park on a Bank Holiday Sunday

Other facilities, such as leisure centres, have a **physical carrying capacity** (see Chapter 5, p. 39), which is the maximum number of people that can use the squash courts etc. at any one time. Their **throughput capacity** is the maximum number of people per booking period multiplied by the total number of booking periods. Car parks too, have a physical carrying capacity.

Perceptual and environmental carrying capacity, however, are harder to measure, because they depend on people's perceptions and judgement.

One option to control numbers within the intended carrying capacity is pricing. A second option is to control the movements of vehicular traffic and people.

?

11 Suggest a technique to measure:
a the perceptual carrying capacity of a National Park (Fig. 7.17).
b the environmental carrying capacity of a National Park.
Give an example of how you might use each technique.

12 Describe a recent outdoor recreation trip when the carrying capacity of the environment or facilities you were using were being exceeded (note which *aspects* of carrying capacity were being exceeded and how you became aware of this).

The Pennine Way

Opened in 1965, the Pennine Way was the first National Trail (then known as a 'long-distance route'). It runs north–south along the length of the Pennines for 402km from the Scottish Borders to Derbyshire (Fig. 7.14). It winds along mountain ridges, across open moors, through forests and river valleys, but the central idea is one of *challenge* (Fig. 7.15).

The Pennine Way is the best known and most used of all the National Trails, and there has been growing concern about erosion and crowding along some sections in the summer, especially in the south. However, this popularity also brings income and jobs to communities along and near to the Pennine Way. In order to find out who uses the path, how much they spend, and what they spend money on, a survey was carried out between April and October 1990 at a number of points along the route. The patterns of usage are summarised in Figure 7.18.

One important finding is that the trail is used in a variety of ways. Two main user groups are identified: long-distance walkers, and day walkers. Each of these groups is then divided into sub-groups.

?

13 Surveys of other National Trails have made similar findings to the Pennine Way survey. Use the information in Figure 7.18 and the method in Question 1 to write profile descriptions of the two user categories of National Trails.

This is useful information because each of the groups and sub-groups has distinct needs and motivations, makes different impacts and has different spending patterns. An equally important finding of the survey is that the levels of usage are distributed unevenly along the trail. This distribution is determined largely by the location of (*a*) access points and (*b*) key attractions such as waterfalls, viewpoints etc. From this finding it is possible to propose a general model which states that it is around these accessible and attractive 'honeypots' that problems of management are most likely to occur (Fig. 7.19) .

Figure 7.18 Use of Pennine Way, April–October 1990

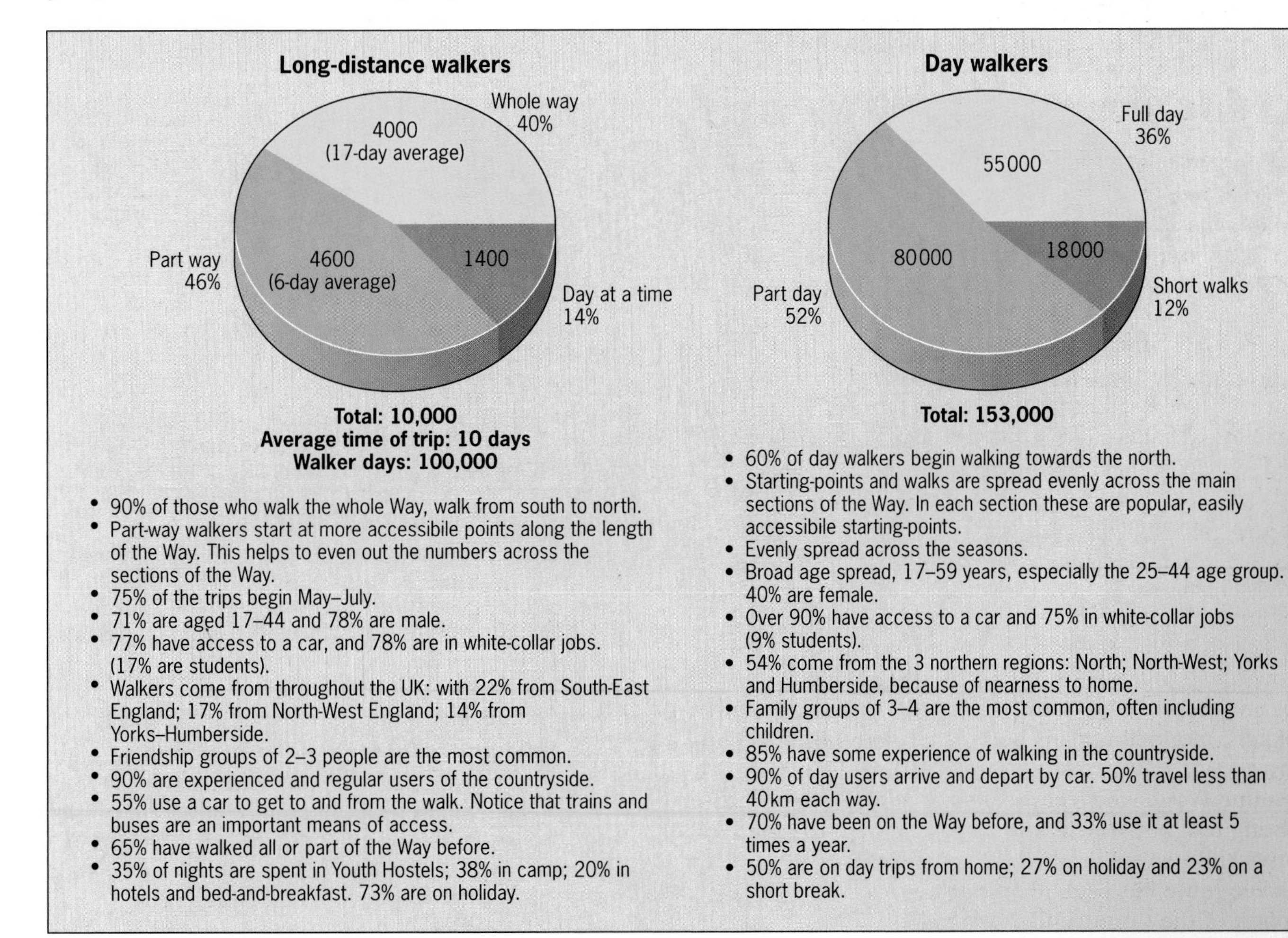

The Pennine Way

Impact and erosion

Levels of impact and erosion are not determined solely by numbers of walkers. It is true that along the Pennine Way the two most seriously eroded sections are also among the most popular: Edale to Kinder Scout (A in Figure 7.14) and across the flanks of Pen-y-Ghent (B in Figure 7.14). The crucial factor is, however, the fragile nature of the surface materials. These are peat bog areas, where the mat of surface vegetation is easily broken up by walkers' boots. Once exposed, the soft peat is very susceptible to erosion during rainstorms and snowmelt periods. Walkers continue to churn up the peat, erosion accelerates, and, as walkers detour around these quagmires, they steadily expand the eroded, boggy surfaces, which can exceed 20m in width. Along other stretches of the trail, where the surface is more resilient (i.e. resistant to impact), the carrying capacity is much higher. Good examples are the better-drained areas crossing limestone and sandstone without a peat blanket (e.g. over Cross Fell).

Controlling erosion

Both of the seriously eroded sections of the trail are in **National Parks** (Peak District and Yorkshire Dales), and since 1988 a series of projects, which will finally cost over £2 million, has been in progress over at least 60km of the trail. Their aim is to control erosion and increase the carrying capacity of the eroded, intensively used sections of the trail. There is general agreement that this is a 'good thing', but much disagreement about how it should be done, especially inside National Parks. The ideal is to retain the 'naturalness' of the Pennine Way, and use natural materials such as local stone for the path surface, or perhaps wooden logs laid across the peat. However, because of their lower cost, ease of laying and durability, a variety of plastics and aggregates have been tried – even tarmac. Critics claim that such artificial surfaces lower both the quality of the environment and the experience of the walkers (Fig. 7.20).

A radical solution?

Despite such efforts to reduce erosion, the pressures on the Pennine Way continue to mount, and it has become known, half jokingly, as 'the M25' of National Trails! Not only do more walkers want to use it, but also pony trekkers, mountain bikers and trail bike enthusiasts. The most radical solution is the proposal for a second 'Pennine Way', which runs roughly parallel to the existing trail but which is in fact a bridleway usable by horses and two-wheeled vehicles, as well as walkers. A possible route has been identified and has the general support of the Countryside Commission.

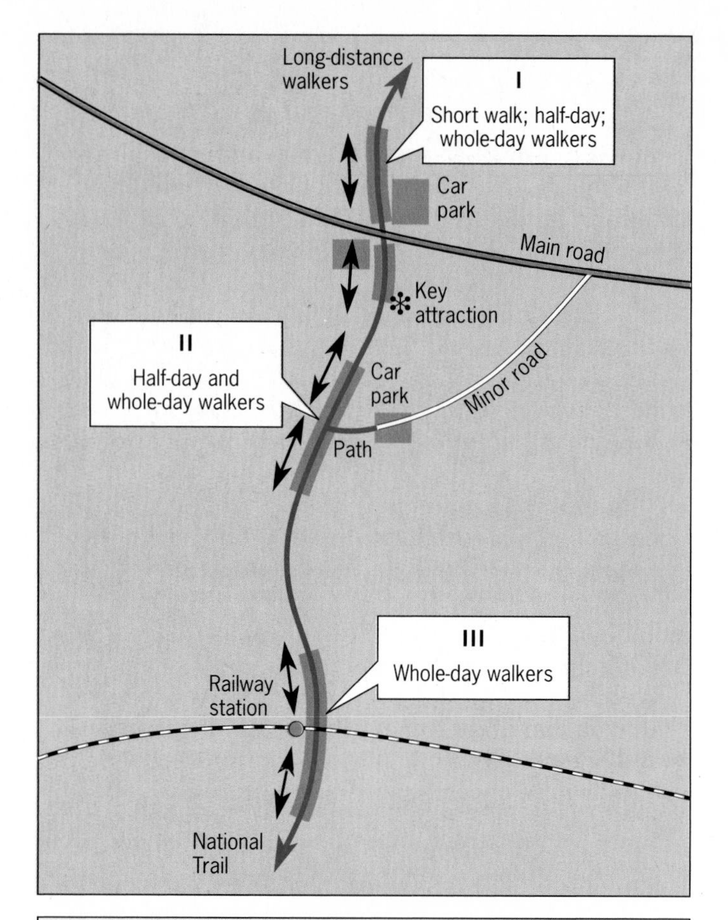

I A mingling of all walker types, and likelihood of greatest use and impacts. 'Car-and-stroller' visitors venture as far as the 'key attraction', stay a short while, perhaps picnic, then drive off. They use the locality differently from more serious walkers, who move through with only brief stops. Main user concentrations are within 1 km of the access point.

II Walkers must leave their vehicles some way from the trail and approach it on foot before fanning out for up to 10km in either direction. Walker densities are lower and visitor types less varied than at access point **I**.

III These are full-day walkers, arriving by a morning train and leaving in the evening. The train times limit access and so the number and type of visitor. They are usually serious walkers who fan out at fairly low densities for up to 15km, thus the impacts around the access point are not severe.

In general, impacts and potential conflicts decline from **I** to **III**.

Figure 7.19 Model of usage patterns along a National Trail

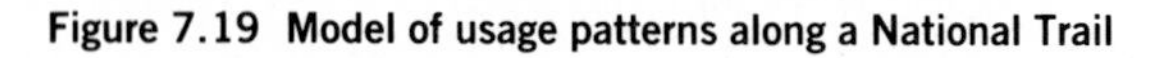

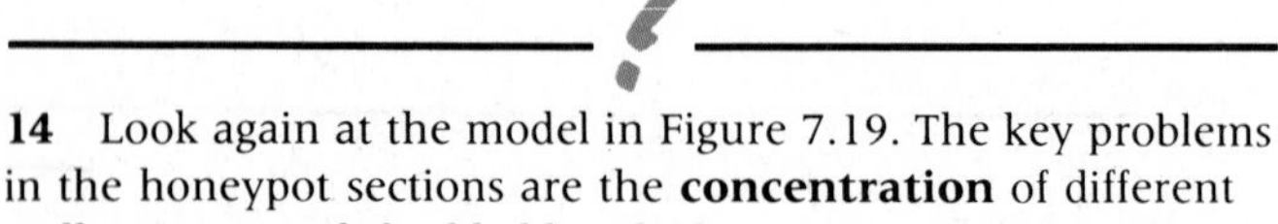

14 Look again at the model in Figure 7.19. The key problems in the honeypot sections are the **concentration** of different walker types and the likelihood of erosion. Suggest methods:

a for reducing the level of concentration and mixing of the walker types.

b for controlling erosion.

Major airlift to save trail

Lancashire mill flagstones were airlifted to four problem sites along the Pennine Way in a determined effort to repair eroded parts of Britain's famous long-distance trail.

A helicopter used self-emptying steel tipper pallets to lower the recycled flagstones at strategic places on sites in Northumberland, Durham, Calderdale and the Peak National Park. The flagstones, from demolished cotton mills, were then put into position, creating traditional 'causeway paths'.

Almost 600 tonnes of flagstones were dropped: 300 tonnes along the Border Ridge near Blindburn in Northumberland National Park, 60 tonnes in Teesdale near Cauldron Snout and Bleabeck Force, 65 tonnes at Calderdale, near Longfield Common, and 135 tonnes in the Peak National Park near Bleaklow.

The airlift will lead to the building of 3 km of path at an average cost of about £30 per metre, with the whole operation being funded by the Countryside Commission.

Figure 7.20 Report on airlift to save parts of the Pennine Way path (*Source*: *Countryside*, 1992)

15 At which of the three honeypots in Figure 7.19 (I, II, III) is the problem likely to be most difficult to solve? Why?

16 What additional information would be helpful in your response to question 14?

17 In your opinion what matters most – the 'naturalness' of the appearance of the Pennine Way or its carrying capacity, no matter how it looks?

18 Essay: Use the information in Figure 7.21 to assess the case for a management policy that supports:

a the provision of more money to maintain the trail.

b giving priority in the plan to long-distance walkers.

(The term 'assess' means you need to consider the benefits and costs and the possibilities of alternative policies.)

Figure 7.21 Economic impacts of the Pennine Way (*Source*: Countryside Commission, 1992b)

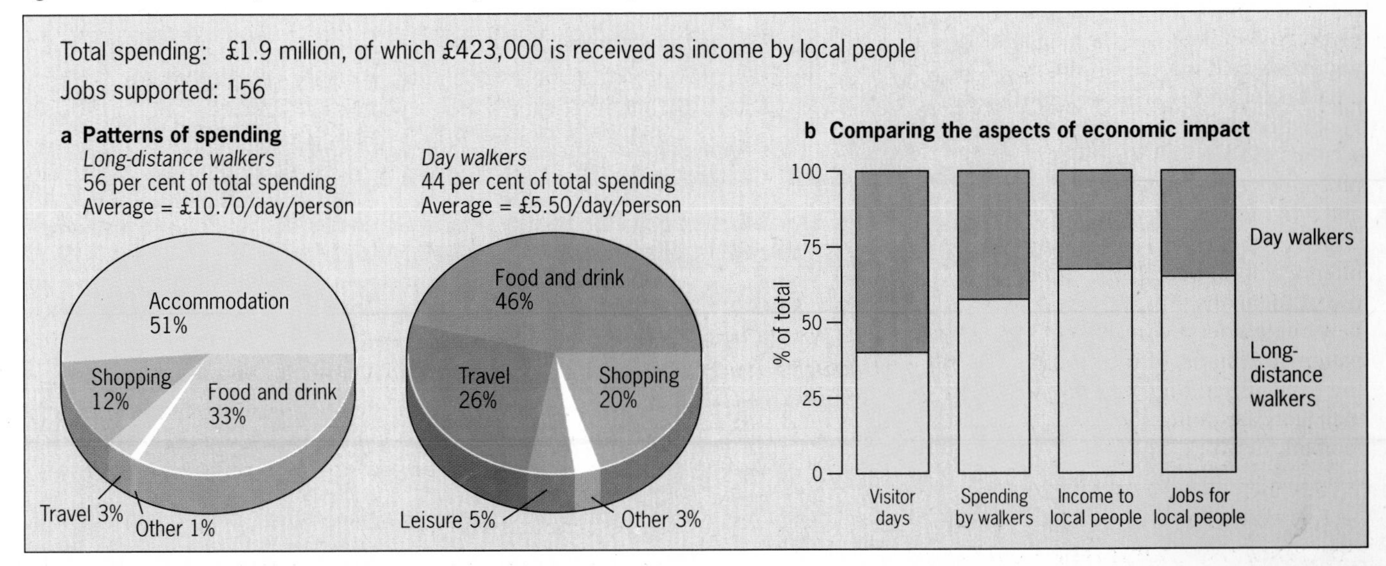

?

19 Use the information in Figure 7.22 to draw two diagrams:
a A flowchart to show the sequence of events.
b A spider diagram to show the links between the organisations taking part. In a different colour, add notes about the flows of money and equipment.
c Evaluate the strengths and weaknesses of each type of diagram.

20 Parish footpaths survey.
a Select a rural or urban fringe parish accessible to you.
b From the relevant 1:25 000 OS sheet, on tracing paper: draw the parish boundary; shade in the main settlement nucleus; and draw in the footpaths marked.
c Make copies of your base map.
d Carry out a field investigation into footpath status, using colours and symbols for the following classifications:

1 Path accessible and used

2 Path accessible but little sign of use

3 Line of marked path not visible

4 Obstruction across path

5 Signpost, stile, or other management input

6 Path visible but not marked on OS map

7 Signs of vandalism

e Locate the definitive map and compare it to both the OS map and your own field map. If possible, ask a parish councillor – preferably the Footpaths Officer – to show you sections of path that have had problems or experienced changes, and why. (If time permits, you may wish to either observe usage, or interview local people about their use of the paths.)
f Write a brief report on the pattern and status of the footpaths, the main issues, and what the local managers are doing about the footpath network.

Staffs move yields path dividend

Staffordshire County Council operated a rights of way maintenance agreement whereby participating parish councils were paid a fixed sum per mile of path.

But the take-up was poor, says Staffordshire's rights of way project officer, Alice Coleman. So a new 'community paths initiative' was devised.

'We wanted to encourage those wanting to do more than just keeping the same paths clear,' says Alice Coleman. Parish councils, and local groups or individuals working in consultation with their parish council, were invited to apply for grants of up to £2000 to carry out a paths survey, produce a local walks leaflet, organise a refurbishing project or do anything else that benefited walking or riding in their area.

The scheme galvanised parishes into action, so that 21 different projects shared a total of £9000 in 1991/92.

Typical of those taking advantage is the Gnosall parish council. When parish councillor Bob Southern took over as Gnosall's local footpaths officer a year ago, the paths network around the village was mostly overgrown, blocked and inaccessible.

'The new scheme concentrated the minds of the parish council on the rights of way, and what we wanted to do to open up the local footpaths,' he says. He organised a local footpaths survey. This was followed up with a programme of footpath clearance and renovation, based on creating circular walks around the most attractive routes.

These are advertised through leaflets available in local pubs (which are particularly popular with boaters using the nearby Shropshire Union canal), articles in the parish magazine and a central information board and map in the village community centre.

But by the end of 1992, the parish council hopes to have another four or five circular walks set up in the area. As well as making use of money from the community paths initiative, it is also involving an Employment Action team to clear paths and install stiles, bridges and waymarking, using kits and materials supplied by the county council.

Figure 7.22 Report on a community paths initiative by Staffordshire County Council (*Source*: *Enjoying the Countryside*, Spring 1992)

Summary

- In the UK, eight out of ten people make some use of the countryside for leisure.
- There is a huge and growing demand for an ever-widening range of leisure activities, which is putting increasing pressure on countryside resources.
- Different user groups make different demands and impacts upon resources and facilities.
- The supply of leisure opportunities is the outcome of interactions between resource owners, developers, special-interest organisations and government agencies.
- Access and accessibility have an important influence upon leisure participation.
- Rights of way, especially footpaths, play a vital role in providing access to privately-owned countryside, but are under threat from both overuse and development pressures.
- An important countryside management task is the reorganisation of the UK footpath network to fit modern recreational needs.
- It is important to involve local communities in the management of leisure resources and facilities.

8 Managing leisure in the changing countryside

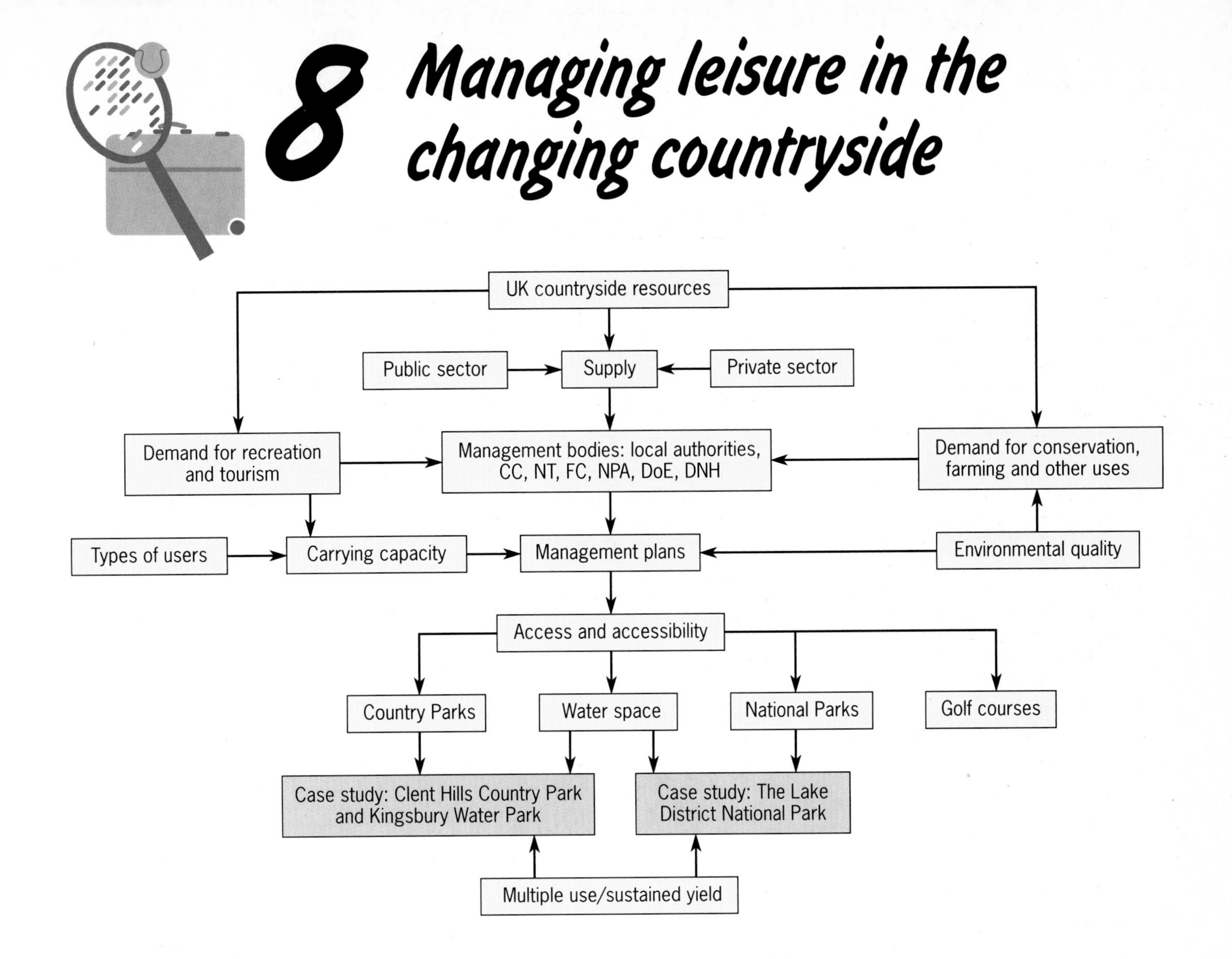

8.1 Introduction

In the countryside, as in cities, **leisure** must compete with other users for space and resources – farming, industry, housing, transport. This competition involves a constantly shifting balance between **supply** and **demand**. If we are to avoid chaos, then changing provision has to be managed. **Management** involves the thoughtful allocation of resources according to selected criteria and priorities. As you follow the issues raised in this chapter you will find these underlying principles recurring: first, the balancing of private and public rights; second, the management of resources for **multiple use** and **sustained yield** (i.e. meeting the diverse demands without degrading the resource base over time). So, will the attractive mix of farming, homes, woodland and open fell shown in Figure 8.1 still be there to be enjoyed in 50 years' time?

Figure 8.1 The Blencathra massif and the Greta Valley, Lake District National Park

8.2 Finding space for leisure near cities: the case of Country Parks

Although open spaces for informal leisure – picnics, walks, rides etc. – within easy reach of cities have a long history, the formal category of **Country Parks** was not created until the Countryside Act 1968. Local authorities 'were given powers to provide Country Parks and picnic sites – places in country surroundings, not necessarily beauty spots, for the enjoyment of the countryside by the public' (Open University/Countryside Commission, 1985). Notice that they were 'given

Figure 8.2 Guidelines given to local authorities on Country Parks. The photograph shows Queenswood Country Park, Dinmore Hill, Herefordshire

Guidelines on Country Parks

1 To encourage the provision of Country Parks where the present facilities are inadequate. Indicators of need are:

   a a deficiency of recreation areas within easy reach of large urban populations,

   b pressures of use on existing facilities,

   c growing traffic congestion and damage to the countryside environment, e.g. between Liverpool and Manchester.

2 To encourage the improvement of areas already in use for recreation which could be converted into Country Parks without too much expense, e.g. Lickey Hills and Clent Hills, West Midlands.

3 To encourage the development of Country Parks on land at present derelict or under-used, particularly where publicly owned. The use of high quality agricultural land should be discouraged, e.g. Kingsbury Water Park, Warwickshire and Pugnetts Park, Wakefield have both been developed from disused gravel workings.

powers', but provision was not compulsory. By 1991 there were more than 300 Country Parks across England and Wales, mostly within 25km of cities and between 10 and 1000 hectares in size. The key features are, therefore, free **access** and easy **accessibility**, with the supply being located as close to the demand as possible (i.e. **demand-based** rather than **resource-based** locations). The purposes of Country Parks are set out in Figure 8.2. These are the guidelines given to local authorities hoping to locate Country Parks.

Country Parks are **public sector** facilities in that they are managed by metropolitan and county councils, with funding support and policy guidance from the Countryside Commission. However, the land and water resources are often owned by the **voluntary sector** (e.g. the National Trust), other public bodies, (e.g. the Forestry Commission), or private individuals (in some parks, the land may be leased to farmers who continue to graze animals).

Two important objectives have been, first, to take pressure off **National Parks** by making opportunities available nearer to the origins of demand, and second, to reduce the impacts of trespass and disturbance on farmers and residents in intensively used areas around cities. So, if you feel like a day or half-day out, you need not drive all the way to a National Park or risk trespassing. Because Country Parks are relatively small and are near large numbers of people, they must be managed for high-density use, and users of the parks must expect to meet lots of people, especially at weekends.

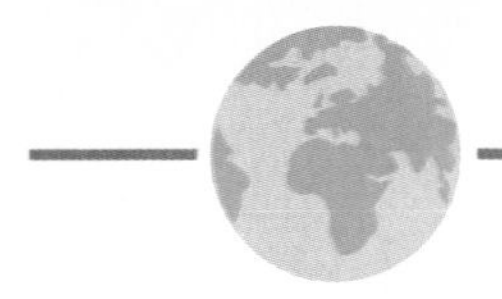

Clent Hills and Kingsbury Water Park

The Clent Hills

The Clent Hills are an excellent example of all that Country Parks are meant to be – and of the impact problems associated with intensive use (Figure 8.3). They lie along the south-west edge of the West Midlands conurbation and have been a popular 'green lung' for the urban population for at least 100 years. The built-up area extends to the foot of the hills, and main roads give easy access. The two elongated ridges that make up the park (Walton Hill and Adams Hill) provide contrasting views over the conurbation to the north and the Worcestershire countryside to the south. Although the ridge-tops are open and often crowded, the flanks are cut by thickly vegetated small valleys that create a sense of quiet and relaxation. Clent Village, at the southern edge of the park, is the traditional entrance, but the park managers have attempted to disperse the impacts of visitors by developing two car parks and **facilities** on the northern edge of the park. Most of the land is owned by the National Trust (voluntary sector) but the Worcester and Hereford County Council (public sector) manages the park.

The two hills of the park are separated by a valley with a lane. Access is controlled by three peripheral car parks, and motor vehicles are banned within the park. A dense network of footpaths fans out from these access points. The visitor numbers have caused extensive impacts on vegetation and erosion, especially near car parks and along the ridge tops, where the bare surface sometimes extends to 50m. To reduce conflict and impacts, separate bridle paths for horses have been marked out. Mountain bikes are also causing concern. A gently-graded path with hand-rails improves accessibility for people with disabilities. There is a permanent orienteering course.

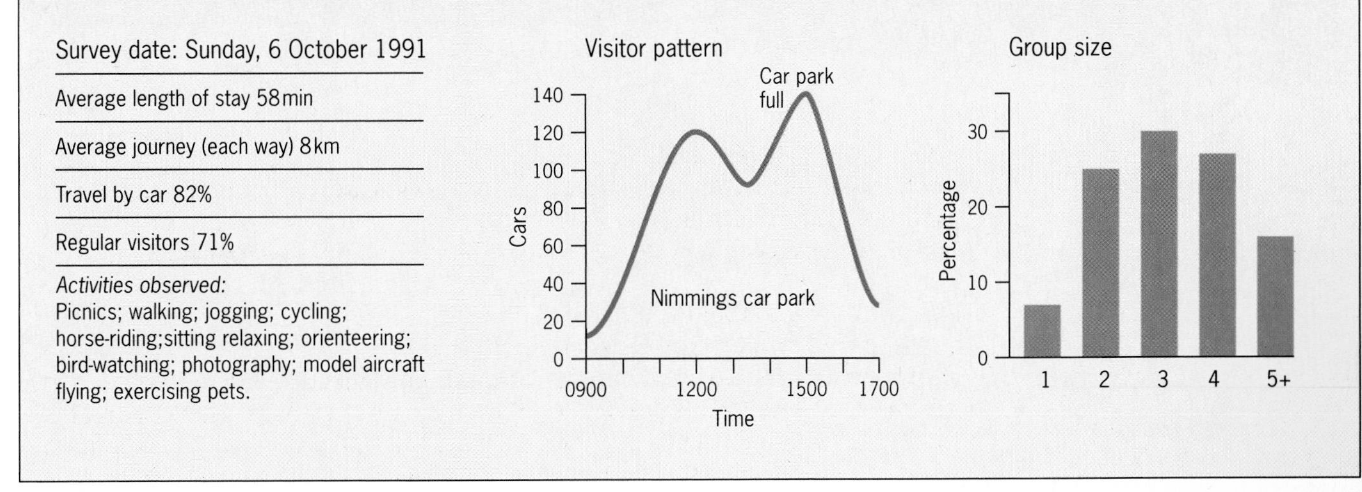

Figure 8.3 Intensive use at Clent Hills Country Park

Kingsbury Water Park

Kingsbury Water Park represents the other extreme to Clent Hills – it is a new **recreational** resource created from derelict land for mainly water-based activities. Warwickshire County Council have taken control of extensive disused gravel workings which, as they lie in a flood-plain, had filled naturally with water. The designers have divided the area into two main **zones**. The first is a series of small lakes, each designated for a particular water-based activity, such as windsurfing, dinghies, remote-control model boats etc. (Fig. 8.4). Around the lakes, where there has been a regeneration of scrub and woodland, car parks, trails, picnic areas and children's activity areas for informal recreation have

Clent Hills and Kingsbury

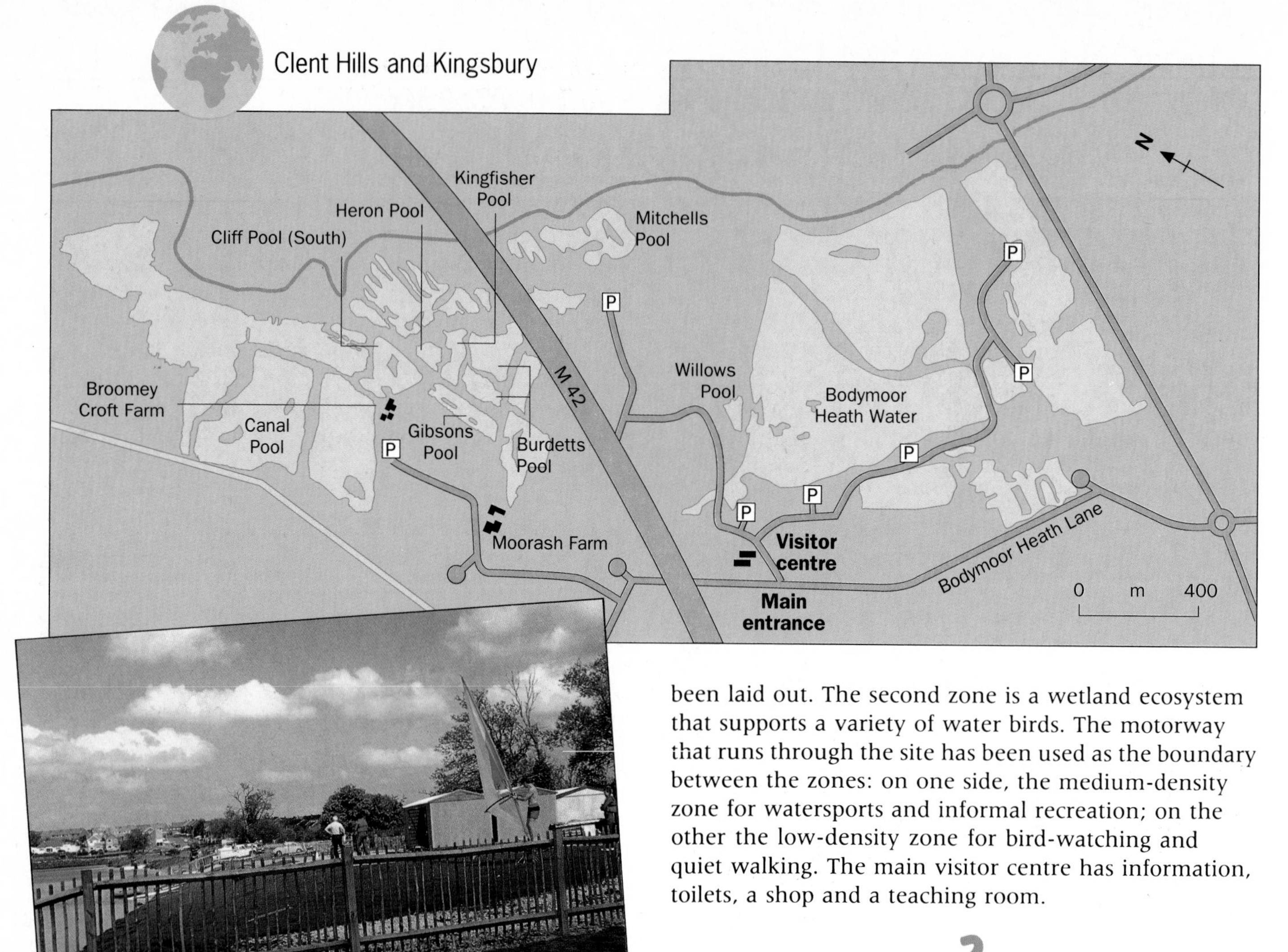

Figure 8.4 Kingsbury Water Park

been laid out. The second zone is a wetland ecosystem that supports a variety of water birds. The motorway that runs through the site has been used as the boundary between the zones: on one side, the medium-density zone for watersports and informal recreation; on the other the low-density zone for bird-watching and quiet walking. The main visitor centre has information, toilets, a shop and a teaching room.

?

1 Essay: In what ways do the Clent Hills and Kingsbury Parks illustrate the diverse purposes and character of Country Parks?

8.3 National Parks

National Parks make up the high-order category of the park hierarchy. They are relatively large, widely though irregularly spaced, and fulfil distinctive recreational and **conservational** functions (Fig. 8.5). Their boundaries enclose landscapes that are given a special status because they are regarded as precious, in need of protection and careful management (Fig. 8.6).

World–UK comparison

Throughout the world, National Parks are an important element in countries' policies for conservation, recreation and **tourism**. The world's first National Park was Yellowstone in the USA, designated in 1872 ('designation' is the term used to mean the formal giving of the title and status). By the early twentieth century, countries such as Australia and New Zealand had National Parks. Yet Britain's first National Park, the Peak District, was not designated until 1951 (as one of the outcomes of the National Parks and Access to the Countryside Act 1949). A further nine National Parks were established during the 1950s, but

Table 8.1 Land ownership (%) in National Parks, 1990 (*Source*: National Park Authorities, in Edwards, 1992)

	Brecon Beacons	Broads	Dartmoor	Exmoor	Lake District	Northumberland	North York Moors	Peak District	Pembrokeshire Coast	Snowdonia	Yorkshire Dales
Private	69.6	90.8	57.3	79.1	58.9	56.4	79.9	72.3	85.7	69.9	96.2
Forestry Commission	8.0	0.2	1.8	1.8	5.9	18.9	16.6	0.5	1.3	15.8	0.0
Ministry of Defence	0.1	0.0	14.0	0.0	0.2	22.6	0.5	0.3	4.6	0.0	0.3
Water companies	4.0	1.5	3.8	0.6	6.9	1.2	0.1	13.0	0.0	0.9	0.3
National Trust	3.5	3.0	3.7	10.1	24.2	0.7	1.2	9.6	4.2	8.9	2.5
Nature Conservancy Council	0.8	4.0	0.3	0.0	0.0	0.0	0.0	0.1	0.5	1.7	0.4
National Park Authority	13.0	0.5	1.4	4.4	3.9	0.2	0.6	4.2	2.3	1.2	0.1
Other	1.0	0.0	17.7	4.0	0.0	0.0	1.1	0.0	1.4	1.6	0.2

British definition of a National Park

'An extensive area of beautiful and relatively wild country in which, for the nation's benefit and by appropriate national decision and action, [i.e. government policy] the characteristic landscape beauty is strictly preserved, access and facilities for public open-air enjoyment are amply provided, wildlife and buildings and places of architectural and historic interest are suitably protected, while established farming use is effectively maintained.'

(National Parks and Access to the Countryside Act 1949)

International definition of a National Park

'A relatively large area (1) where one or several ecosystems are not materially altered by human use and settlement; (2) where plant and animal species, geomorphological sites and habitats are of special scientific, educational and recreative interest, or which contains a natural landscape of great beauty; (3) where the government of the country has taken steps to prevent or eliminate, as soon as possible, use or settlement in the whole area and to enforce the respect of ecological, geomorphological or aesthetic features, which have led to its establishment; and (4) where visitors are allowed to enter under special conditions.'

(United Nations, 1977)

2 For each of the landowning groups shown in Table 8.1, suggest what their main objectives are (e.g. the main objective of water companies is to produce an ample supply of drinkable water at reasonable cost).

3 Look again at the British definition for National Parks and identify those owners in Table 8.1 whose objectives:

a best fit the aims of a National Park

b are most likely to clash with the park aims.

4 List the elements of the international definition of a National Park that would *exclude* any British National Park. This is an important understanding because some 'world lists' of National Parks do not include Britain's 'National Parks'.

the 11th (the Norfolk Broads) did not arrive until 1989, and a 12th (the New Forest) is to be added during the 1990s. That will bring approximately 12 per cent of England and Wales within National Park boundaries. As yet, Scotland has no National Parks, although there are strong campaigns supporting the designation of the wild uplands of the Cairngorms.

The two most important points to understand about National Parks are first, that most countries use them primarily for conservation reasons rather than as recreational 'playgrounds', and second, that Britain's National Parks differ from those in most other countries. Although the British definition of National Parks stresses their wild and natural character, they are, in reality, cultural and economic landscapes – the result of centuries of human settlement and land management. About 260 000 people live within Britain's National Parks.

Equally important, these National Parks do not 'belong' to the nation. As Table 8.1 makes clear, the land and water resources are mainly privately owned or owned by organisations whose priorities are not focused upon recreation, (e.g. the Ministry of Defence). In contrast, most parks in other countries are publicly owned through the national governments. For example,

National park	Confirmation of designation	Area sq.km 1990	Population 1991 (rounded)
Peak District	17 April 1951	1404	38100
Lake District	9 May 1951	2292	42100
Snowdonia	18 October 1951	2171	26300
Dartmoor	30 October 1951	945	31500
Pembrokeshire Coast	29 February 1952	583	23800
North York Moors	28 November 1952	1432	25000
Yorkshire Dales	13 October 1954	1760	19100
Exmoor	19 October 1954	686	10000
Northumberland	6 April 1956	1031	2200
Brecon Beacons	17 April 1957	1344	32200
Norfolk and Suffolk Broads	15 March 1988[1]	288	5500
Total		**13936**	**255800**

[1] Date of the enactment of the Norfolk and Suffolk Broads Act 1988

Figure 8.5 The National Parks of England and Wales (*Source*: Countryside Commission)

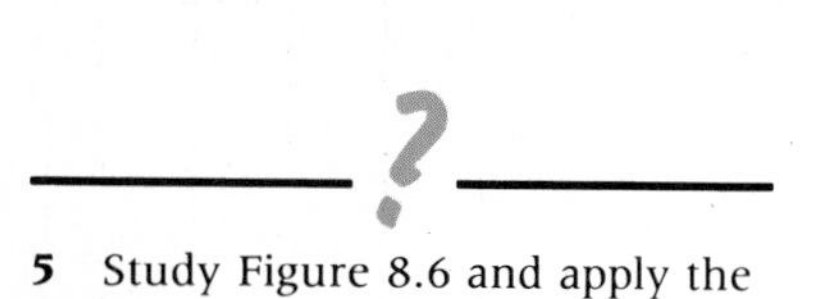

5 Study Figure 8.6 and apply the following evaluation technique on the landscape shown.

The landscape evaluation technique sees the landscape as containing a set of items (e.g. trees, hills, buildings), and asks you to assess their value in terms of:

Impact on the landscape (I)	*Score*
Stands out very strongly	+2
Stands out	+1
Makes little impression	0

Contribution to the landscape (C)	*Score*
Excellent	+2
Good	+1
Neutral	0
Poor	−1
Very bad	−2

a Identify the main components in the landscape.
b Complete a copy of Table 8.2 for each item that is present. For instance, if you think the walls 'stand out' and make an 'excellent' contribution to the landscape, the scores for this item would be: I = +1; C = +2 ; T (Total) = +3.
c Sum each section and overall total scores. (NB The higher the total score the more 'valuable' is the landscape).
d Discuss briefly your findings. How do they explain why the landscape has been designated as worthy of National Park status?

Figure 8.6 The Peak District National Park – a view to Castleton

all but 1000 hectares of the 309 000 hectares of California's great Yosemite National Park are owned by the US Federal Government and administered by the National Park Service.

By some measures, therefore, British National Parks are neither 'national' nor 'parks'. This distinctiveness stands out when we compare the two definitions on page 79 – notice particularly how the international definition emphasises the absence of human impacts and focuses upon the removal of any such impacts where they presently exist.

Table 8.2 Landscape evaluation form

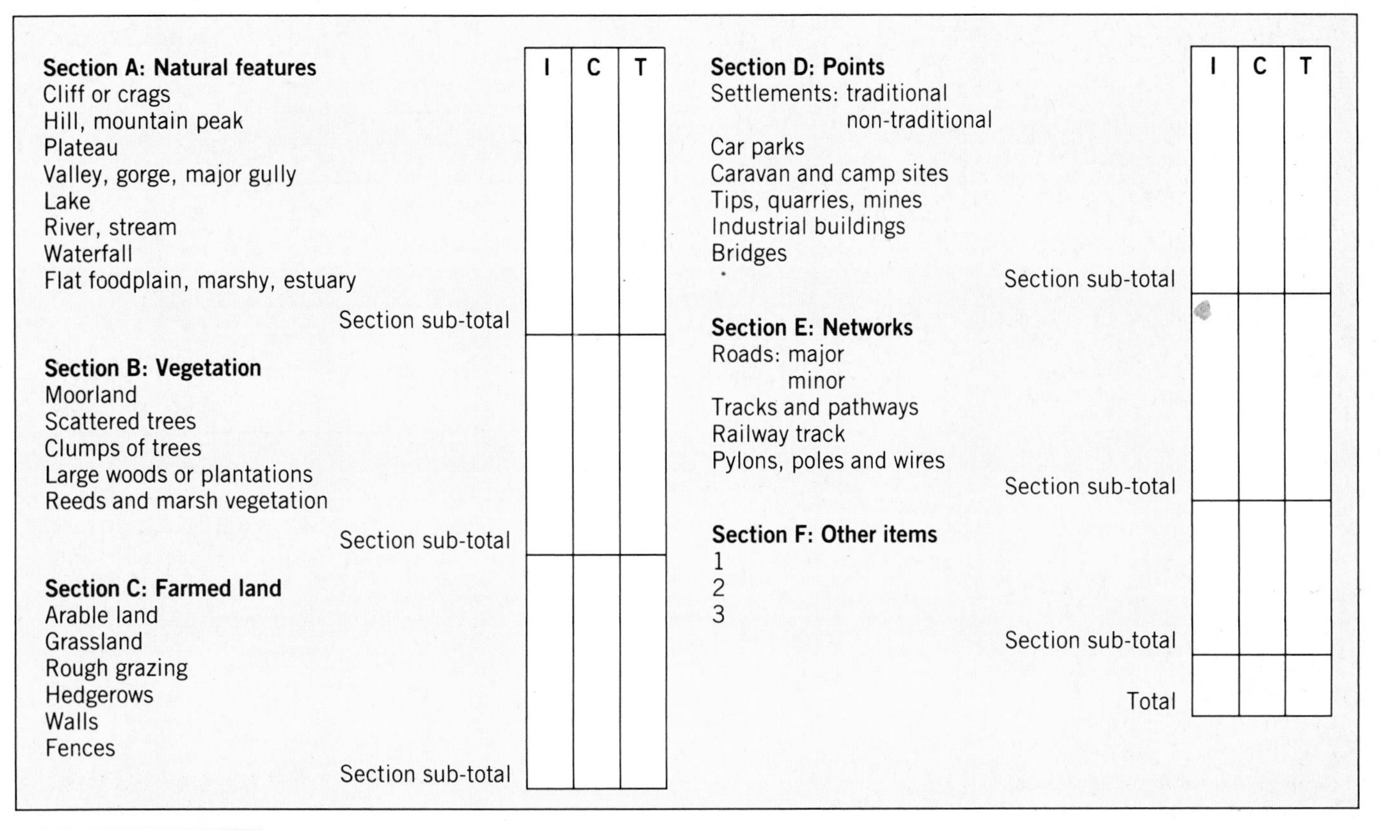

Section A: Natural features	I	C	T
Cliff or crags			
Hill, mountain peak			
Plateau			
Valley, gorge, major gully			
Lake			
River, stream			
Waterfall			
Flat foodplain, marshy, estuary			
Section sub-total			
Section B: Vegetation			
Moorland			
Scattered trees			
Clumps of trees			
Large woods or plantations			
Reeds and marsh vegetation			
Section sub-total			
Section C: Farmed land			
Arable land			
Grassland			
Rough grazing			
Hedgerows			
Walls			
Fences			
Section sub-total			

Section D: Points	I	C	T
Settlements: traditional			
non-traditional			
Car parks			
Caravan and camp sites			
Tips, quarries, mines			
Industrial buildings			
Bridges			
Section sub-total			
Section E: Networks			
Roads: major			
minor			
Tracks and pathways			
Railway track			
Pylons, poles and wires			
Section sub-total			
Section F: Other items			
1			
2			
3			
Section sub-total			
Total			

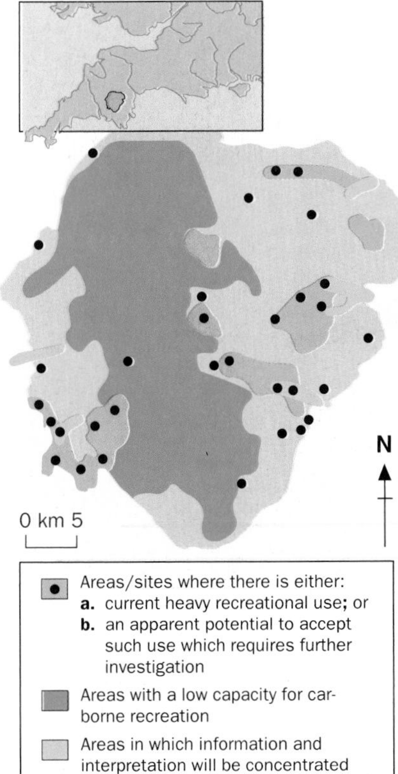

Figure 8.7 Planning for leisure: a proposal from the Dartmoor National Park Authority. The park is divided into two main zones, for conservation and recreation (*Source*: Dartmoor NPA, 1977)

Making decisions

Decision-making in Britain's National Parks is not a simple process. Each park is managed by a National Park Authority (NPA), with key decisions being made by a committee or planning board. However, it is important to remember that the NPA does *not* replace the county councils within a park boundary. Therefore, the NPA has limited powers: it produces a structure plan that sets out how it believes the aims of the park can be achieved, but it must then obtain the agreement of both the county council and the various landowners if the plan is to work. Furthermore, the plan has to be approved by central government – the Department of the Environment (DoE), the Department of National Heritage (DNH) and the Countryside Commission. Figure 8.7 shows how the Dartmoor National Park planners have suggested that recreational traffic access and opportunities should be managed. A core area is to be protected from dense traffic movements, with car-based visitors focused on managed **honeypots** around the fringes. To achieve this objective, the planning and highways policies of Devon County Council must agree with this idea of zoning. Each NPA has four main tasks:

1 To conserve the precious environments of the park.

2 To enable access and opportunity for a wide range of outdoor leisure activities.

3 To support jobs, the economy (especially farming) in the park.

4 To protect the local people's quality of life.

These tasks demand that the resources of a park are used in quite different ways, so tensions and conflicts are inevitable. The NPA becomes a persuader and negotiator rather than a director of what happens in the park. All National Park

Planners 'stifling' Brecon Beacons

By JOHN YOUNG

MORE than 10,000 people, about a quarter of the adult population of the Brecon Beacons national park, have signed a petition expressing no confidence in the park planning authority.

They claim that people wanting to start businesses, including farmers who are being encouraged by the government to diversify, are unable to do so due to excessively restrictive planning policies.

The petition calls for a referendum on whether some areas should be removed from the jurisdiction of the park committee, including the town of Brecon, where the council has passed a resolution supporting 'independence'.

The Brecon Beacons is one of the 11 national parks in England and Wales established under a 1949 Act of Parliament, and its dismemberment would be legally and practically almost impossible, but the petition organisers have asked Richard Livsey, SLD MP for Brecon and Radnor, to present the document to David Hunt, the Welsh secretary, in the hope that he will intervene in the dispute.

Ashford Price, who has won three Prince of Wales Awards for Enterprise, is a former farmer who now runs the Danyrogof Caves, said to be the largest complex in Western Europe and an important tourist attraction. He is anxious to expand his equestrian interests, including the breeding and training of shire horses, but has been unable to obtain planning permission.

'I have found no difficulty in working with other authorities like the Nature Conservancy Council and the Mid-Wales Development Board,' he said. 'But with the national park committee it is absolutely impossible.

'Farmers can't diversify. Many are selling up and their children are leaving the area. There must be changes which will allow people to earn a living or the place will end up as just one giant holiday home.

'What we are really concerned about is the off-hand attitude of planning officers. They are not really concerned about people and they seem to be keen on saying no to everything.'

Gwyn Gwillim, a member of the park committee and a Powys county councillor, claims that if everyone in the area had been approached the number of signatories could have been doubled.

'One of my complaints is that we are not consistent,' he said. 'We tend to put stricter controls on small individuals than on large bodies like British Coal, British Telecom and the electricity board, which is allowed to clutter up the countryside with pylons.

'We gave permission to the water board to put up a filtration plant, which is a real eyesore and looks horrible in a very sensitive area, yet ordinary people have to bother about whether they have the right coloured tiles or slates on the roof of their home.'

Martin Sitton, the newly appointed national park officer, said he was aware of the problems and recognised that communications in the past had been unsatisfactory. Since taking up the post at the beginning of this year he was determined to change things and intended to start planning 'surgeries' where people could come with complaints and had already attended a number of public meetings.

About 70 per cent of all planning applications were passed, which was in line with the national average, but some schemes would still have to be refused and that was the problem. Until now overall responsibility for the national parks had rested with the Countryside Commission, but from April the three parks in Wales will come under a new Welsh authority.

Figure 8.8 Objections to the Brecon Beacons National Park policies (*Source*: *The Times*, 16 February 1991) © Times Newspapers Ltd 1993

?

Use Figure 8.9 to answer questions 6–8.

6 Take each of the planning issues in turn, and build up a table, using the following headings:
Who applied?
What for?
Who opposed?
Why was the proposal rejected?

7 In order to examine impacts, draw a matrix like the one below. Assess each proposal according to the four aspects listed, using these symbols in the matrix boxes: Benefit +; Loss –; No effect 0.

	1	2	>
Leisure			
Conservation			
Local economy			
Local people			

8 Which of the planning issues involve leisure activities in the parks and which have both benefits *and* losses for leisure opportunities?

Snowdonia: A property developer applied to turn the disused gold mine at Clogau near Dolgellau, into a 'living museum' providing up to 60 jobs and attracting ¼ million visitors a year, plus a cable car up the mountain. Although supported by the Snowdonia National Park Authority, it was opposed by the Countryside Commission, the Council for National Parks and the Snowdonia Society (the last two are voluntary action groups). At appeal the application was rejected as it would be 'undesirable and incongruous in the tranquil Mawddach estuary and would seriously affect the privacy of residents in the quiet village'. It was in conflict with the 'beauty, peace and quiet', which attracted so many visitors.

Northumberland: The National Park Committee has rejected an application by Tilcon to extend Harden Quarry on the southern edge of the Cheviot. It is a hard, decorative stone. The existing quarry has a 'life' of 39 years. . . . The extension would add 30 years and extend across four acres. The rejection was principally because of the 'unacceptable level of visual intrusion into the landscape'.

Pembrokeshire Coast: The Secretary of State for Wales has turned down a developer's proposal for 150 holiday cottages on a cliff-top site at Amroth, which would replace a static caravan park. The Inspector expressed concern at the *precedent* of converting caravans to permanent buildings and that 'the proposed buildings would be obtrusive and alien, spoiling the character of the locality'.

Dartmoor: A management agreement has been reached to avoid the ploughing of 300 acres on Hangar Down near Ivybridge. The permission to allow ploughing was given in 1987, but the National Park has paid a block sum and provided for 'no ploughing and for access in perpetuity'.

Peak District: The National Park Committee has turned down an application by a London development company to build a luxury hotel and time-share holiday complex at Litton Mill in the Wye Valley. It contravened the Structure Plan and 'the scale and form of the development would have a seriously adverse effect on the appearance and cultural heritage of the mill, the local community, and the enjoyment of visitors'. Litton Mill is a Site of Special Scientific Interest (SSSI), and the development would impact wildlife.

Brecon Beacons: Sun Valley Poultry Limited has opened a new turkey processing plant at Abergavenny, just outside the National Park. This has led to several applications from farmers within the park for turkey-rearing units. Sun Valley says the plant needs 90 units, each 80m by 20m, for 7000 turkeys, plus traffic generation and soiled litter disposal. The National Park Authority feels such developments are incompatible with park objectives and policy.

Figure 8.9 Development pressures in National Parks

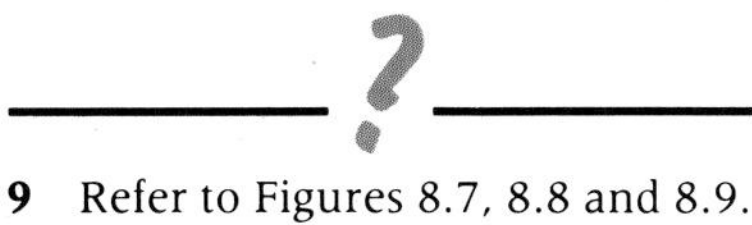

9 Refer to Figures 8.7, 8.8 and 8.9. Suggest two ways in which National Park planners are controlling **carrying capacity**.

10 Give two examples of positive management techniques and two examples of negative management techniques in National Parks.

structure plans are based upon the principles of multiple use and sustained yield – the resources of the park will be used for a variety of purposes in ways which will sustain their quality and quantity over time. These are ambitious aims, and it is hardly surprising that National Parks are not always popular (Fig. 8.8).

Pressures for development have been steadily growing, despite a very tight planning policy. Between 1980 and 1990, the number of planning applications per year made in the 10 parks rose from around 4500 to over 5500. In the Lake District National Park alone, there were regularly more than 1000 planning applications per year. A continuing rise in recreational demand is only one developmental pressure, as the sample of planning decisions for 1991 shown in Figure 8.9 illustrates.

Visitor usage of National Parks

Leisure is only one component of managing National Parks. British parks have also been successful in increasing opportunities for recreation and tourism. (Table 8.3). Indeed, the parks have in some ways become victims of their own success, with widespread evidence of overcrowding and overuse of some sites, especially during the summer months. However, it is not only the growth of visitor numbers which is causing alarm, but changes in the *type* of visitor and what they want to do. Figure 8.10 illustrates these changes as four major waves or surges that have swept over the parks during the past 40 years. Remember, each wave has not replaced the earlier one, rather it has been placed on top of it, resulting in the continuing growth of total numbers.

Table 8.3 Visitor days in National Parks (*Source*: Edwards, 1992)

	Visitor days* (millions)
Brecon Beacons	7
Broads	3
Dartmoor	8
Exmoor	3
Lake District	20
Northumberland	1
North York Moors	11
Peak District	20
Pembrokeshire Coast	13
Snowdonia	8
Yorkshire Dales	9
Total	**103**

*Figures are the latest available from National Park Authorities.

Although these waves of change have occurred across the countryside as a whole, they have been especially intense within the National Parks because of the attractive resources and the relatively widespread access. While about 80 per cent of all visitors arrive by car, the resource demands and impacts of different visitor types vary enormously inside a park. It is this diversity that creates critical problems for National Park managers. For example, if you decide to go for a day's walking in the Yorkshire Dales National Park, you arrive by car or mini-bus and park your vehicle all day at the access point for the paths or moorland you intend to use. Then, perhaps at the end of the day you may visit a café or pub. On the other hand, if you decide to 'go for a drive in the Dales', then you may make use of several car parks, toilets, picnic spots, shops, cafés, pubs, themed sites (old woollen mills, steam railways etc.), short-walk opportunities, and so on. And if you want to jet-ski, or enjoy your trail bike, then your resource demands and impacts will be different again (look again at Figure 7.8).

Management issues

An NPA has to cope with both the continuing growth of total numbers and the ever-widening range of activities, while still conserving the quality of the environment and caring for the interests of the local people. The crucial questions facing British National Parks, therefore, are:

1 Can and should the parks continue to provide free and unlimited access to growing numbers of visitors?

2 What types of recreational activities/experiences are appropriate?

3 How can the tensions and conflicts between leisure and other **values**, and between different types of leisure be reduced?

4 Who should manage and pay for the provision of leisure opportunities and conservation?

5 Do we need more National Parks, and if so, where should they be located?

6 Should the aims of National Parks be changed?

Figure 8.10 Waves of growth in National Parks

1950s
Continued growth in the popularity of 'traditional' outdoor activities for which the parks were originally intended, e.g. walking, climbing, camping, wildlife observation, etc.

1960s and 1970s
The surge in the arrivals of car-bound, less active visitors which enveloped the parks in a deluge of mass recreation and tourism, e.g. the 'car-and-stroller', the picnicker, the 'gift-shop browser', etc. Development pressure particularly for caravan parks, road improvements and parking.

1980s
Growth in the popularity of 'action sports' such as hang-gliding, water-skiing, sailboarding, orienteering, horse-riding, mountain-biking and other off-road vehicles, etc. As a National Park Officer said in 1990: 'A shift from passive to active – gawping to walking; from walking to riding – two feet to four; feet to wheels.' Development pressures for facilities and access permission for these activities.

1990s
Rapid growth in the private commercial leisure industry which has realised the development potential of the National Parks with their attractive environments and visitor popularity. This has resulted in a serious increase in planning applications for large-scale projects such as time-shares, hotels with golf, riding and sailing facilities, theme parks, health spas, etc.

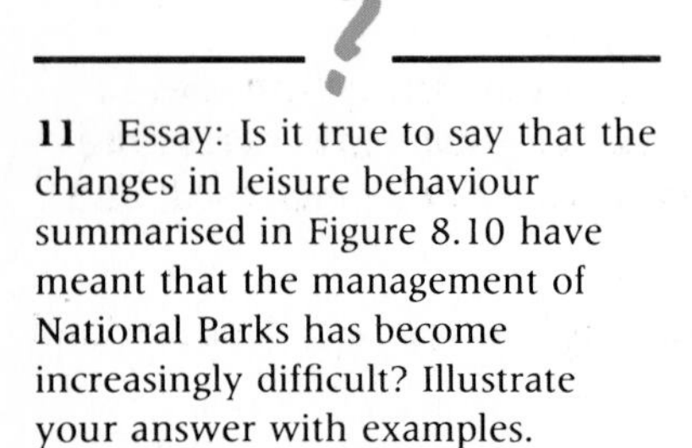

11 Essay: Is it true to say that the changes in leisure behaviour summarised in Figure 8.10 have meant that the management of National Parks has become increasingly difficult? Illustrate your answer with examples.

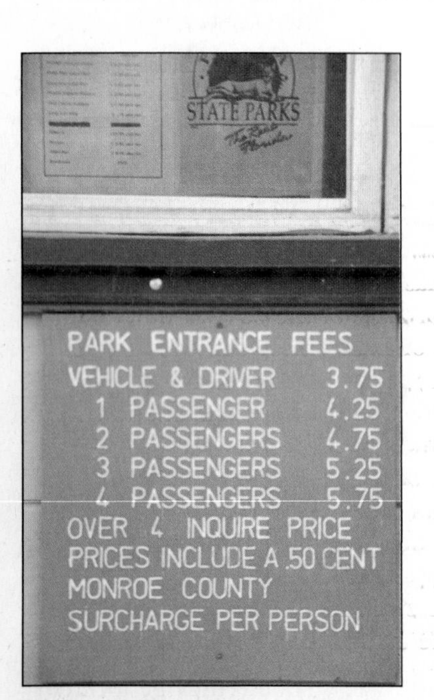

Figure 8.11 Fee-charging in Long Key State Park, Florida, USA

Management plans are usually based on the idea of carrying capacity (see p. 70): how many visitors can be absorbed without too much environmental damage, and before the quality of the visitors' experience begins to decline. One method of making numbers fit in with the intended carrying capacity is pricing. This has the advantage of bringing in income, i.e. economic benefit. Many countries do charge entrance fees (Fig. 8.11) but this would be difficult in Britain because of the many entrances, the number of people who live in the parks and the volume of traffic coming and going which is connected with their economic life.

An alternative, therefore, is to control the movements of vehicular traffic and people. One extreme form of this type of control is to use modern technology to regulate access, as is common in Switzerland (Fig. 8.12); another is to exclude all private vehicles and provide public transport on extremely restricted routes

Figure 8.12 Easy access to mountain tops in Switzerland, where a variety of trains, chair and gondola lifts have a capacity to carry over 1 million people on to mountain tops in an hour! The photo shows the Rigi Mountain Railway above Weggis

Figure 8.13 Leaving your car outside: shuttle buses take visitors along the single road in Denali National Park, Alaska

(Fig. 8.13). When you examine a scheme at any scale, from a park as a whole to a picnic site, you will find that the park planners have asked, and attempted to answer, the following questions:

1 What is the character of the attractive resource (e.g. moorland, river valley, lake, 'pretty' village, native woodland etc.)?

2 What is the carrying capacity of the resource (i.e. how many visitors and what type of activities can it absorb before the environment deteriorates and visitors begin to feel dissatisfied); how can carrying capacity be increased, and should it be?

3 How do visitors want to use the resource and how should they be permitted or enabled to use it (i.e. what is the appropriate use)?

4 How can traffic and people be managed to fit the carrying capacity of the resource (i.e. how many vehicles and people, what range of activities, and where)?

The Lake District National Park

The Lake District has to cope with at least 20 million visitor-days each year. Over 80 per cent arrive by car and coach, and three in every four come between April and September. Surveys show that the most attractive resources are the lakes, the uplands and mountains, and the traditional settlements such as Keswick and Hawkshead, as well as nineteenth-century **resorts** such as Ambleside. By far the largest number of visitors are car-bound, informal recreationists who make heavy use of the road network, parking and picnic sites, toilets, viewpoints, accessible short walks, and settlements for food, drink, shopping and browsing. However, because of the growing popularity of watersports and the widespread access rights for walkers and climbers, the lakes and the uplands are under considerable environmental pressure. Erosion, pollution and crowding have become increasingly common.

The response to visitor demand

Figure 8.14 shows how the park planners' response to this diverse demand has been based upon four key ideas: (1) the setting aside of parts of the park as 'quiet areas'; (2) the concentration of high visitor densities into a small number of honeypots with high carrying capacities; (3) the protection of the central and northern uplands from penetration by vehicles – access will, wherever possible, be based on the 'walk-in' principle; (4) the management of lakes according to a hierarchy of usage levels, from 'developed' to 'natural'.

The principal honeypots are focused along the two entrance routes to the park, both leading from the M6: the Kendal–Ambleside axis in the south (B) and the Penrith–Keswick axis in the north (A).

The heavily used A591 road between the Ambleside and Keswick honeypots has been upgraded and provided

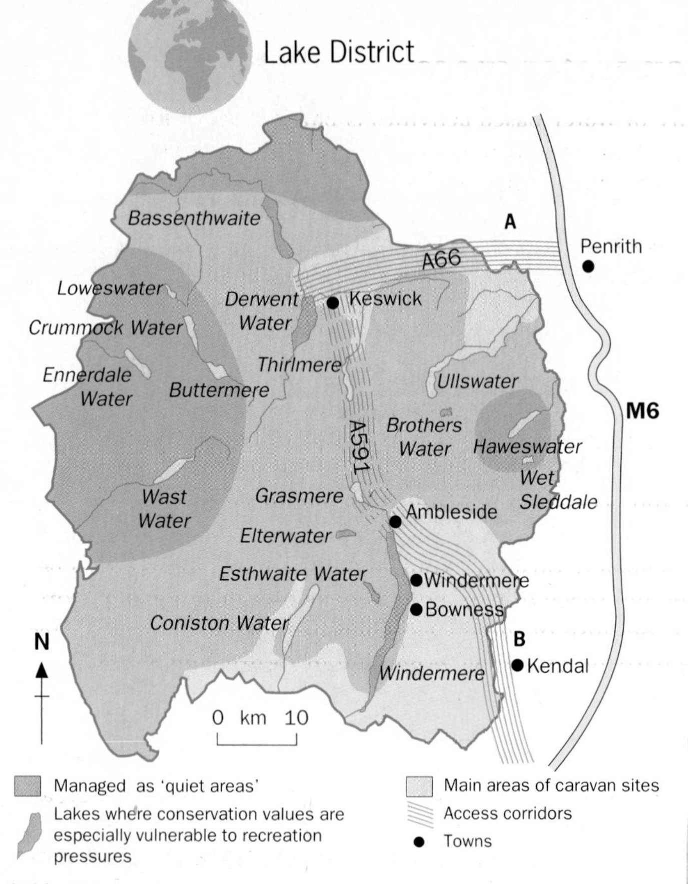

Figure 8.14 Balancing recreation and conservation: zoning of leisure activity in the Lake District National Park

with additional parking capacity to produce an efficient corridor through the heart of the park. Also, HGVs are banned, except when they have business in the area. In these sections of the park, therefore, access, accessibility and carrying capacity have all been improved by positive management inputs.

The distribution of caravan sites in Figure 8.14 illustrates this policy clearly. As caravanning has grown in popularity, so farmers and landowners have made increasing numbers of planning applications for caravan sites. However, the National Park Special Planning Board have worked hard to contain the sites within the two main entrance axes and to restrict sites to a capacity of below 7000. This policy restricts traffic movements along the generally narrow, winding lanes, and limits the areas where clusters of caravans are highly visible in the landscape.

Controlling the lakes

The policy for the use of the lakes has been linked to the honeypot/quiet-area zoning principle. Lake Windermere, the largest lake, has the Ambleside–Windermere–Bowness honeypot along its north-east shore and has a long history of recreational boating use. The NPA has accepted this reality and permits a wide range of uses, including powerful boats for waterskiing. This is the only fully developed lake, yet even here a zoning system operates (e.g. waterskiers are restricted to a zone near their launching point at Lowwood).

On all the lakes the key controls are, first, that all boats must be registered and, second, a speed limit of 16km per hour must be observed. The only exception to this limit is the waterskiers' zone on Windermere. However, the NPA is trying to have all such powered boat activities removed from *all* the lakes, as it regards them as inappropriate in a National Park.

At the other extreme, the 'natural' lakes, on which no use of the water surface is allowed (except for lakeside owners), lie within the 'quiet areas' (e.g. Wastwater and Ennerdale Water in the west and Haweswater in the east). These are managed at low carrying capacities, to give low-density, quiet leisure experiences. In such areas, negative planning techniques are used to restrict accessibility and hence to control numbers of visitors (e.g. *not* upgrading the narrow, winding roads over the passes from the honeypots; *not* providing more parking spaces and facilities).

Between the two extremes are those lakes with moderate development levels, (e.g. Lake Coniston), on which there is considerable activity, but the only powered vessels permitted are a few tiny hire boats and a cruise 'gondola' which provides trips along the length of the lake (Fig. 8.15). Coniston Village is a popular honeypot that has large caravan and camp sites, outdoor pursuits centres and stretches of free launching shore that benefit from the availability of the lake.

Figure 8.15 Lake Coniston

?

12 How have the managers of the Lake District National Park tried to provide for a range of high-quality recreational experiences, while conserving the quality of the environment? List as many measures as you can.

13 A watersports club in Manchester wants to persuade the Lake District planners to allow the use of a lakeside site and water space for jet-skiing in the National Park. Write two brief reports:

a In support of the proposal;

b In opposition to the proposal.

14 Essay: Describe the benefits and disbenefits of planners in National Parks such as the Lake District supporting a policy in favour of concentration of recreational activities rather than dispersal.

Figure 8.16 Yacht Club, Pittwater Bay, Sydney, New South Wales

8.4 Pressures on water space

The growing popularity of water-based activities is part of the 1980s boom in 'action sports' (e.g. the number of windsurfers in the UK increased at least fivefold during 1980–90). Across the world watersports are 'fashionable' in terms of status, image and healthy lifestyles – notice how often they are used as the setting for the advertising and marketing of products. One result of this has been a continuing pressure of demand on the limits of the supply of opportunities.

Water use and access

Three key understandings are (*a*) the enormous range of activities involved – from canoeing, through scuba diving to waterskiing and yacht racing; (*b*) the different resource, equipment and facility demands made by these various activities; (*c*) the two aspects of resource access required, namely, the use of the water space itself and access to the water frontage for launching, landing and mooring etc. For instance, if you live near the coast, then you have plenty of water available immediately offshore. Your main problems are likely to be access to the shoreline and space to park your vehicle and to moor (i.e. store your boat) (Fig. 8.16). Because of the development pressures on coastal sites, planning controls are particularly strong, especially in resorts and along Heritage Coasts with high conservation values.

Inland water

Away from the coast the pressures on both shore and water access are great. One aspect which complicates the issue is that the owners of the water and of the surrounding land may be different. Thus, even where there is a traditional right of navigation along a river or a lake, you may be able to reach the water at only very restricted points. It is not surprising, therefore, that, where there is a combination of (*a*) available water and (*b*) landowners interested in providing access and facilities for profit, intense use has often resulted. Even though there are planning controls, piecemeal growth may lead to overuse and environmental problems.

Waterhead, Ambleside, at the north-east corner of Lake Windermere (Fig. 8.17) is the classic example of a waterside honeypot. With direct access from a main road, it has become a principal public launching point, a boat hire and lake cruise centre, as well as being a favourite spot for the 'car-and-stroller' visitor who makes a brief stop to feed the ducks and swans, walk the dog, visit

Figure 8.17 The Waterhead 'honeypot', Ambleside, Lake Windermere

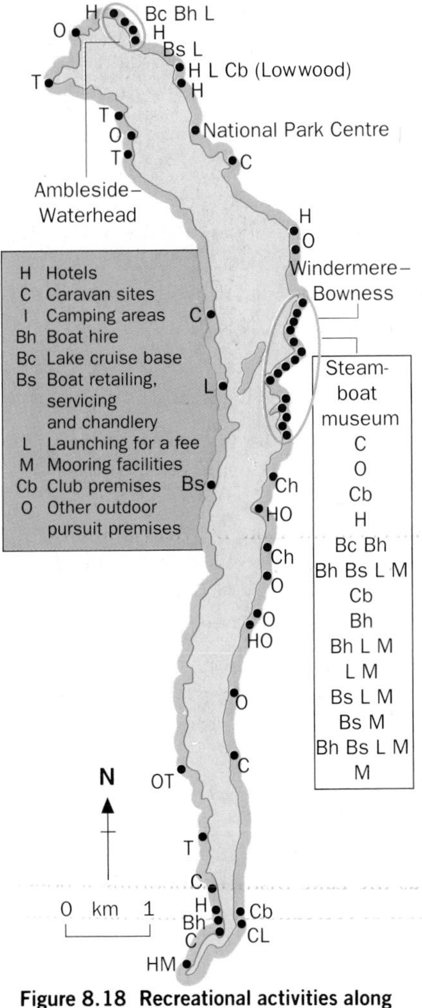

Figure 8.18 Recreational activities along Lake Windermere

Figure 8.19 The Bartley Green Watersports Club, Birmingham. This private club has been developed on a main reservoir for Birmingham's water supply. The clubhouse, boat storage and launching area can be seen on the far shore. The site lies at the junction of the urban built-up area and the Green Belt

Table 8.4 The history of a watersports club

Location: Bartley Green Reservoir, on the southern fringe of Birmingham. Owned by Severn Trent Water plc.

1920s	Dam and reservoir is built to store water for Birmingham.
1920s–70s	No recreational use of the reservoir, owned by the Severn Trent Water Authority (STWA).
1978–82	A 'pressure group' of local enthusiasts negotiates with the STWA to allow a private club (voluntary sector) to use the reservoir and build a shore facility.
1982	Dinghy sailing begins for club members, with the club paying rent to the STWA.
1985	The club obtains a grant and loan from the Sports Council to build a clubhouse and improve the storage facility. The club continues to enlarge the membership and to raise funds.
1985–7	Pressure from windsurfers to be admitted.
	Initial opposition from many sailing members and from STWA. The sailors think there would be crowding and safety problems; the STWA are concerned about water pollution.
From 1987	Windsurfers allowed, they bring in extra money without demanding extra storage space.
From 1990	The owner is now a commercial plc (due to privatisation of the water industry) and the club is concerned about rising rental charges.
1992–3	New slipway and boat storage area come into use. Over 400 sailing and 200 windsurfing members, with waiting lists. Local schools and university rent times to use the facilities.

the café, gift shops and the toilets, and gaze at the boats on the lake. The National Park planners have attempted to disentangle this mixture of users and control the use of the lake with speed limits, zoning, and the provision of a separate powered-boat facility, i.e. Lowwood (Fig. 8.18).

Supply of water space

The public sector has helped to increase the supply of water space, for instance, by creating water parks near to large urban centres as part of the Country Parks policy (e.g. Kingsbury Water Park, Warwickshire [pp. 77–8]). The voluntary sector too, has been very active in putting pressure on owners to allow private clubs to use reservoirs or lakes. In many cases this has meant negotiating with Regional Water Boards, which before 1990 were government 'quangos' and are now **private commercial** companies. Figure 8.19 and Table 8.4 summarise a typical story.

Figure 8.20 Declining traditional rural industries (*Source*: *Guardian*, 28 November 1992)

8.5 Countryside change and the opportunities for recreation: the example of golf

From 1945 to 1985, agriculture was given top priority in terms of how the countryside was used and managed. Government support, in the form of money and planning policy, favoured landowners who wished to modernise their techniques and the farming landscape. Permission for other land uses was much more difficult to obtain. Since the mid-1980s, these policies have begun to change, caused by:

a Agricultural overproduction and the resultant huge expense for the EC Common Agricultural Policy, leading to reduced financial support for farming.

b Growing evidence of unemployment and poverty in rural areas (Fig. 8.20).

c People's increasing concern for the environment (e.g. 'green issues').

d Continuing development pressures for housing, industry and roads, especially in the Midlands and South-East England.

e The growth of countryside recreation demands, especially for activities that

Figure 8.21 Private sector developers move in on the countryside: sign advertising land for holiday cottages

are new and very popular, e.g. golf, fishing (conversion of small valleys to 'fishing lakes' by earth dams), off-road vehicle activities, orienteering, hang-gliding and a variety of other 'action' activities.

The results have been, especially since 1987: (*a*) a loosening of district planning committees' guidelines about what they should allow, and (*b*) encouragement of farmers and landowners to diversify outside agriculture. (By the year 2000, up to 2 million hectares of land are likely to be taken out of production.) Because of the growing demand and the limited supply, leisure, including outdoor recreation and sport, has emerged as an attractive option for the private sector (Fig. 8.21). In 1990, the president of the Country Landowners Association stated: 'Sport is the farm crop of the future.'

As profitability is a key motive for landowners and developers, activities for which people will pay to take part, and to which other money-spinning facilities can be attached are particularly attractive. Golf is an outstanding example of this explosion in leisure development.

None the less, not everyone is happy about such changes, as the example in Figure 8.22 illustrates.

Figure 8.22 Report on objections to a golf course in Devon (*Source*: Sheila McNamara, *Observer*, 2 June 1991) © The *Observer*

THE CAMPAIGNER

David Bourne sees golf courses as case of rural vandalism

David Bourne is secretary of the Sampford Courtenay Action Group, formed to fight plans for a top-of-the-market golf course development over three farms and 350 acres of land in an untouched area of Devon. Bourne, a freelance chartered surveyor, moved to the area eight years ago. Villagers learned of plans by Fairway International to construct a 150-bedroomed hotel, 120 time-share houses, two 18- and one nine-hole golf course development – essentially for the American and Japanese market – at a meeting called by the parish council.

Bourne admits that the village is now going over to the 'country cottage' set, but is adamant that most opposition to the scheme comes from people who live and work in the area, and not just from the weekenders who want to preserve its 'chocolate-box' charm. Predictably, the plan has caused divisions. 'Between those who think they will make money out of it and those who prefer things the way they are,' he says. 'It all got very nasty. One businessman said people who didn't like the idea had moved once, and they could move again.'

Why golf?

The first boom in golf popularity lasted from 1890 to the 1930s, and the majority of golf courses in use in 1990 were laid out in this period. Yet from the 1970s, a second golf boom has been under way, helped by increasing TV coverage of competitions. Despite this growth in demand, the difficulty of obtaining planning permission to convert farmland into golf courses meant that developers showed little interest. Demand so exceeded supply that, by 1990, the average waiting-list time for membership of clubs was 5–10 years and there were regularly long queues at public courses. In England and Wales, 1700 private clubs catered for 900 000 members, leaving a further 1.6 million players to squeeze on to around 300 municipal courses. In Scotland, where golf has long been a 'national' sport, the public provision is much better. A national survey carried out in 1989 showed that the UK needs 700 additional courses by the year 2000. This is based upon demand forecasts and the Sports Council recommendation that there should be one 18-hole course per 25 000 people.

This combination of a large unsatisfied demand, the loosening of planning restrictions, and the ready availability of money in the late 1980s generated a lot of new activity by developers and landowners. For example, during 1989, 25 new courses were approved in Essex and Surrey alone; and in 1991, there were 48 planning applications in Surrey and 35 in Kent. Although costs vary according to course location and type, the figures can be very high. As an 18-hole course, with associated facilities, may take up 60–80 hectares, just buying the land may cost £500 000. At 1991 prices, to design and lay out the course will cost £700 000–£1 350 000 (£40 000–75 000 per hole). In 1993, the average cost of a golf course with incorporated hotel was £1.3 million *without* the land costs! On the other hand, a practice driving range may require only 10 hectares, a 9-hole course only 20 hectares, and courses for beginners and casual players can be laid out relatively cheaply.

Location and impacts

The central issues that arise from such demand focus upon location, accessibility and access. Surveys have shown that golfers prefer not to have a journey time each way of longer than 30 minutes, so the supply needs to be near to the demand. The most accessible and attractive locations are, therefore, the fringes of large urban populations and near to motorways (e.g. between 1972 and 1992, 38 new golf courses appeared or were planned within 15km of the line of the M25). These are zones which are, of course, in great demand for other

Manicured greens and sandy bunkers are alien features in landscapes designated for their scenic beauty

The fairway code

The Countryside Commission wants any plans for golf courses in areas designated for their scenic beauty to be bunkered. In a position statement, published as an advisory booklet for planning authorities and golf course developers, the Commission recommends a general presumption against new courses in: national parks, including the Broads, Areas of Outstanding Natural Beauty, Heritage Coasts, historic parklands, and the New Forest.

In other areas the go-ahead should be given only where such a development would contribute to and enhance the character of the landscape. And it should proceed only after a thorough environmental assessment of the likely impact, says the Commission.

Manicured greens, contouring, planting of often alien species, sandy bunkers and the removal of hedgerows and stone walls can give an 'imposed' look which would conflict with beautiful landscapes – especially as, on average, an 18 hole golf course spreads over 50 hectares of land. There are fears, too, that such a facility could be the thin end of the wedge, with clubhouses, hotel accommodation, roads and other development following. But the Commission is not against the idea of golf course facilities in less sensitive areas of the countryside.

Preference should be given, it says, to locating them where they can make a positive contribution to the area – for example, within degraded landscapes, such as those affected by mineral workings or where intensive agriculture has already left its mark.

The 12 new community forests being planted in different areas of England, or the New National Forest being created in the Midlands, could make suitable locations for new golf courses, it suggests.

But, says the Commission, in all circumstances where golf courses are allowed, consideration must be given to their effect on the conservation of wildlife and historic features, as well as on local communities. Furthermore, appropriate management of new or retained landscape elements should be a condition of any planning permission, together with arrangements for the provision of public access to the countryside.

The Commission, with the help of consultants, is later this year to publish an advisory booklet on the subject, giving guidance to local authorities and golf course developers on the way in which the principles should be applied. It will cover matters such as environmental and landscape factors to be taken into account when considering a new course, design guidance for landscape treatment and enhancement, and opportunities for creative conservation, together with guidelines for future management and after-care.

Figure 8.23 Report on the Countryside Commission's guidelines for golf courses (*Source*: *Countryside*, March/April 1992)

developments and public open space, and so planning decisions are often difficult.

From the viewpoint of the landowner and the private developer, the location must be profitable (i.e. income from membership and playing fees must pay back the cost of **investment** and yield a profit). The basis for such a calculation is the physical carrying capacity of the course: an 18-hole course can accommodate about 150 rounds in one day, or 50 000 rounds a year.

Because of their size, the ways in which they change the landscape and the traffic they generate, golf developments have considerable environmental impact. Local communities and conservation organisations are raising increasing objections, especially where the proposals are in scenically and ecologically sensitive settings. As a result, the Countryside Commission has issued guidelines (Fig. 8.23). On the other hand, conservationists do see well-planned golf courses as having an important role to play in habitat and wildlife conservation – trees, ponds, streams, rough vegetation etc.

Alternative courses

Criticism has been growing too, over who has access to these space-consuming developments. Because of the high costs involved, most of the proposals have been from private sector companies. They see their best chance of profits from high-quality, membership-only clubs. But this does not solve the problem of the 2 million beginners and casual players who simply want to enjoy regular rounds with their friends, and are prepared to pay about £10 a round to do so. Local authorities have not had the money to increase the numbers of municipal pay-as-you-play (PAYP) courses, so a recent trend has been for farmers to set up very basic courses (Fig. 8.24). Planning committees have encouraged such initiatives by giving planning permission for change of use of farmland, unless it is Grade I quality, or protected for conservation values. For example, the Six Hills Golf Club in Leicestershire began in 1986 when the farmer obtained planning permission to convert cattle pasture with a good meadow grass cover to a 9-hole course. The fairways and greens were simply marked and mown across the meadows, and a portable cabin was bought cheaply to serve as a clubhouse and shop. The course operates on a PAYP basis and profits are put into improving the course and facilities (Fig. 8.25).

Figure 8.24 A basic PAYP golf course, Bodenham, Worcester and Hereford. This 9-hole course opened in 1992 by a farmer, using two fields, operates on an easy-access pay-as-you-play basis. Once planning permission for change of use has been obtained, the modifications are not expensive: mown fairways, small bunkers, tree landscaping, a simple clubhouse and car park, immediately beside a road for accessibility

A final aspect of concern is that some commercial developers submit a planning application for a golf course, but hidden within it there are 'ancillary

THE FARMER

Golf is more profitable than crops for Elwyn Harris

For more than 40 years Elwyn Harris rode by tractor across the 250 acres of Dewstow Farm, five miles west of the Severn Bridge in Gwent. Today he goes by golf buggy. His 100 beef cattle, 200 ewes and lambs are all sold. He no longer plants 100 acres of corn.

Declining fortunes convinced him there was no future in agriculture, but immense potential in golf. 'I ended every year with a £5,000 deficit and finally an overdraft of £80,000. There wasn't much point in passing that on to my sons.'

In 1987, before the government Set Aside scheme was devised to pay farmers to turn their land to other uses, his plans were revolutionary. But Harris, a shrewd and canny businessman and a keen golfer, knew that 50 acres of his land, in a lightly wooded valley, was perfectly suited to a nine-hole course. All Gwent's 12 courses had waiting lists.

Using farm labour, he and his sons built the course on pastureland at a cost of £50,000. They continued farming 200 acres and his wife Margaret could not anticipate the way life would change. 'I thought we'd have a wooden hut to collect the green fees. I didn't want a lot of change. Now I wish we'd done it 20 years ago.' The clubhouse, which was built by contractors, has a lounge bar, restaurant, changing rooms and a shop. Dewstow Golf Club has 500 members who pay £60 subs, no joining fee and green fees of £5 per round (visitors pay £9). There is an average of three enquiries per day for membership. Later, they made a nine-hole course on a further 50 acres, leaving 150 acres to farm. The final winter beet crop has just been harvested. The Harris family (son Mark, daughters Jackie and Sarah are also involved) now have permission for a further, 18-hole, course, and employ a staff of 43.

Around the course they have planted 3,000 native greenwood trees, plus a few conifers, and put in four ponds. They use almost no sprays, water the greens by means of a bore hole. Wildlife is encouraged. 'But it needs cover, which balls get lost in. That holds up the game.'

Their only grant has been £8,000 through an Agricultural Diversification Fund. There is still an overdraft, since bank loans topped a quarter of a million at one point, but a full car park and busy lounge confirm that deficits are a distant memory.

Figure 8.25 Report on a farmer making his land profitable (*Source*: Sheila McNamara, *Observer*, 2 June 1991) © The *Observer*

developments' which are stated as vaguely as possible. These may be acceptable facilities such as a clubhouse, but they may also include conference centres, executive housing, hotels etc. The company submitting the application knows it would be unlikely to get planning permission for such profitable developments on their own but hopes to slip them in under the 'golf umbrella'! Equally, planning committees may seek 'planning gain' by insisting upon improved landscaping, such as the setting-up of conservation areas, or improved roads, before giving permission.

One response from county planning departments has been to set out clearer and firmer guidelines against which applications will be evaluated.

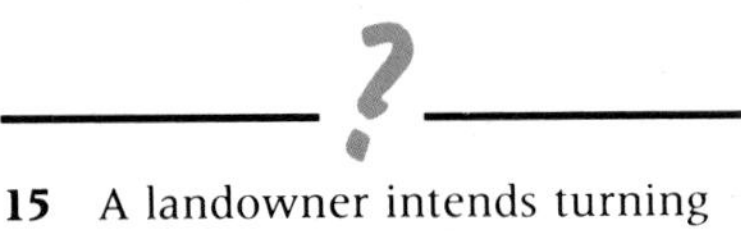

15 A landowner intends turning part of her land into a golf course and sees two alternatives:

- To sell to a large commercial development company that wishes to build a full 18-hole course with clubhouse, hotel, landscaping etc., to be run as a members club;
- To retain ownership of the land and develop a low-cost 9-hole course and simple clubhouse to be run on a PAYP basis.

Write two persuasive statements:

a From a development company stating why she should support their proposal and sell.

b From a group of local residents and golfers who want her to go for the PAYP development.

16 Essay: Is golf course development the most useful way of making more countryside resources available for outdoor recreation? Discuss.

Summary

- Leisure must compete with other users for countryside resources.
- Countryside resources are managed for multiple use and sustained yield.
- Country Parks have been located near urban populations to provide easily accessible opportunities for informal recreation.
- The land and water resources of UK National Parks are mainly under private ownership and are cultural, not natural landscapes.
- National Parks are coming under severe pressure from increasing visitor numbers and an ever-widening range of recreational activities.
- Multiple ownership of resources in National Parks makes decision-making complex.
- The rapid growth in the demand for water-based activities has placed serious pressure upon the supply of water space.
- The shift in priorities for countryside management is providing new opportunities for recreation provision and for building up supply to meet demand for popular activities (e.g. the golf-course boom).

9 Travel and tourism in the United Kingdom

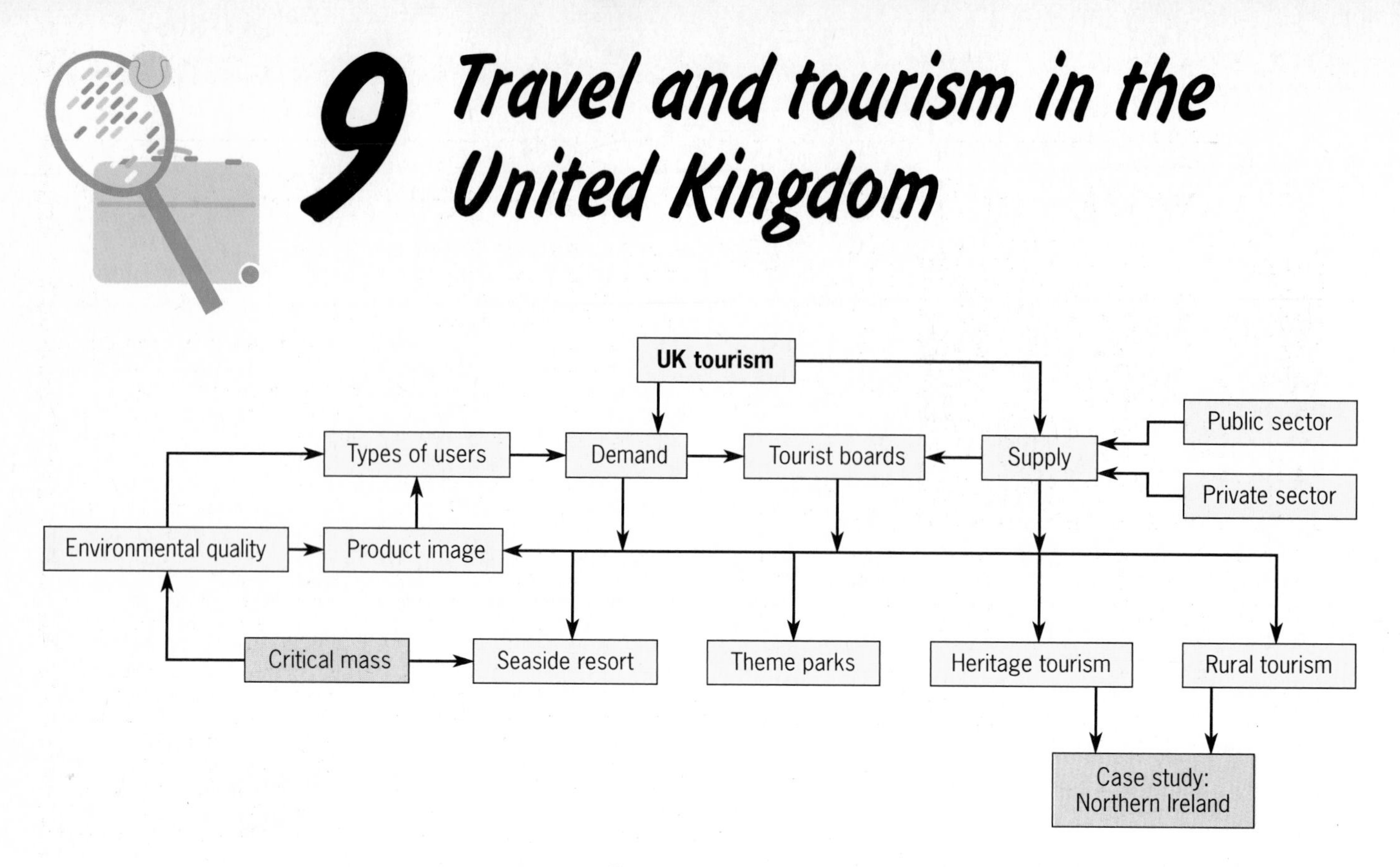

9.1 Introduction

The graph in Figure 9.1 shows very clearly that domestic **tourism** (i.e. holidays in the UK by UK residents) has changed fundamentally over the past 25 years. Between 1972 and 1992, domestic tourism declined by approximately 8 million holidays. In 1989, for the first time, British tourists spent more on foreign holidays than on holidays in the UK. This chapter examines the effects that this revolution has had upon the UK tourism industry, the regions that depend significantly upon tourism, and the responses they are making.

A second theme of the chapter is to seek reasons for the changes, a search that is continued when we look at global tourism in Chapter 10. By comparing holiday experiences in Scarborough and Majorca, the examples in Figure 9.2 help you to begin to understand the revolution and to think of what British **resorts** must do to compete.

Study Figure 9.2.

1 List three reasons (*a*) for choosing, and (*b*) for *not* choosing Scarborough for a holiday.

2 Repeat the exercise for Majorca.

3a As one of the Kenyon family, write to the Lombards, trying to persuade them to go to Scarborough.

b As one of the Lombard family, write to the Kenyons, stating why you prefer Majorca.

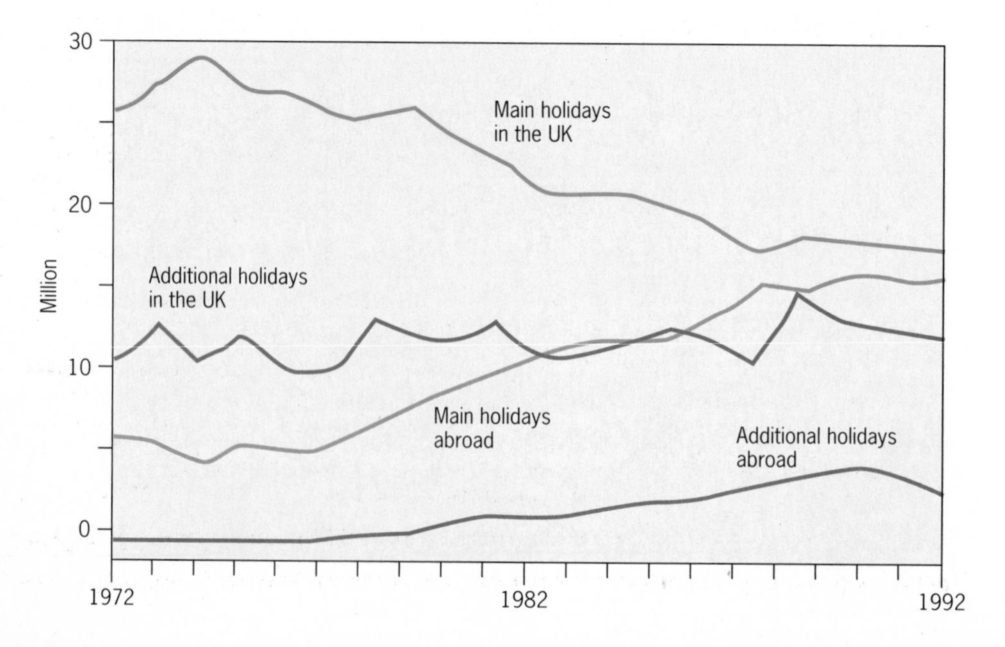

Figure 9.1 Holidaymaking trends of UK residents, 1972–92 (*Source*: *Travel News* and BTA, 1991–3)

Two weeks in Scarboro' v. Two weeks in Majorca

Tony and Carol soaked beside the sea

By Colin Wright in Scarborough

THE KENYON family huddled in a Scarborough sea-front café over a warming cup of hot chocolate and reflected on their decision to take a holiday in Britain instead of heading for warmer climes.

'Well, you can't complain, can you?' said Carol Kenyon. 'There's not much you can do about the weather and, anyway, the sun came out yesterday and it was beautiful.

'We all got out on the beach for the first time and I even managed to get my shoulders burned.'

This at the end of a week of virtually unremitting rain, wind and drizzle. The Kenyon family's resolve to enjoy themselves, come what may, was strangely touching.

They were sitting in the warmth of Paccitto's ice cream parlour and tea rooms watching fellow East Coast holidaymakers pass by swathed in plastic macs and clutching umbrellas.

Over the road on the sand the Kiddyland carousel was deserted. A large stack of deckchairs, tied down against the wind, told their own story.

Carol, 31, a mail order firm enquiries clerk, and her husband Tony, a 30-year-old van driver, had travelled with their children Kara-Rose, three, and Kyle, five, from their home in Plungington Road, Preston, Lancs, for a seven-day taste of the wonders of the Yorkshire coast.

They had been staying in a seven-berth caravan, which had cost them £220, savouring fish and chips, trying to keep dry and thoroughly enjoying themselves.

'The whole thing has been great. Nothing wrong at all. The scenery is beautiful, there is plenty to do at the camp where we are staying and we couldn't really have asked for anything more,' said Tony.

'All right, the weather hasn't been so great — but what do you expect on a holiday in Britain? You know before you come that it might rain and then you just have to get on with it.'

The Kenyons, eight years married, had been confirmed continental package tourists until the birth of their son: Ibiza, the South of France on a budget.

They say the delights of abroad now hold no great appeal. They feel the children are a bit too young for air travel (Kyle has sensitive skin anyway and does not like too much sun) and believe that Britain has plenty to offer.

For the past five years they have regularly taken two weekly holidays in resorts throughout Britain — one in June and the other September. Wales is next on the agenda.

It is said that when it rains and you have children in tow, the cost of a British holiday rockets — much to the benefit of amusement arcade owners.

Since they had not been on the beach due to the autumnal conditions, Mr Kenyon reckoned to have spent around £500 in seven days.

He was pleasantly surprised when he totted things up: £220 for the caravan (booked in January); £50 on petrol travelling to Whitby, Robin Hood's Bay and Filey; £60 on food for the four; £10 on amusements and rides; and £50 or £60 on drinks.

'That's not bad at all is it?' he said. 'It would cost more than that just to travel abroad.'

...as John and Sue soak up the sun

By John Harlow in Majorca

THE LOMBARDS may be the only people in Upper Elmers End Road with a suntan when they fly home from Majorca tomorrow to face the rigours of this soggy British summer.

This time last year the talk among their neighbours in Beckenham, south London, was of the greenhouse effect and a shortage of water, suntan lotion and ice cream.

Now it is of the prospect of a washed-out Wimbledon and further central heating bills.

But for another 24 hours the gloom will not be shared by John Lombard, his wife Sue and their children Kara, 10, and Tom, six.

The Lombards paid £1,600 for two weeks half-board at the Hotel Playa, Camp de Mar, a tiny resort on a white-sanded horseshoe bay. Their booking was made as soon as the 1990-91 Thomson brochure was published in October.

Sue stayed at the hotel with her mother-in-law three years ago, while her John was building up his plumbing business.

On Friday, relaxing in 86° heat by the Playa pool, John and Sue judged the £4,000 earmarked for the two weeks holiday a better investment than an umbrella.

With some package holidays costing only £150, the bill seems high, but the Lombards are unexceptional. Surveys show that Britons pay least for their basic package deal, but spend most on extras.

Sue said: 'I spent £1,000 on clothes and other things in the four months before the holiday, but much of it would have been spent anyway. We have brought about £1,500 spending money, and may go home with £200.'

About £700 of the pre-trip spree goes on the children, whose clothes fill two of the three suitcases. Both have six swimming costumes, four new bought at around £10-£15, four pairs of shoes at £3 to £18 and many T shirts. Underwear alone cost £40.

They will each use a bottle of sun-tan lotion, and drink a bottle of mineral water a day. Apart from a lunchtime snack, that is about it for extra spending.

A pair of sandals for John cost £60, and Sue has her evening dresses, but they spend only £50 on alcohol, probably 75 per cent less than the average youth 30 miles away in Magaluf.

There are a couple of 'extras' — car hire to visit John's brother on the other side of the island cost £18 a day, but cheaper than an around-the-island excursion selling for £80. The only one set-piece entertainment was a Pirates show which cost the four around £60.

The most expensive single items were gifts for their 'tribe', like a set of plates and salad bowl and locally made baby clothes together costing nearly £200. And there are gifts for themselves, like nougat or a bottle of 103 Black Label brandy or Tia Maria at £7 each.

Down in the market, negotiating a soft-leather handbag for £20, is where the Lombards notice the falling pound. In 1988, the exchange rate was 220 pesetas. Now it is 180. But the Lombards don't seem to mind.

Sue said: 'We have never found anywhere in England which could offer as much. I feel sorry for Scarborough — how can it compete?'

Figure 9.2 Comparing a family holiday in Scarborough with one in Majorca (*Source*: *Daily Telegraph*, 24 June 1991) © The Telegraph plc, London, 1991

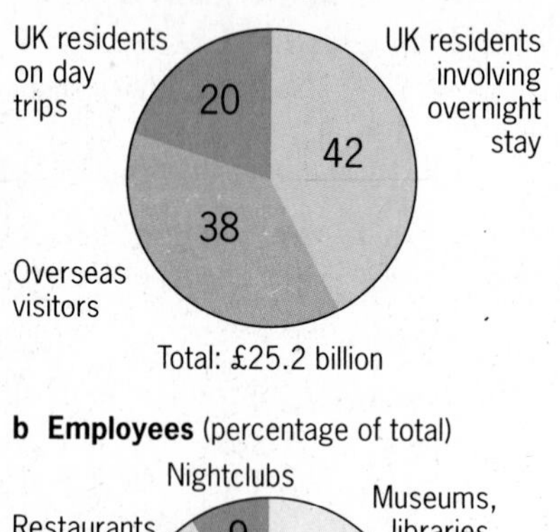

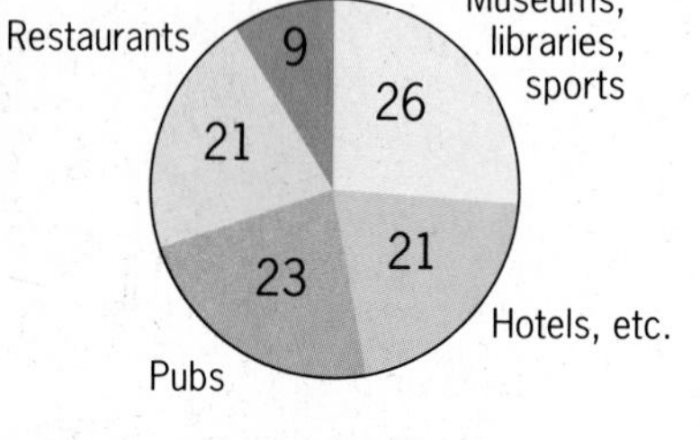

Figure 9.3 The economic impact of tourism in the UK, 1990 (*Source*: *Employment Gazette*, September 1991 © Crown Copyright)

Table 9.1 Central government support for tourism, 1993–4 (*Source*: BTA, 1993)

Agency	**£** (millions)
British Tourist Authority (BTA)	32.0
English Tourist Board (ETB)	14.2
N. Ireland Tourist Board (NITB)	11.9
Scottish Tourist Board (STB)	13.7
Welsh Tourist Board (WTB)	14.0

?

4 Obtain a map of your area (e.g. an OS map, or one from a road atlas). On a tracing paper overlay, mark the places that you think are or could be tourist attractions. Classify them by type (e.g. historical site). Comment on your map.

5a Study the photograph of Minehead in Figure 9.5 and identify as many features on it from the morphology map in Figure 9.4 as you can.

b How far does Minehead follow the model of a 'traditional seaside resort', shown in Figure 9.6a?

9.2 The tourism industry in the UK

Two initial understandings are important. First, you become a 'tourist' if you stay away from your usual home for at least one night. Otherwise, you are a 'day-tripper' or 'excursionist'. None the less, with the exception of the accommodation element, both categories use the same set of resources and **facilities**. Second, the resources and facilities are enjoyed by both domestic tourists and foreign visitors to the UK. So the decline in domestic holidays shown in Figure 9.1 does not necessarily mean a decline in the tourism industry: more of us are enjoying day excursions and 'short breaks', while numbers of foreign tourists have been increasing.

In consequence, as Figure 9.3 shows: 'Tourism is the UK's most important industry, earning £25 billion a year – more than food manufacture, motor vehicles or aerospace. . . . Tourism employs 1.5 million people. . . . The growth in tourism employment over the past 10 years has run at an average of more than 20 000 new jobs each year' (ETB, 1991). By 1993, income from tourism was estimated to be at least £27 billion. Each year there are at least 25 million domestic short breaks (1–3 nights), 18 million domestic long holidays (more than 3 nights), 12 million trips involving accommodation, 22 million visits to friends and relatives, and 18 million foreign visitors.

In 1990, income from foreign visitors was around £9 billion, 28 per cent of this from business travellers. In 1992, London alone attracted 6.5 million visitors from the rest of the UK (excursionists and tourists), bringing in £1 billion, and 9 million foreign visitors who spent £3.6 billion. At least 7 per cent of London's workforce is employed in travel and tourism. As capitals and historic cities, Edinburgh and Cardiff are also important tourist centres – Belfast's attractiveness is at present reduced by 'the Troubles'. All three sectors – **commercial**, **voluntary** and **public** – are involved in providing the **supply** of opportunities. Central government acts as a promoter by issuing guidelines, encouraging initiatives and by funding organisations that support the tourism industry (Table 9.1).

The tourist boards

The purpose of the British Tourist Authority (BTA) is signalled by the title of its 1992 report, *Selling Britain to the World*: 'In accordance with the Development of Tourism Act 1969, the BTA works to strengthen the performance of Britain's tourist industry in international markets by encouraging people to visit Britain and encouraging the improvements and provision of tourist amenities and facilities in Britain' (BTA, 1992).

The tourist boards support the tourism industry within their own parts of the UK, through a regional structure (e.g. the Heart of England Tourist Board serves central England). You will be most aware of their work through advertising, seeing promotional stands at exhibitions and shows, and in Tourist Information Centres (TICs). Most TICs are run by county and district councils with funding support from the tourist boards. They are a vital link connecting the **demand** with the supply, by holding accommodation lists, maps, brochures etc. Thus, if you run a guest-house, a falconry etc., you place your advertising brochure in the TIC for tourists to pick up.

This promotional and co-ordinating role is important because the tourism industry is very fragmented – at least 200 000 enterprises are involved. Thus, although transnational giants such as Forte and Grand Metropolitan dominate certain aspects (e.g. luxury hotels), a distinctive feature of the industry is the large number of small companies and family enterprises. Many such firms have been given start-up support by government schemes that have seen the potential of the growing and diversifying tourism industry for economic development (e.g. bed-and-breakfast, craft industries, activity centres). All councils, too, offer a range of opportunities, from deck-chair rental and putting-greens to 'heritage experiences'.

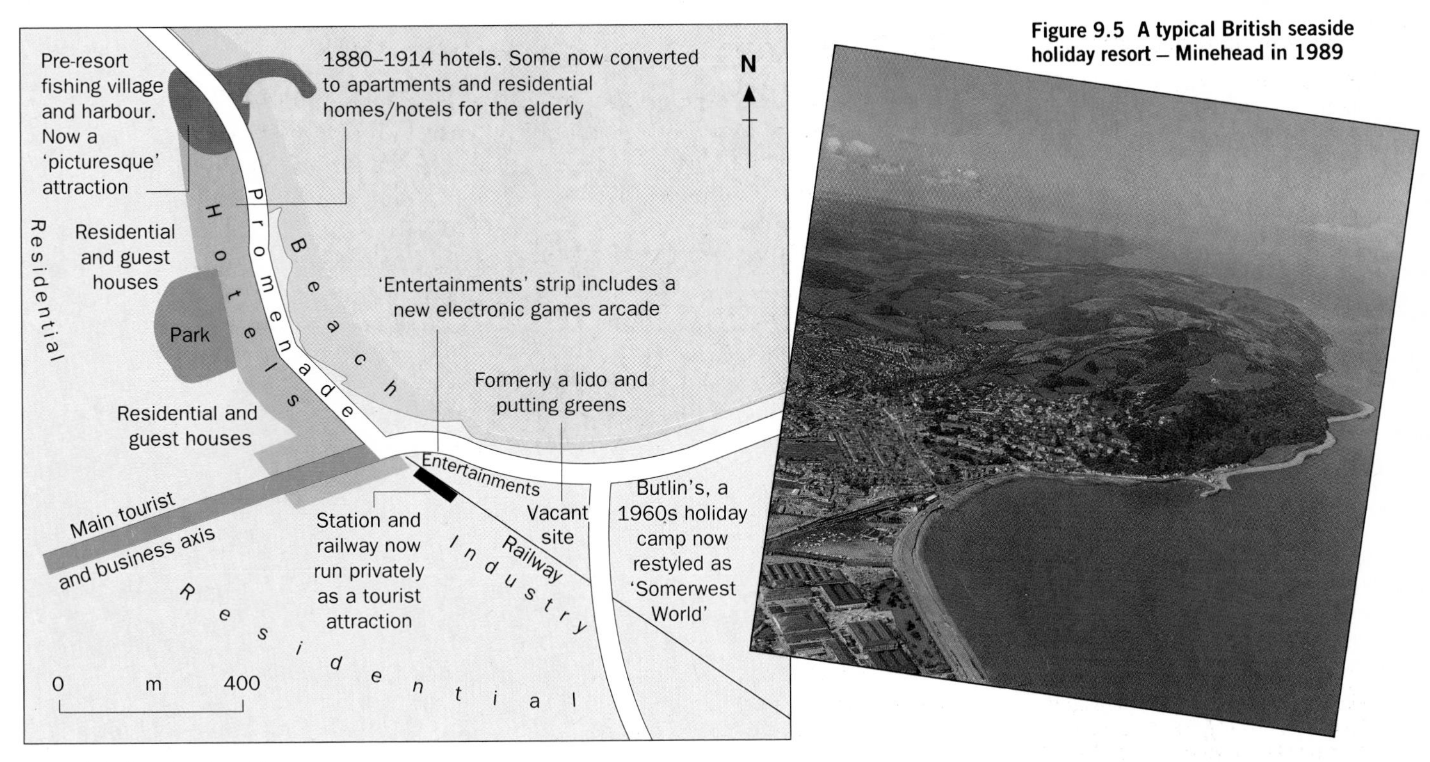

Figure 9.5 A typical British seaside holiday resort – Minehead in 1989

Figure 9.4 Minehead: outline morphology of a 'bucket-and-spade resort'

9.3 The story of the British seaside resort

Despite all the changes in the ways we enjoy our holidays, at least 70 per cent of all domestic main holidays are still based at least in part beside the sea (Figs 9.4 and 9.5). The traditional week or fortnight 'at the seaside' has produced a distinctive type of urban settlement – the resort. It is distinctive in its *location* – backing an accessible and attractive beach; in its main *function* – serving the accommodation, entertainment and activity needs of the holidaymaker; and in its *morphology* – a linear and crescent form giving maximum **accessibility** to the attractive resources, namely the beach and the sea (Fig. 9.6a).

Some resorts have grown around pre-existing settlements (e.g. Great Yarmouth), but many others have evolved only as tourism has developed (e.g. Blackpool). Although parts of individual resorts have been planned (e.g. older areas of Brighton), they are essentially settlements that have emerged piecemeal, growing and being modified by internal and external pressures over

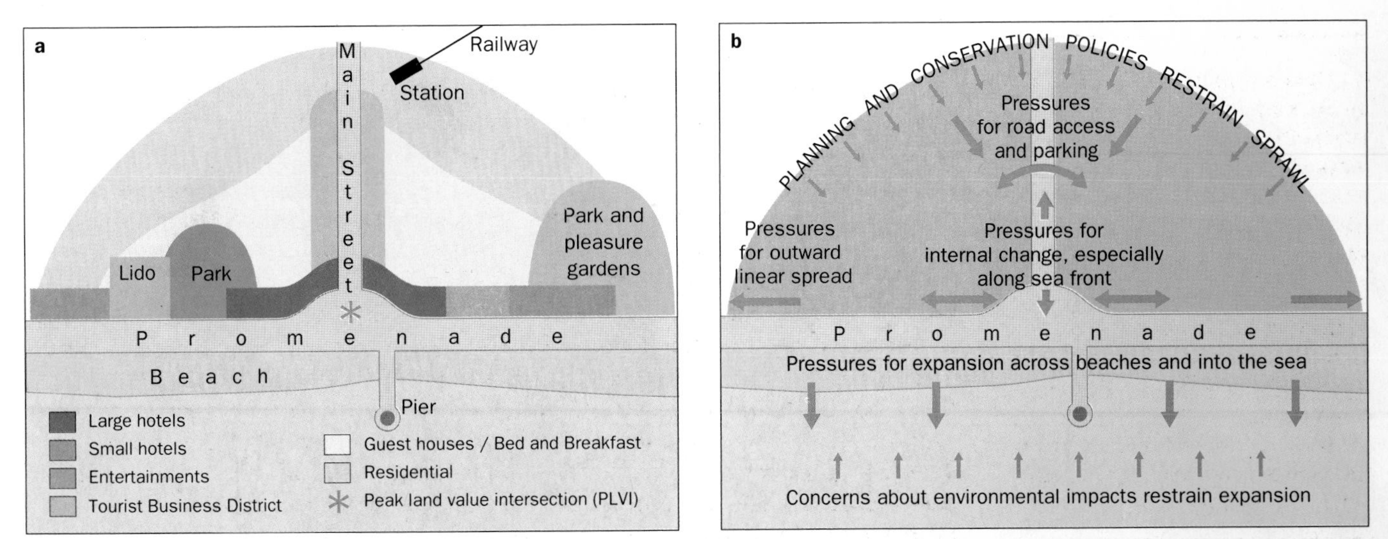

Figure 9.6 (a) A simple model of a traditional seaside resort and (b) pressures at work in seaside resorts

Table 9.2 Resort responses to change

- Indoor leisure and entertainment complexes to combat the erratic British weather (e.g. Rhyl).
- Rising costs and the popularity for self-catering accommodation have brought widespread conversion of hotels to self-catering apartments.
- Extensive caravan and campsites on the peripheries, again to cater for the boom in 'do-it-yourself' holidays and the spread in car ownership.
- Replacement of traditional swimming pools ('lidos') by elaborate leisure pool complexes (e.g. Blackpool).
- The upgrading of existing facilities, from shopping parades, eating places, parks to beach management, in response to demands for better quality provision.
- New facilities to modernise and diversify the product (e.g. marinas).
- Strategies to lengthen the season and to give a distinctive identity. The classic example is Blackpool and its 'illuminations'. Many resorts have copied this and have off-season festivals, 'Weekend Breaks' etc.
- Conversion of buildings to retirement and nursing homes, or to educational establishments. Seaside resorts are popular retirement locations and offer attractive environments and spacious buildings for, e.g. language schools.
- Road improvement, traffic control and parking schemes which allow car-bound visitors access while protecting pedestrians. This car–pedestrian conflict is particularly intense along the promenade or esplanade. Where the railway has closed, its land may be converted to road and parking use, or the railway itself becomes a tourist attraction (e.g. Minehead).

time (Fig. 9.6b). There are more than 100 such settlements dotted along the British coastline, many with well-developed regional **catchment areas**. For instance, Margate and Southend are traditional destinations for Londoners; Llandudno and Southport draw visitors from Liverpool and Manchester; Yorkshire people go to Scarborough and Bridlington; Tenby and Barry Island have long been popular with people from the South Wales valleys; Belfast people visit Bangor.

The origins of UK resorts lie at the beginning of the nineteenth century, when the Prince Regent became convinced of the health-giving properties of sea water and sea air, and built the Royal Pavilion at Brighton. Fashion and status have always been important factors in the spread of tourism, so it is not surprising that the rich and famous quickly took up 'seabathing'. By the 1840s fashionable resorts such as Brighton and Scarborough were well established. During the second half of the nineteenth century, trips to the seaside became possible for increasing numbers of people. By 1900 the railway network, cheap excursion tickets, slowly improving pay and the availability of cheap accommodation in 'boarding houses' enabled urban working populations to enjoy day-trips and short holidays at the seaside. Some resorts, such as Bournemouth, retained their 'middle-class' image, while others, such as Margate and Blackpool were, from the start, 'working-class' resorts. A few managed to combine various social groups, especially where there was more than one stretch of beach (e.g. Scarborough, Newquay).

By the 1920s almost all of these 'bucket-and-spade' resorts were in full swing – a distinctive feature of British tourism is that very few new coastal resorts have appeared since that time. Since the 1940s the combination of planning restrictions and the changing nature of demand for holidays has limited developments largely to specialist projects such as holiday camps and marinas.

In many ways the period 1945–65 was the high point of 'the great British holiday'. Post-war enthusiasm, increasing prosperity, more holidays-with-pay entitlements, efficient and cheap rail and coach systems, a broader choice (from elite hotels, through boarding houses to the popular holiday-camp packages of Butlins and Pontins) and improved marketing and selling techniques all contributed to this boom. Since the mid-1960s, however, British resorts have faced a tough struggle to maintain their share of the market. This is because the spread of car ownership has improved personal mobility and holidays abroad have become increasingly available and popular. The battle has been particularly difficult where the holiday 'product' is beach-based: the Mediterranean, the Caribbean etc. can offer guaranteed sun–sea–sand, but British resorts cannot.

Resort responses to change

Resorts have fought hard to adapt to demand, and there have been significant changes in land use and the facilities offered. When you visit a British resort, look for the signs listed in Table 9.2.

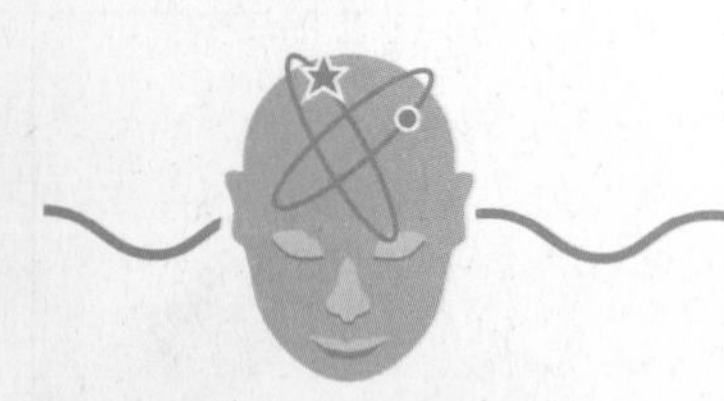

Critical mass

Too many resorts are chasing a declining market for domestic tourism. An American, Donald Lundberg, has put forward the idea of **critical mass** (Fig. 9.7). He states that for a traditional resort to survive and thrive it must attain a certain mass. This 'mass' can be measured not only in the quantity of attractions but also by their range, character and quality. Once this critical threshold of size, quality and range of product and image is achieved, then the resort's attractiveness in itself remains powerful enough for success. Below the threshold, the magnet becomes steadily weaker. Resorts such as Blackpool seem to have achieved this critical mass (Fig. 9.8) while smaller and less high-profile resorts such as Minehead continue to struggle (Fig. 9.9).

Spruced up tower counters attraction of EuroDisney

ENGLAND'S riposte to EuroDisney officially opened yesterday with 10,000 perspiring school-children consumer-testing the £13 million refurbishment of Blackpool Tower.

The first part of a two-stage development ultimately costing £23 million, the investment is designed to secure the Lancashire town's position as Europe's most popular holiday destination.

Representatives of First Leisure Corporation, the owners of the 518ft 9in tower and a large slice of the rest of Blackpool's rumbustious attractions, refused to put the boot too heavily into their cross-channel rival.

'I am sure it will be extremely successful,' said Roy Page, divisional managing director, 'once it has overcome some inherent problems.'...

A PR company discreetly circulated statistics demonstrating that a family of four could have three holidays in Blackpool for the price of one Chez Mickey.

First Leisure's designers have been engaged in what Mr Page called a balancing act. Part of the £13 million has been spent in resurrecting the Victorian character of The Stick, as the hundred-year-old structure is known locally, part on luring punters less impressed by rococo carpets and aqua-marine tiling.

The principal white-knuckle rides will probably be the two high-speed lifts to the summit.

Last year a million people visited the tower, which also features a circus and a grade 1 listed ballroom. Mr Page hopes to boost that to 1.7 million.

Figure 9.8 The opening of the refurbished Blackpool Tower (*Source*: *Guardian*, 15 May 1992)

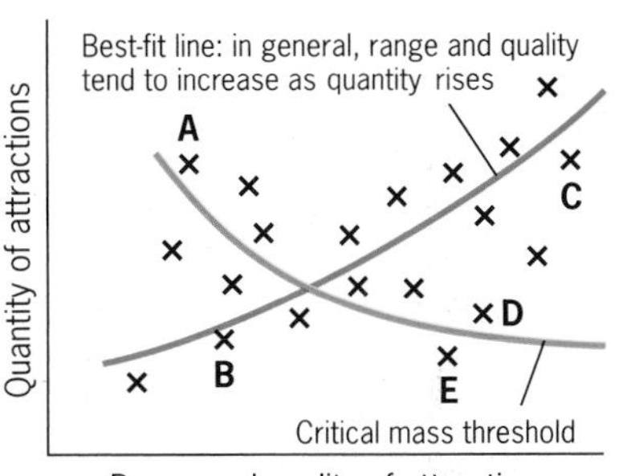

A High quantity, low range/quality – moderate attractive power, above the critical mass threshold but *struggling*

B Low quantity, low range/quality – weak attractive power, below the critical mass threshold – *declining*

C High quantity, high range/quality – strong attractive power, above critical mass threshold – *successful broad-based resort*

D Low quantity, high range/quality – strong attractive power, above the critical mass threshold – *fashionable, élite, specialist resort*

E Low quantity, high range/quality but too few to sustain critical mass as a specialist élite resort – *declining*

Figure 9.7 The critical mass concept of resorts

?

6 Which of the signs of change listed in Table 9.2 can you identify from the information on Minehead given in Figure 9.4 and 9.9?

7 Essay: Suggest the specific criteria you could use to measure the 'mass' of a resort, and assess the usefulness of the idea of 'critical mass' in a study of resorts, using Blackpool and Minehead as examples.

Reviving the seafront. The wide promenade remains with only minor changes, but the older seafront buildings are struggling to survive. The old building with the spire remains as an amusement arcade, but in Spring 1993 was adjoined by a row of empty commercial premises. Part of this pre-1914 strip has been redeveloped as the 'Carousel', a hall given over to electronic games, as an attempt to attract young people.

Butlin's: Built as a typical 'Hi-de-Hi' holiday camp in 1960, this has suffered from the changes in holiday fashions. Like other Butlin centres, it has been restyled and marketed as a 'World', in this case 'Somerwest World' with a western/cowboy theme. It is a self-contained resort accommodating 9000 holidaymakers, many self-catering, plus day visitors, and employs 1300 people. It is of major economic significance to the Minehead district.

The original resort owed its growth to the coming of the railway in the 1880s. This provided access from Bristol and the industrial towns of the Midlands. The station stands at the heart of the resort, at the junction of the promenade and the main commercial street, a sign that when it was built the settlement was very small. The line was closed in the 1960s but has reopened as a private leisure venture, running excursions almost to Taunton. The old steam engines, rolling stock and station fittings are an important tourist attraction.

Figure 9.9 The changing face of Minehead

Revival of hustle in Hemsby

Hemsby grew up in an unplanned sort of a way between the wars. There are no hotels, just lots of caravans and chalets as well as two Pontins holiday centres.... Next door is the smaller, but similar, resort of Newport. Both enjoy miles of wonderful sandy beaches. Hemsby and Newport are not everybody's idea of a perfect holiday destination. They are very unsophisticated – 'You either love it or you hate it' says Mervyn Bevan, Chairman of the *Hemsby 2000* group and Local Area Initiative (LAI) leader.

Hemsby is six miles north of Great Yarmouth and is within the Great Yarmouth borough. It is, however, a self-contained holiday village. Between the caravans and the beach are the dunes. As well as being important as a sea defence, the dunes are also of considerable environmental importance for their rare sand orchids and other unusual plants. But, although Hemsby remains popular, with most holidaymakers returning year after year, the village was getting a bit bedraggled and there were fears that a new younger generation of families might not be as loyal to it as had been their parents. So, the Borough Council and the East Anglia Tourist Board have put together a unique plan to give the village a face lift.

With a basic budget of around £140,000 over the three years of the initiative, Hemsby, with advice from the East Anglia Tourist Board and with the enthusiastic support of local businesses, has come up with a design plan which will improve the quality of the Hemsby experience and give the village a sense of its own identity. The plan includes flags, bright colours for facades and lots of benches, tables, umbrellas, flower baskets and flower tubs on fresh red tarmac. The centre of Hemsby is getting a continental touch.

Out on the dunes, erosion is gradually being halted. New boardwalks lead through the dunes to the beach, making it more easily accessible. Chalets and caravans are being upgraded. Among next season's planned innovations are diplays of fluttering flags and lots of 'welcome' signs.

Figure 9.10 An LAI scheme to boost the attraction of Hemsby, Norfolk to tourists (*Source*: *Tourism Enterprise*, English Tourist Board Nov./Dec. 1992)

?

8 From the information in Figure 9.10, list the objectives of the LAI plan, and state how such initiatives might encourage tourists.

Responses to economic conditions

A further problem is that the tourism industry is sensitive to economic conditions – when times are hard, we spend less on holidays. Thus, the recession of the early 1990s meant reduced business for resorts. This may seem a little strange, for we might suppose that when money is 'tight', more people would opt for holidays in Britain. Yet regions such as Devon and Cornwall, where tourism is important to the economy, suffered badly. Central government, as part of its economic development policies, provides grant-aid support to smaller districts that are struggling to adapt their tourism products. One promising scheme, the Local Area Initiatives (LAI), begun in 1991, helps local communities to help themselves (Fig. 9.10).

9.4 Broadening the base of tourism

Product and image

Adapting the product and the image to reflect changing demand are clearly two keys to success. For instance, the Butlins organisation have not only closed several locations but have dropped the 'all happy campers together' image in favour of themed 'worlds' (Fig. 9.9). The Center Parcs organisation has adopted a more radical strategy: it accepts that it cannot compete with sun-drenched Mediterranean beaches, and so a main factor of location – **access** to a beach – is removed. Once you build indoor facilities to overcome the disadvantages of British weather, then you have a wider locational choice, i.e. your industry has become more **footloose**. Also, it is easier to obtain planning permission for inland sites. As a result, the two UK Center Parcs resorts, in Suffolk and Nottinghamshire, have inland locations, shielded in woodland settings and offer inclusive family holiday experiences (Figs 9.11 and 9.12).

Figure 9.11 Key features of the Center Parcs concept

- A self-contained custom-built resort: an integrated holiday enclave
- High-quality woodland settings and facilities for family holidays
- Accommodation in self-catering bungalows spread in a woodland setting
- A wide range of outdoor and indoor facilities to make enjoyment independent of the weather. The centrepiece is the glass dome sheltering an elaborate leisure pool complex
- All-year availability
- Cars are excluded; bikes and walking are encouraged
- Inland locations, bringing the supply nearer to the demand

Environmental quality

Equally important alongside product and image is **environmental quality**. For any seaside region this applies crucially to the two essential attractive resources – the sea water and the beach. Concern over water pollution and beach conditions has grown over the past decade. In consequence, a number of schemes have emerged to encourage and enforce improved standards (e.g. the EC 'Blue Flag' awards, the 'Keep Britain Tidy' campaign and many local schemes run by individual resorts).

All the fun of a holiday camp in a huge glass bubble

Center Parcs is Butlins brought up to date – less regimentation, but a giant holiday camp nonetheless. It can also be tremendous fun.

There are two of the Dutch-owned centres in Britain, at Sherwood Forest in Nottinghamshire and Elveden Forest in Suffolk, which is where we went. A third is due to be built on the Longleat estate in Wiltshire, although this depends on the outcome of a planning enquiry.

If you have children and are wondering, as we were, how to stop them driving you up the wall during the half-term holidays, Center Parcs is one answer. It takes a little while to get over the strangeness of the place. But soon even the strangled Tarzan cries which accompany the switching on of the wave machine in the 'sub-tropical swimming paradise' seem quite normal, and like everyone else you find yourself rushing into the water to be buffeted by 10ft waves.

The secret of Center Parcs is that it appeals to the kid in all of us. Splashing around in water all day, rushing through warm water rapids which go out into the sub-zero temperatures outside the bubble, cold plunges, hot tubs, Jacuzzis, water slides, and all the time nobody is particularly interested in the fortysomething paunch.

The bubble in the forest houses the swimming complex, which also has safe areas for toddlers and young children who cannot swim, and envelopes a sports complex, bars, restaurants, a supermarket and of course the shops.

All the facilities in the swimming complex are free, but everything else costs. To hire an indoor tennis court costs £10.50 an hour, while a squash court is £2.35 a half-hour.

Center Parcs boasts an astonishing 99 per cent occupancy level and although Elveden Forest, which accommodates 6,000 visitors at a time, was full with half-term visitors like us, it did not feel particularly crowded. However, if you are going at the most popular times – notably school holidays – and want to use the sports facilities, it pays to make the bookings the minute you arrive. We wanted to go bowling but there was not a spare half-hour for the entire weekend.

Eating in the restaurants, all of which cater for families, can make the holiday much more expensive, so we took food with us and as a result spent very little in addition to the basic cost.

A weekend break or short mid-week holiday is probably the best way to enjoy Center Parcs. I can't imagine spending an entire week there. And it is probably a nicer holiday in the winter, when lounging around in swimming costumes in the water complex, amid sugar cane and papaya trees, can be quite pleasant. The temperature is maintained at a constant 84°F.

The accommmodation is in hundreds of one to four-bedroomed bungalows arranged in a perfectly logical sequence around lakes and streams in the forest.

The bungalows themselves are comfortable, and our four-bedroomed version easily accommodated two families – four adults and five children. Each has a well-equipped kitchen, fireplace and television with satellite channels. Babies are catered for with a cot and high chair in each bungalow; baby-sitters can also be arranged.

Cars are banned in the forest other than for unloading and loading luggage outside your bungalow. Many families use bicycles to get around the forest – an adult bike costs £3.60 a day to hire, £2.30 for children.

Figure 9.12 Center Parcs: a fresh approach to the holiday resort (*Source*: *The Independent*, 29 February 1992)

Rural tourism and heritage tourism

Two factors that are helping to sustain the UK's domestic tourism market are (*a*) it is less dependent upon the traditional seaside resort and (*b*) it has introduced new tourist products and experiences. As more people travel by car, even though they may use a resort as a base for accommodation, they spend significant parts of their holiday touring the surrounding countryside. In response to this greater mobility, the **private** and **public sectors** are offering an ever-widening range of experiences. This, in turn, encourages the visitors to explore their destination region even more. Two good examples of the expansion of demand and supply are **rural tourism** and **heritage tourism** (Figs 9.13 and 9.14).

Figure 9.13 Principles of rural tourism (*Source*: Ryan, 1991, pp. 104–5)

Principles of rural tourism

a The promotion of tourist enjoyment of the countryside should be primarily aimed at those activities which draw on the character of the countryside itself, its beauty, culture, history and wildlife.

b Tourism development in the countryside should assist conservation and recreation, by bringing new uses to historic buildings, supplementing the income of farmers, and aiding the reclamation of derelict land.

c The planning, design, siting and management of new tourist developments should be in keeping with the landscape, and wherever possible, seek to enhance it.

d Investment in tourism should support the rural economy whilst encouraging a wider geographical and temporal spread so as to avoid problems of congestion and damage through over-use.

e Those who benefit from rural tourism should contribute to the conservation and enhancement of the countryside.

f The tourist industry itself should seek to develop the public's understanding and concern for the countryside and of environmental issues generally.

Figure 9.14 Examples of rural and heritage tourism

?

9 For each of the advertisements in Figure 9.14 identify:

a the provider.

b the attractive resources/facilities offered and where they are located.

10 On the map you compiled for Question 4, identify and describe one example of each of a rural tourism and a heritage tourism attraction, and one that combines both aspects.

Northern Ireland

'Different places, different perceptions: in Britain, the whole of Northern Ireland is seen as dangerous; on the north coast, the city of Belfast is regarded with alarm; in Belfast centre, it is West Belfast the citizens regard as a virtual no-go area.' (Fred Mawer, *The Independent*, 12 June 1993).

Outsiders' perceptions of a place strongly affect its potential for attracting tourists. The low point for tourism in Northern Ireland was in the early 1970s, when 'the Troubles' began. Since then, the number of people visiting the province has been on the increase, slowly but surely. In the early 1990s, Northern Ireland received about 250 000 visitors a year. But compared with Scotland, which received over 10 million tourists, the numbers are still very low. How can it attract more tourists?

The reputation that Northern Ireland has for bad weather, along with the ever-present threat of terrorist activity, undoubtedly continue to depress visitor numbers. One of the few attractions that remains comparatively busy throughout the year is the Giant's Causeway on the north coast. Not surprisingly, it is the isolated rural beauty of the countryside that the tourist brochures emphasise – the quiet, empty beaches and the remote landscapes (Fig. 9.15); they make no mention of 'the Troubles'.

Figure 9.15 The rural beauty of Northern Ireland, the High Mournes, Co. Down

11 Jot down five words that describe the image you have of Northern Ireland. Compare your list with those of other students. Divide the lists into words that are 'negative', 'neutral' and 'positive'. Comment on the image that comes out of your lists.

12 Use Figure 9.15 to write a paragraph for a tourist brochure to attract visitors to the area.

13 The material in Figure 9.16 is part of the 'Walking and Cycling Guide' to 'The Linen Homelands' in Northern Ireland. The brochure is one of a series produced by three local councils – Banbridge, Craigavon and Lisburn – with funding from the EC Marketing Development Support Scheme. Make a list of the attractive resources and tourist opportunities being promoted. Identify separately:

a natural heritage attractions
b human heritage attractions

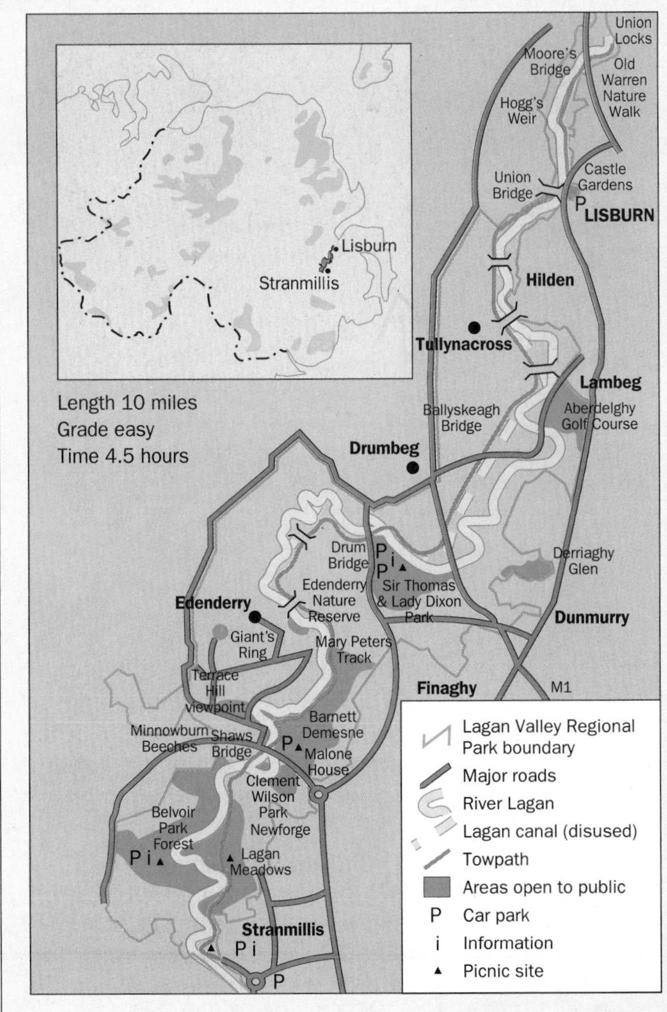

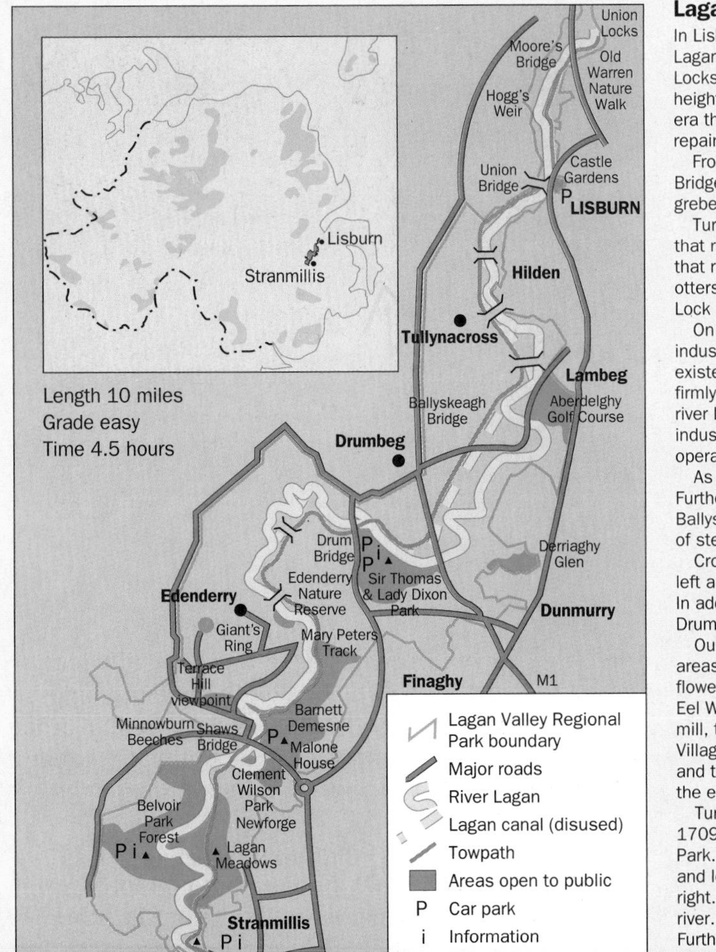

Lagan Valley Regional Park Towpath – Lisburn to Belfast

In Lisburn, join the towpath at Moore's Bridge. On the opposite side of the River Lagan you can see a site of industrial archaeological importance, known as Union Locks. This impressive feature consisted of four locks that lifted the barges a height of over 26 feet within a distance of less than 100 yards. During the canal era this area included the canal manager's residence, a lock-keeper's house, repair workshops and stables.

From here you head towards the centre of Lisburn, passing under Moore's Bridge built in 1825 and on to Hogg's Lock. Here you will find mallard, little grebes and swans dabbling for food.

Turn right and cross Union Bridge. Castle Gardens, high up on your left, is all that remains of what was known as Lisburn Castle, destroyed in the great fire that ravaged the town in 1707. Keep a sharp eye out for the shy and elusive otters that frequent the Hilden area. This stretch includes the remains of Hilden Lock and the large premises of Barbour-Campbell Threads Limited.

On then towards Lambeg where it is said that the Northern Ireland linen industry was born, and certainly as early as 1626 a bleach green was already in existence. Even by the time the Huguenots arrived in 1685 the industry was firmly established, although these settlers did bring new methods and ideas. The river Lagan and Canal played an important part in the development of the linen industry throughout the Lagan valley area, with nearly all of the merchants operating a private quay.

As you head towards Ballyskeagh, Lambeg Village and church sit on your left. Further along as you round a corner you will find the red sandstone arches of Ballyskeagh High Bridge. It is rumoured that the last man to hang, for the offence of stealing sheep, did so from this bridge.

Cross the river via a small footbridge. Sir Thomas and Lady Dixon Park on your left and St Patrick's Church, set back on your right, are both well worth a visit. In addition, from the towpath, you can see the restored lock-keeper's house at Drum Bridge.

Our journey towards Shaw's Bridge passes through one of the most scenic areas of the Park. Mature trees and woodland, together with a variety of wild flowers, provide an array of colour during the changing seasons. Soon you reach Eel Weir Picnic Site, whilst the small secluded village of Edenderry and former mill, that grew out of the linen industry, are visible on your right. Access to the Village, Edenderry Nature Reserve, Minnowburn Beeches, Terrace Hill viewpoint and the Giant's Ring is provided via the Gilchrist Bridge. Malone House, built in the early 19th century, is visible on the horizon.

Turn right and cross Shaw's Bridge, the famous old bridge that was built in 1709. Beyond this point, on the opposite side of the river, lies Clement Wilson Park. The path then follows a dry section of the old canal to as far as No. 3 lock and lock-house. Pedestrian access to Belvoir Park Forest is provided on your right. Shortly you will reach the Red Bridge that enables the towpath to cross the river. The trees overhanging the river on your right are part of Belvoir Park Forest. Further along on your left you will find a number of access points to Lagan meadows. Your journey finishes at Stranmillis car park. You are now less than 2 miles from the commercial heart of the city of Belfast.

Figure 9.16 Part of a brochure advertising walking and cycling routes in 'The Linen Homelands' of Northern Ireland

Figure 9.17 Heritage tourism; an advert for the Beamish Industrial Museum

9.5 The theme-park boom

Wildlife and heritage attractions

'Themed' attractions have a long history. After all, zoos and safari parks use the 'wildlife' theme, although their popularity is decreasing as fashion shifts, people show greater concern about the enclosure of wild creatures, and costs involved in meeting expectations keep rising. As a result, in 1991 the Windsor Safari Park closed and in 1992–3 the famous London Zoo in Regent's Park was fighting closure despite its attractive and accessible location. In contrast, the wave of modern **theme-park** developments is one of the success stories of the 1980s (e.g. the Windsor Safari Park site is now to be the home of the first Legoland outside Denmark). We must remember too, that heritage tourism is all about 'theming', such as the very high-quality Ironbridge and Beamish Museums with their industrial heritage themes (Fig. 9.17).

What is a theme park?

In contrast to such heritage attractions, however, most true theme parks are private commercial ventures and very expensive to develop. 'To qualify for theme-park status . . . a park must be built around one or more fantasy or historical themes, charge some form of all-inclusive entry fee, and offer a broad enough range of facilities and attractions to occupy a family for the whole day (rides, playgrounds, scenic displays, some indoor entertainment, shopping and catering)' (Tucker, 1991).

By this definition, although the UK has literally thousands of 'themed' attractions, only about a dozen qualify for full theme-park status (Table 9.3).

Of course, the majority of visitors to theme parks are excursionists rather than tourists, but market researchers believe that the tourist component is essential for the success (i.e. economic profitability) of these large parks. Although the first full theme park in the UK, Thorpe Park, did not open until 1969, in 1992 total attendances exceeded 8 million, with an average admission price approaching £10.

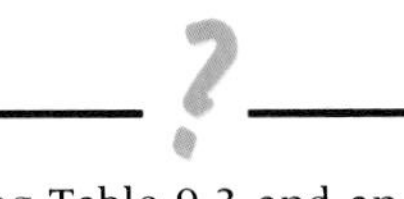

14 Using Table 9.3 and an atlas, plot the location of the seven biggest theme parks on a map of the UK. Shade the conurbations that are likely to be the main sources of visitors. Is it possible to identify a catchment area for each theme park?

Table 9.3 'The Magnificent Seven': theme parks with more than 500 000 visitors, 1990 (*Source*: Tucker, 1991)

Park	Location	Owners
Alton Towers	Staffordshire	Tussauds
Chessington	London (Surrey)	Tussauds
Thorpe Park	Surrey	RMK
Frontierland	Morecambe (Lancs)	Thomson
American Adventure	Derbyshire	Granada
Camelot	Chorley (Lancs)	Granada
Pleasurewood Hills	Lowestoft	RMK

More quality, more excitement

However, by the early 1990s there were signs that the market was levelling off. To remain competitive and retain their share of the market, owners constantly add more quality, more excitement and originality: bigger and more terrifying 'white-knuckle' rides mean huge **investments** (Fig. 9.18). The upgrading of Chessington in 1987 cost £10 million and since then a further £8 million has been spent on the Transylvania themed area. The new Pleasurewood Hills at Cleethorpes, opened in 1990, cost £12 million (this is a major additional attraction to add to the 'mass' of a struggling resort). The Tussauds organisation have a £50 million scheme for Woburn Abbey, and there is an ongoing planning battle over Rainham Marshes in Essex, where the **transnational company** MCA wants to build a £2.6 billion 'film studios' project. It is not surprising, therefore, that this is one area of tourism that is controlled by a small number of huge companies, and where a location with access to large markets is vital.

Figure 9.18 The Thunder Looper, Alton Towers: opened in 1990, this 'death-defying' ride reaches 97km/h in 2.8 seconds, loops a 23m looper twice and suspends passengers at 37m

Euro Disney® Resort

The 'gold standard' for all UK theme-park developers is, of course, Euro Disney Resort outside Paris, opened in 1992 (Fig. 9.19). The Walt Disney Company evaluated sites in several countries (including the UK) before choosing France. As their intended catchment area is the whole of western Europe, they made accessibility in relation to transport networks and to centres of population very important in their locational decision. To attract the millions of visitors necessary to be profitable, such fully **integrated resorts** must have associated provision for hotels, restaurants etc. The sheer scale of such a project as Euro Disney Resort brings inevitable environmental impacts and the company has made great efforts at landscaping and environmental enhancement in the surrounding districts. For instance, the traffic (generated by the combination of more than 10 000 employees, service vehicles and the cars and coaches of the visitors) puts enormous strain upon the existing transport infrastructure and will affect the quality of life of communities over a wide area. In recognition of this The Walt Disney Company has jointly funded, with the French authorities, large-scale improvements to the regional road and rail networks.

Such statistics lead some market researchers to calculate that a small and crowded country such as the UK, with high land prices and restrictive planning policies, can support only one Disney-scale park/resort project. Remember, too, that developers require accessible locations (e.g. 20 million people live within a 2-hour drive of Alton Towers), and large sites of at least 300 hectares. However, it is possible to develop a theme park within an existing facility (e.g. Woburn or Beaulieu), or to upgrade derelict land. This was the case with Thorpe Park, which was built on disused sand and gravel workings. The crucial element that changes an attraction from a large theme park mainly for excursionists to an integrated resort that draws large numbers of tourists is the addition of hotels and other entertainment facilities (e.g. Alton Towers is adding an accommodation element).

Figure 9.19 Euro Disney Resort: the scale of large theme parks

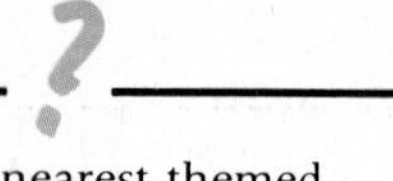

15 Name the nearest themed attraction to where you live which comes within the definition of a theme park given on page 102.

a What is its theme?

b What type of experiences does it offer?

c How far is it from where you live?

d How often have you visited it, and who with? If you have not visited it, why not?

e Are there additional **leisure** facilities that are there because of the park?

9.6 Foreign tourists in the UK

Where do they come from?

The graphs in Figure 9.20 show very clearly the scale and importance of foreign visitors to the UK. The nearness and business contacts of EC countries combine to make them the main source of visitors. For example, in 1991, for the first time, France overtook the USA as the leading country of origin for tourists to the UK. The overall trend is one of growth, but dips in the graphs illustrate how political and economic factors can affect tourism. For instance, the fall-off in arrivals in 1986 was caused mainly by the drop in the numbers of Americans travelling abroad as a result of terrorist attacks upon US airlines and citizens. The dip since 1989 has been caused by the economic recession, with cutbacks in both business and holiday travel, which has affected a number of the main countries who provide tourists to the UK. As a result, less has been spent in the UK, which has had a knock-on effect on employment (e.g. jobs in the leisure industry fell in 1992 for the first time in a decade).

Once in the UK, foreign visitors differ markedly from domestic tourists. They stay an average of 11 days, although the purpose of the trip makes a difference: business trips average 6 days; visiting friends and relatives (**VFR**) 15 days; holidays 10 days. Business travellers spend most per day and VFR tourists spend least. Around 40 per cent of all bed-nights are spent in London, where most trips begin and end. A further 50 per cent are spent in the rest of England, leaving 10 per cent spread through Northern Ireland, Scotland and Wales.

Where do they go?

At least 80 per cent of foreign visitors arrive through the airports and ferry terminals (and from 1994, the Channel Tunnel) of South-East England. Once they leave London, they tend to follow touring itineraries. These may be organised coach tours or independent trips by rental car or public transport. Such tourists make less use of seaside resorts than do domestic holidaymakers, but they do focus heavily upon a small number of internationally known **honeypots**: Stratford-upon-Avon, Oxford, Windsor, Stonehenge, Edinburgh, York, the English Lake District, the Scottish Highlands. The resulting impacts of this concentration are causing growing tensions in these destinations (Fig. 9.21). This is one of the reasons why tourist boards are encouraging the dispersal of visitors to less usual attractions, such as the rural beauty of Northern Ireland (Figs 9.15 and 9.16), urban and industrial heritage attractions such as Wigan Pier and the Beamish Museum (Fig. 9.17), and 'Big Pit' in South Wales.

Figure 9.20 Foreign tourists in the UK (*Source*: BTA, 1992)

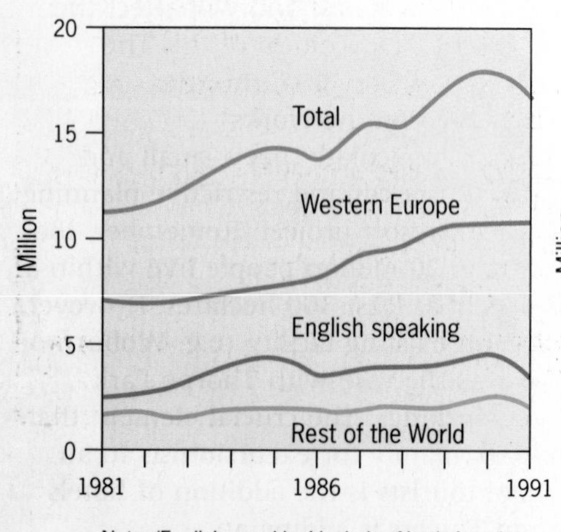

Note: 'English speaking' includes North America

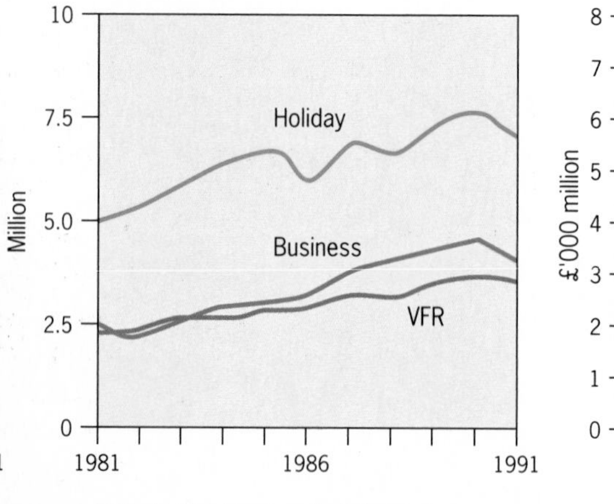

VFR = Visiting friends and relatives

c Spending

£'000 million

8 7 6 5 4 3 2 1 0

North America

European Community (EC)

Other Western Europe

Rest of the World

1987 1990 1991

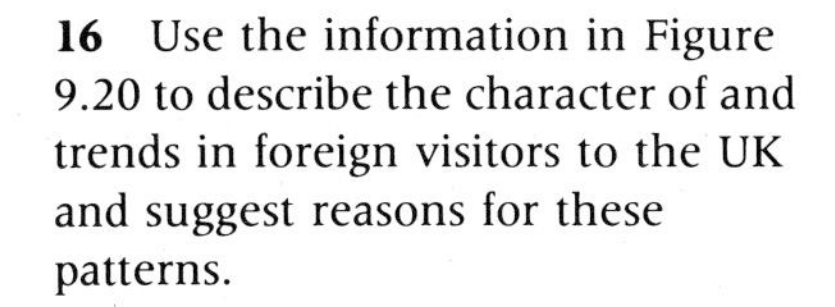

16 Use the information in Figure 9.20 to describe the character of and trends in foreign visitors to the UK and suggest reasons for these patterns.

17 Essay: Discuss which policy is better: (*a*) the continued concentration of foreign tourists or (*b*) their greater dispersal through the UK.

18a Visit your nearest TIC, or one when you are on a trip, and collect three brochures about different attractions.

b Analyse what they offer, who provides them and who you think they hope to attract.

19 Group Project: You have been asked by a large leisure company to propose a site in your local region suitable for the development of a theme park. Identify a site and write a report setting out your decision. (1:25 000 OS maps are the best basis for your search, with 1:10 000 sheets for more detailed site analysis.) In your report:

a Consider site size, location, character (drainage, present use), ownership, transport infrastructure and access, neighbouring settlements and land uses, and landscape character. (Local newspapers and estate agents may allow you to make an estimate of land costs.)

b List the competition from existing developments.

c Identify existing support facilities (e.g. hotels, restaurants).

d List the advantages and disadvantages of the site.

e Identify who would be likely to support and to oppose the development.

f Carry out a simple environmental impact assessment (i.e. the impact on the local community, economy and environment that the project would have). Include 'costs' and 'benefits'.

Overwhelming enthusiasm as four-hour culture hunters land in Bard's honeypot

The super-comfort land-liner with dark glass windows slides gently to a halt, touching down like an alien spaceship. Inside, its cargo yawn as they struggle off Pringle cashmere sweaters and put on 'Shakespeare Lovers' baseball caps.

Bailing out of their air conditioning, they arrive into the warmth of morning in Stratford-Upon-Avon, and minutes later are heading in an orderly crocodile for breakfast at McDonald's.

Within the hour, the citizens of Osaka shuffle reverentially around the half-timbered house in Henley Street where, 426 years ago, the world's most famous dramatist and most consistent tourist attraction was born.

Four hours later, these Shakespeare enthusiasts are back on the road, this time their objective being to go to 'Edinburgh, Scotland'.

Stratford tourism is a bit like that: a short, concerted invasion; then an orderly retreat,

But business people of Stratford do not complain, when the tourist trade accounts for around a quarter of their local economy. Stratford's experts would like more encouragement given to their tourists, rather than them being sent to alternative attractions.

The tourist trade recognises places like Stratford as 'honeypot' locations.

Roger Thompson, managing director of a town-tour company, Guide Friday, is concerned about the ideas being discussed, including the fear that Stratford, like so many other 'honeypots', is in danger of being environmentally overwhelmed by tourist hordes.

Mr Thompson, who is chairman of the Shakespeare Country Association of Tourist Attractions, is anxious that the trade is not seen as anti-green. But in a letter to Alan Howarth, Stratford's MP, he warned of the possible damage that dispersing tourism away from Stratford and similar attractions could cause.

August is Stratford's busiest month, when the pressure of visitors, that each year adds up to 2½ million tourists, is at its peak.

Figure 9.21 Newspaper report on tourist pressures on Stratford (*Source*: *Guardian*, 2 August 1990)

Summary

- Patterns of British tourism have changed greatly as domestic holidaymaking has declined and foreign holidays have increased.
- Tourism is the UK's most important industry, involving the commercial, voluntary and public sectors.
- Resorts, located mainly along the coast, are a distinctive category of urban settlement whose main function is the provision of tourist services and facilities.
- Seaside resorts have been forced to adapt and change as tourist demands have changed.
- Survival of traditional resorts depends upon the achievement of a 'critical mass' in terms of quantity and quality of attractiveness.
- The tourism product in the UK is becoming more varied and more widely dispersed as a growing range of attractions competes for the market.
- Themed attractions are a major growth area, but full-scale theme parks require massive investments and have severe environmental impacts.
- Foreign visitors make up an important component of UK tourism and have patterns of behaviour distinctive from domestic tourists.

10 The global explosion of tourism

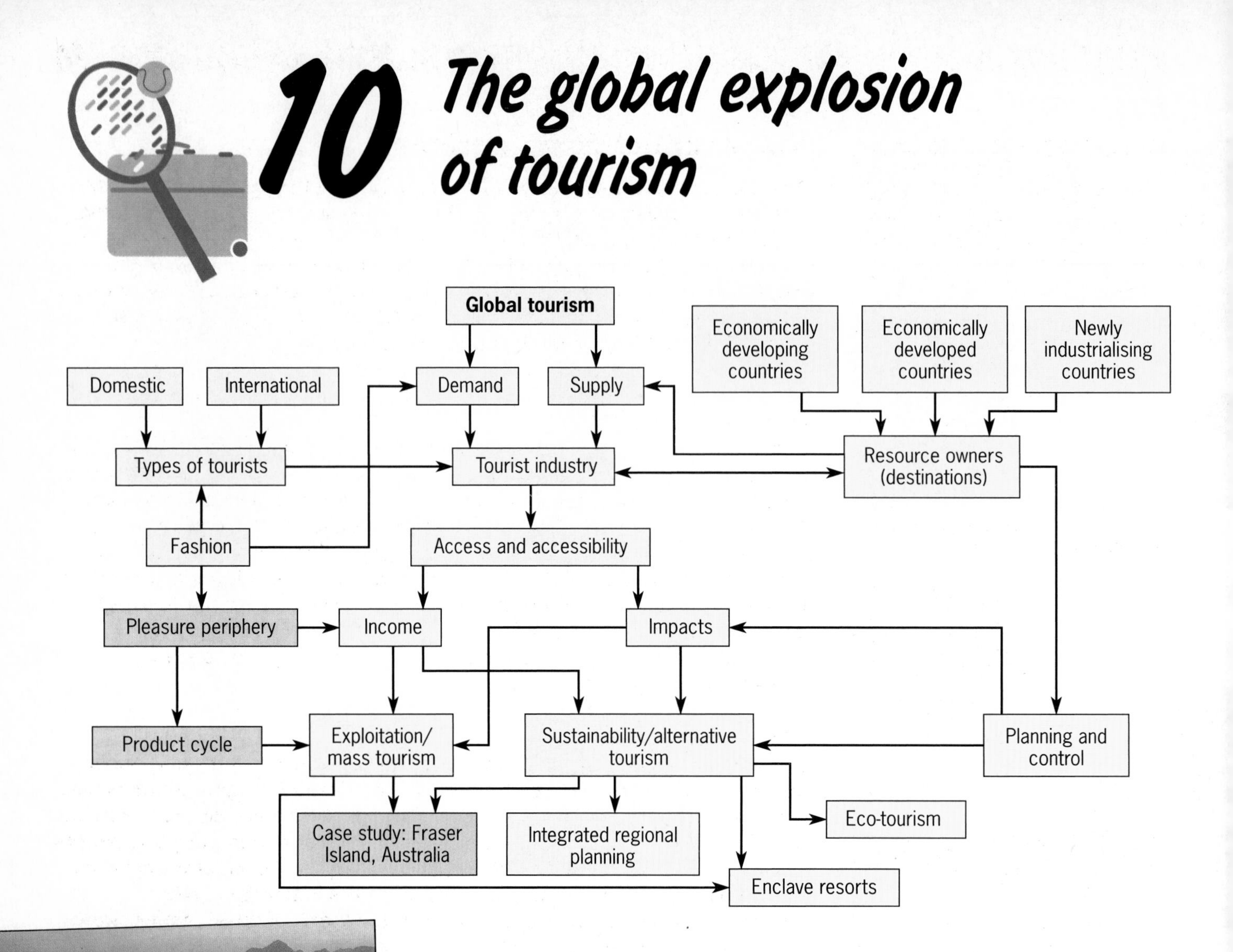

10.1 Introduction

Tourism is in danger of becoming a victim of its own success. It stands today at a critical stage in its evolution: can it continue to improve the quality of life for increasing millions of people (Fig. 10.1), or must it become yet another global environmental problem? This chapter helps you to explore this broad issue by considering a series of more specific questions:

1 Why do people travel for pleasure?

2 How, where and why is tourism growing and changing?

3 How are **demand** and **supply** organised through the tourism industry?

4 Who controls resources and makes decisions about tourism opportunities?

5 What are the positive and negative impacts of tourism, and for whom?

6 Can tourism be developed as a 'sustainable' rather than an 'exploitative' option?

At its most elemental: *is tourism a good thing – and, if so, for whom?*

Figure 10.1 Greetings from a student

10.2 Making travel decisions

'This chapter is being written in a *gîte* (rented cottage) in Brittany, France. My family and I have come here for our summer holiday: my wife wants to relax, read novels under the trees and eat in local restaurants. Our daughter and her friend want to get a tan on the beach, swim, attract the attention of young Frenchmen and get invited to discos. Our son would rather be on a Greyhound bus trek to visit friends and relatives in the USA but cannot afford it, so has rented a bike and has disappeared into the countryside to sketch. I want to spend time with my family, improve my windsurfing and observe tourists "at play", as tourism is my research interest. So, each one of us has different hopes for the holiday' (Fig. 10.2).

Figure 10.2 Holidays as relaxation and for getting a tan

The above is just one of millions of family sketches that could be written all over the world. Increasing numbers of people seem to have a great urge to travel. Indeed, it has been claimed that tourism has become the new global religion (Fig. 10.3). Thus, holidays can be seen as 'pilgrimages' to 'holy' places. Many holidays do improve our spiritual as well as physical well-being. There is no doubt too, that planning, taking and reflecting on a holiday is a major event in the lives of individuals and families. But *why* do we go – what are the motives and factors that influence our decisions? What are our expectations? Look again at the family 'sketch' – one family and one holiday, yet so many motivations and expectations!

Figure 10.3 Tourism as the new global religion – people of all faiths share the belief in the importance of travelling to see famous 'sights'. Tourists from India recording their visit to the Bangkok temples

Why go on holiday?

A holiday or vacation can be defined as a pleasure trip which involves staying away from your normal place of residence for at least one night. (Some official definitions suggest a minimum of four nights.) So, there is always the underlying motive 'for a change' or 'getting away'. This can be seen in terms of **push factors** (getting away *from*) and **pull factors** (getting away *to*). Beyond this, however, people travel for many reasons, and each of us has different motives at different times (Fig. 10.4). This may explain the '*why*?' of travel, but decisions are affected by other elements – *Where to*? *When*? *How much*? *How long*? *Who with*?

This diversity, when added to the huge and growing scale of tourism, means that enormous demands are made on resources, both natural and human-made. It is the issues surrounding these economic, socio-cultural and environmental demands and impacts that make up the central theme of this chapter.

Figure 10.4 Why go on holiday?

?

1 From Figure 10.4 select the motive which most closely fits your last holiday. Summarise where you went, how long you went for and the natural resources, human-made **facilities** and services that you 'consumed'.

2 Suppose you were thinking about your *next* holiday. Select from Figure 10.4 the two most important reasons and the two least important reasons which would influence your choice. Would your motives be mainly 'push' factors or 'pull' factors?

10.3 Tourism demand: scale and distribution

The opening question in any discussion of tourism issues must be: 'How many people are we talking about?' So, this section sets out some numbers as a basis for the rest of the chapter. Remember that most statistics identify three main categories of travel and tourism:

Domestic – trips within the country of origin.

International – where the origin and destination are in different countries (figures may be distorted by the inclusion of involuntary arrivals, i.e. refugees).

Business – where the primary reason for travel is work-related, and which may be domestic or international. (Chapter 9 illustrates the importance of this component in UK tourism.)

Many official figures do not separate out the refugee or business components, and so it may be impossible to say accurately how many travellers are on 'pleasure' trips. For instance, the figures that the World Travel Organisation (WTO) use for 'international arrivals', shown in Figure 10.5 and Tables 10.1 and 10.2 include *all* arrivals. Thus, the country supplying the largest number of arrivals to the USA, after Canada, is Japan, but over 80 per cent of these Japanese are 'business' travellers.

A second important point is that the totals shown on the graphs in Figures 10.5a and 10.5b are *international* arrivals. This explains the huge difference between Europe and North America: people travelling in Europe criss-cross national boundaries easily and frequently. Americans are highly mobile, but most travel is done without crossing an international boundary (almost 50 per cent of all air traffic is generated *within* the US). A family from New York taking a vacation in California will travel farther than a Dutch family holidaying in Greece, but they are recorded as *domestic* tourists. It is worth noting, too, that the 'visits to friends and relatives' (**VFR**) component is often shown separately. This is useful, for as we learned in Chapter 9 (page 94) the economic impact of such travellers is quite distinct. For some countries VFR travel may be significant (e.g. Australia where up to 25 per cent of arrivals are VFR).

The reasons behind the exploding growth rates in all regions of the world are based upon, first, more people in more countries having more time, more money, greater awareness and increased mobility and, second, the growth of international business, facilitated by the revolution in communications and transport technology (Fig. 10.6).

Table 10.1 World totals – millions of international arrivals (*Source*: WTO, 1991)

Year	Number
1950	25
1960	70
1970	160
1980	290
1990	440
1995 (est)	500

Table 10.2 Regional growth rates, 1985–90 (*Source*: WTO, 1991)

Region	Average annual % growth
Oceania	10.5
Africa	9.0
Asia	8.5
Americas	7.5
Europe	5.5

3 From Figures 10.5a and 10.5b construct a table of the *numbers* of arrivals for each region for 1980 and 1990.

a Which two regions had the highest *proportional* increases during that decade?

b Which two regions had the highest *numerical* increases for the decade? (Pay particular attention to contrasts between the **economically developed** and **developing** world.)

4 Summarise what Figures 10.5a and 10.5b, and Tables 10.1 and 10.2 tell you about patterns and trends in world travel and suggest reasons for them.

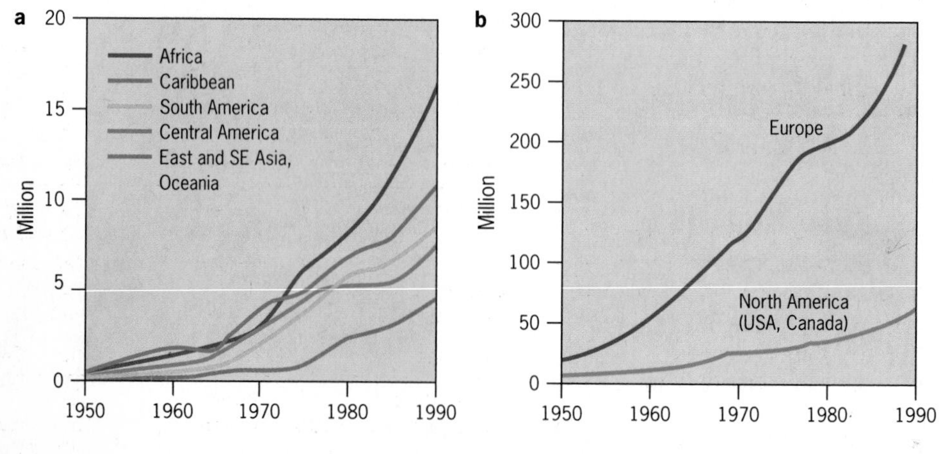

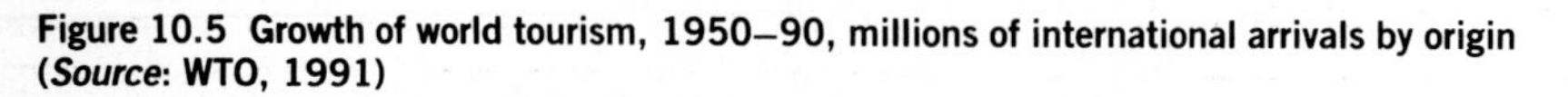
Figure 10.5 Growth of world tourism, 1950–90, millions of international arrivals by origin (*Source*: WTO, 1991)

Figure 10.6 **Making it all possible. Space-consuming, environmentally impactful, but efficient and effective: Dallas–Fort Worth International Airport, Texas, USA. The key to the explosion in world travel has been the revolution in transport technology. Air travel in particular, based on jet aircraft and super-airports capable of handling huge numbers, transports us across great distances with speed, relative ease and surprisingly cheaply**

5 From Table 10.3a, suggest two reasons why so many European countries rank in the top 10.

6 Using Table 10.3b and 10.3c list those countries who are:

a Net earners (earnings greater than spending).

b Net spenders (spending greater than earnings).

Comment on your lists. (NB. If a country appears in only one column then, clearly, that is the greater element.)

7 Using the information in Table 10.4 (and an atlas), give examples that illustrate the following statements:

a Visitors arrive mostly from neighbouring countries.

b Some destinations are dominated by visitors from one other country.

c For some destinations, visitor origins vary widely.

d Visitor origins are influenced by cultural and economic linkages.

e Ease of access is an important factor influencing where visitors come from.

f Some destinations act as 'hubs' or 'stopovers' on long-haul journeys.

g Some destinations are connected strongly with tour operators in specific countries.

Table 10.3 Tourism: The world's 'top ten' – international tourist figures, including business travellers, 1990 (*Source*: WTO, 1990)

a Arrivals (millions)

Rank	Country	No.
1	France	50
2	USA	37
3	Spain	35
4	Italy	30
5	Austria	18
6	UK	17
7	Canada	15
8	Germany	15
9	Hungary	14
10	Switzerland	13

b Earnings ($US millions)

Country	
USA	36
France	19
Spain	18
Italy	13
UK	12
Austria	11
Germany	10
Switzerland	7
Canada	6
Mexico	6

c Spending ($US millions)

Country	
USA	36
Germany	25
Japan	24
UK	16
France	12
Canada	8
Italy	7
Netherlands	7
Austria	6
Switzerland	5

Table 10.4 Origins of tourists, 1989 – 12 countries with popular tourist attractions and the main countries of origin of visitors, percentage of total tourists (*Source*: WTO, 1990)

Spain	%	Mauritius	%	Belize	%	Barbados	%
France	22	East Africa	22	USA	35	USA	33
Portugal	18	France	22	Europe (not UK)	5	UK	26
UK	14	South Africa	14	UK	5	Canada	14
Germany	13	UK	8			Caribbean	14
Netherlands	4	Germany	8			Europe (not UK)	10
Greece	**%**	**Iceland**	**%**	**Mexico**	**%**	**Bermuda**	**%**
Germany	21	Germany	14	USA	87	USA	84
UK	20	Sweden	13	Canada	6	Canada	8
Italy	7	Denmark	12	South America	5	UK	5
France	6	UK	9				
Yugoslavia	5	Norway	7				
Botswana	**%**	**Hong Kong**	**%**	**Cook Islands**	**%**	**Thailand**	**%**
South Africa	45	Japan	22	New Zealand	46	Malaysia	10
Zimbabwe	36	Taiwan	21	Australia	17	Japan	9
UK	4	UK	5	Europe	17	UK	8
Europe (not UK)	5	Australia	5	USA	10	Germany	8
Zambia	4	Thailand	4	Canada	5	USA	6

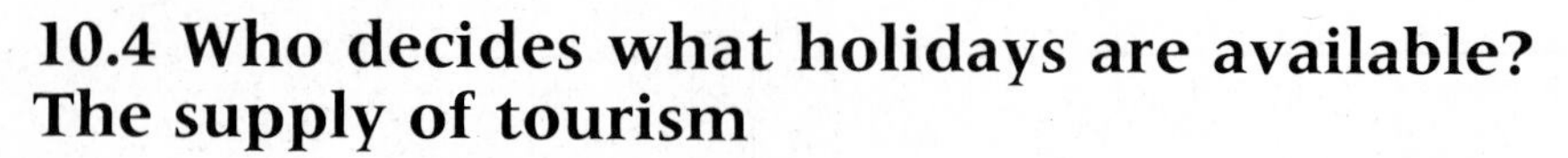

10.4 Who decides what holidays are available? The supply of tourism

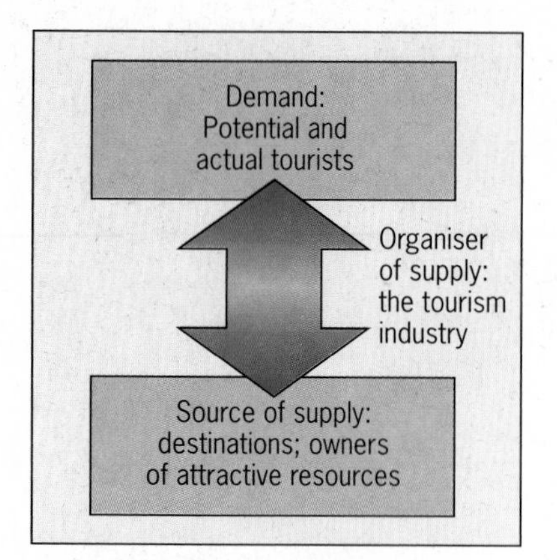

Figure 10.7 The tourism system

Tourism is the world's second largest industry, after oil. It generates over 6 per cent of global **GNP** and 13 per cent of consumer spending. The model in Figure 10.7 shows that the tourism system has three components. First there is *demand* (tourists), second *destinations*, who are the owners of the attractive resources, and third there is the *organiser of supply* – the tourist industry, which brings demand and supply together. The industry provides **access** and **accessibility**.

The power of the tourist industry in the decision-making process is enormous: it influences your experience as a traveller and the extent to which the destinations are permitted to control and develop their own attractive resources. For instance, as a student, you may think of yourself as an 'independent traveller', but to gain access to a Lapp community, an Indonesian volcano etc., you interact almost inevitably with the industry: information, transport, food, perhaps accommodation (Fig. 10.8). Equally, any potential destination wishing to market its attractions as a tourist product can do so only through the network of the industry: advertising, booking, transport etc.

Figure 10.8 Taking a year off before college. Mount Bromo, Indonesia

Economically developing countries

For many **economically developing countries**, connecting with this international network has proved a particular problem. They have, understandably, realised the attractiveness of their resources for tourism – beaches, warm and sunny climates, forests, deserts, mountains, wildlife, 'exotic' cultures, antiquities and so on – and their potential for income and development. To organise and market these resources and products, they have been forced to rely on international systems already in existence, mostly controlled by **transnational companies** based in the **economically developed** world. For example, the eight largest hotel chains in the world are all USA-based companies. Thus, many developing countries have found themselves locked into a dependent status. Indeed, one interpretation of international tourism sees it as 'economic colonialism': the countries of the South have become politically independent, but their resources are still exploited by the economically dominant countries of the North (Fig. 10.9).

Newly-industrialising countries

The group of countries known as NICs (**newly-industrialising countries**) have managed to weaken their dependency ties to wealthy nations and economically developed nations and are increasingly able to raise money internally, to invest in, organise and run their own industries. This progress is well illustrated by the 'Seven Dragons' of South-East Asia (Table 10.5 and Figure 10.10), whose economic growth rates regularly exceed 6 per cent. These countries can raise large sums of **investment** capital. All have increasingly strong policies of tourism development.

Figure 10.9 The Tanjung Aru Hotel, Kota Kinabalu, Sabah, Malaysia. This luxurious resort hotel was originally a government project, but has been sold to a transnational company because of the costs involved

Table 10.5 The 'Seven Dragons' of Eastern Asia

	Population (millions)	1992 Growth of GNP (%)	1991 Tourist arrivals (millions)
Hong Kong	5.7	6	5.5
Indonesia	184.5	7	1.8
Malaysia	18.7	8	4.3
S. Korea	44.3	7	3.0
Singapore	2.8	6	5.0
Taiwan	20.8	7	2.3
Thailand	56.3	9	5.0

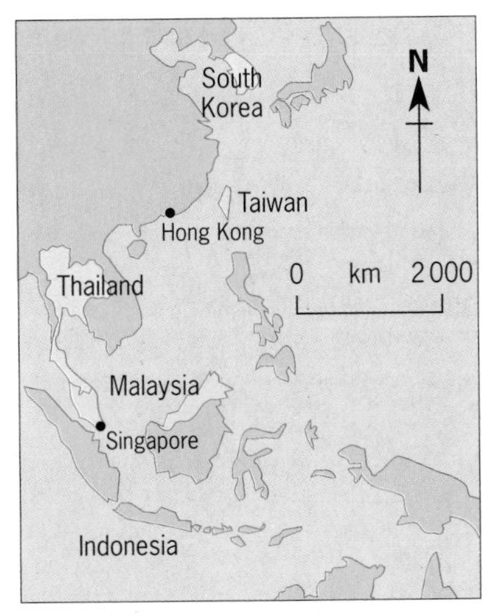

Figure 10.10 The 'Seven Dragons' of South-East Asia

Figure 10.11 Morning rush hour at the Bangkok temples. Each morning, fleets of mini-buses bring tourists from their hotels to the entrances of the temple complexes

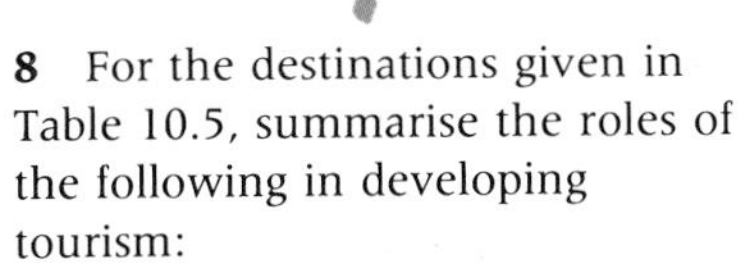

8 For the destinations given in Table 10.5, summarise the roles of the following in developing tourism:

a the public sector in the destination country

b the commercial sector in the destination country

c the international tourism industry

9 Give examples that illustrate the ways in which economically developing countries are 'dependent' upon the developed world (the North) for tourism success.

The policies are a partnership between the government (**public sector**) and **commercial** investment (**private sector**), although government involvement varies. Private enterprise is a combination of internal and external money and companies. For example, the Malaysian government declared 1991 a 'Year of Tourism'. As one element in this campaign, the Malaysia Tourist Board funded and organised promotional events throughout the UK. Displays emphasised Malaysian culture and natural attractions, while Malaysian and European tour operators advertised their 'products'. Problems, however, do remain (Fig. 10.9).

In 1992 the Thai government, in a country with a large tourism industry led by the private sector (Fig. 10.11), ran campaigns to diversify its product and improve its image away from the 'sex and beach' tourism of Bangkok, Pattaya and Phuket. The aim of the campaigns was to disperse the distribution and benefits from tourism more widely through the country. Thus, the Thai International airline (government-owned) was offering special deals involving visits to the system of **National Parks** (i.e. this was a public sector initiative).

10.5 The tourism industry and controlling income

International tourism behaves as an *export* industry. The 'product' of services and goods is sold and paid for in foreign currency (e.g. around £9 billion a year is brought into the UK from foreign tourists). But this product is 'exported' in a peculiar way in that the buyers consume their purchases, i.e. their travel experiences, at the point of production and supply. Thus, countries such as Malaysia and Thailand sell you tourist experiences to gain British currency, create jobs, raise national image etc., like any other export industry, but then you travel to these countries to consume your purchases. For this reason, foreign exchange earnings from tourism are classed in official figures as 'invisible' exports.

Problems of keeping tourism income

The economic benefit arising from this foreign currency has been one of the main driving forces behind many tourism development policies. Not only can the money be invested internally, but it can also be used to buy imported materials, equipment and other goods needed for development programmes. Unfortunately, things are not always this straightforward. Many destinations, especially smaller countries such as the Caribbean islands and Pacific islands, have found that at least 50 per cent of the money earned 'leaks' away.

Figure 10.12 The leakage concept

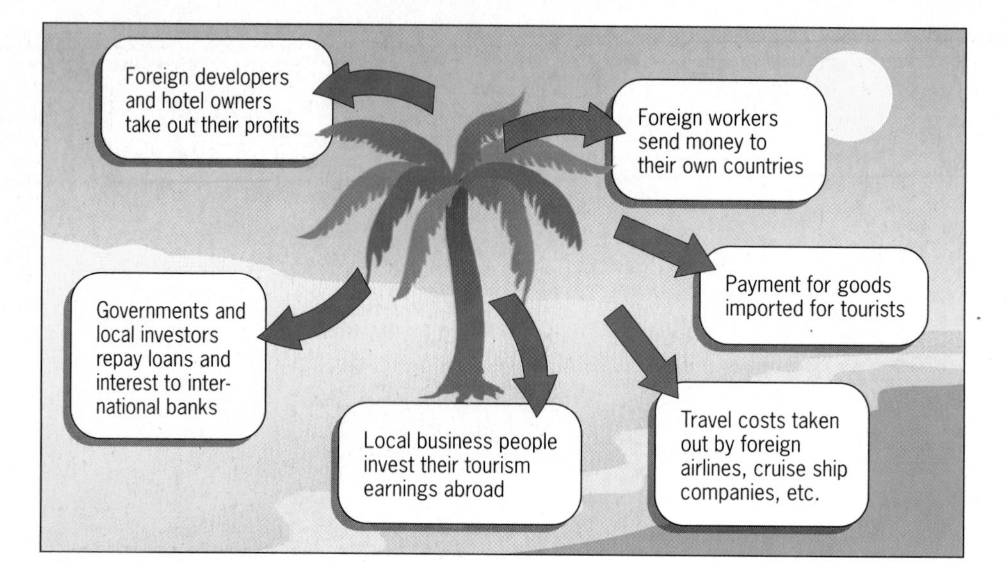

Leakage

Leakage is defined as the proportion of the income that is lost from the destination country and from which it therefore does not benefit (Fig. 10.12). For instance, if you buy a T-shirt in Spain, which has been made in Taiwan, some of your purchase price will not stay in Spain, but 'leaks' to Taiwan to pay for the import of the garment.

This leakage process in turn reduces the potential **multiplier effect** – the benefits from the money circulating through the destination country. For example, if the T-shirt was made in Spain, then Spanish workers will have earned wages which they then spend, which passes the money on through the economy and so on (i.e. it multiplies the benefit of your original spending as the money passes through the Spanish economy). If the money 'leaks', however, there is no such multiplier effect.

Table 10.6 illustrates how a fully inclusive foreign 'package' holiday from the UK may have limited benefit to the destination country. Only one-third of the cost of your holiday price actually reaches the country you visit, and remember, some of the 30 per cent the hotelier receives may then 'leak' to pay for imports etc. Two further points are worth noting: first, the figures exclude your spending while in the country, which may add 20 per cent to the income; second, the 40 per cent taken as the travel component helps to explain why so many countries are keen to develop their own airlines. For example if you fly to Kenya on Kenya Airways rather than British Airways, the economic benefit to Kenya is increased, although airlines are notoriously expensive to run.

Table 10.6 Economics – who benefits? Cost breakdown for a British example of a foreign package holiday; percentage of total cost (*After: Ryan, 1991*)

Retained by tourist-generating country:	
Transport cost	40
Agent commission	10
Publicity	8
Administration	6
Gross profit margin	3
Received by the destination country:	
Hotelier	30
Local services	3

Control

Small countries with narrow economic bases (i.e. few industries), limited capital and lack of a skilled workforce find that they have to borrow capital and use foreign companies to build and manage the developments, especially in the early stages. Much of the food, drink and entertainment has to be imported also. Thus, they have only limited control over their tourism industry. This issue of control is crucial – the greater the control of and involvement in the tourism industry, the greater the economic benefit is likely to be. Tonga, Fiji and the Cook Islands, all tropical island destinations in the Pacific, are good examples of this principle: Fiji has the largest tourism industry of the three, but has the lowest level of local ownership, and loses 60 per cent via leakage; Tonga has a much smaller industry but local people control most of it, so the leakage is only 8 per cent. The 50 per cent leakage from the Cook Islands is due largely to the control of tourism by New Zealand.

?

10 Suggest three ways in which a destination country could reduce 'leakage' of income from tourism.

11 Give three reasons why a tourism destination is more likely to have a higher degree of control over small-scale projects than over large-scale projects.

12 Essay: Suggest reasons why smaller-scale tourism developments may generate less gross income than mega-projects but may result in greater economic benefits to an economically developing country.

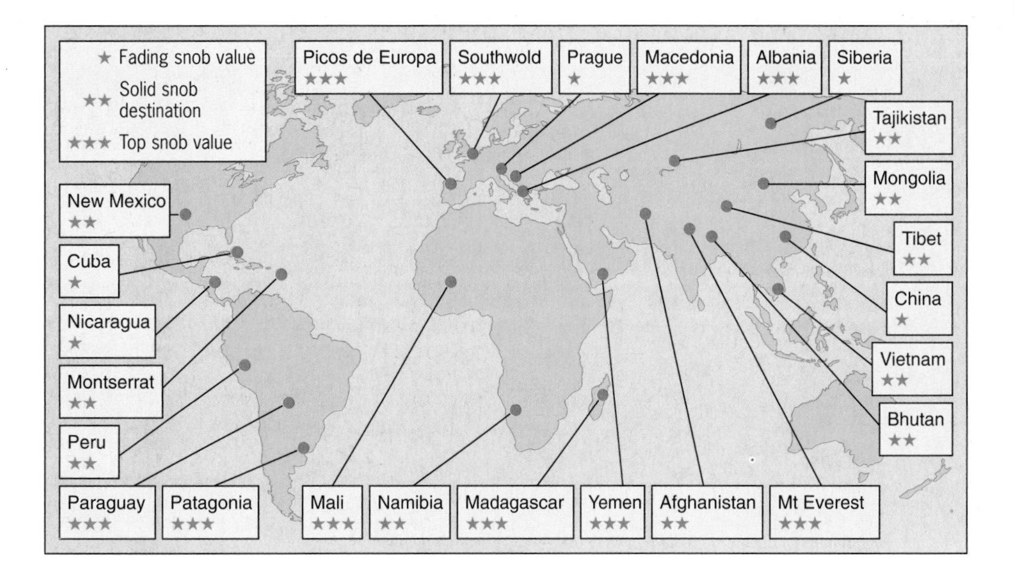

Figure 10.13 Worldwide snob holiday destinations (*Source*: *The Independent on Sunday*, 31 January 1993)

10.6 The impact of fashion

A second and equally important characteristic of tourism is that it is a *fashion* industry. *Status* and *image* are powerful motivators for travel to particular destinations. For instance, it is not simply getting a tan that is important, but *where you acquire it*: Margate is 'out', in the early 1990s even Mali was fading, but Madagascar was 'in' (Figure 10.13)! Where will fashionable suntans come from in 10 years' time? (Or will tans no longer be fashionable? Will natural skin tones be fashionable?)

Tourism marketing plays heavily upon status and image (Fig. 10.14). Fashion trends involve not only destinations (look again at the problems being faced by British holiday **resorts**, pp. 95–7), but also expectations, experiences, types of environment, activity etc. Skiing, for example, has boomed, but downhill skiing is losing some of its glamour to cross-country skiing and heli-skiing. Tourism operates through powerful cultural filters: it is sold to us and we perceive it through a set of cultural **values**.

Figure 10.15 also shows that package holidays are becoming less popular among UK tourists, especially to short-haul destinations such as Europe.

Figure 10.14 Marketing an image. Advert promoting marriage in exotic locations

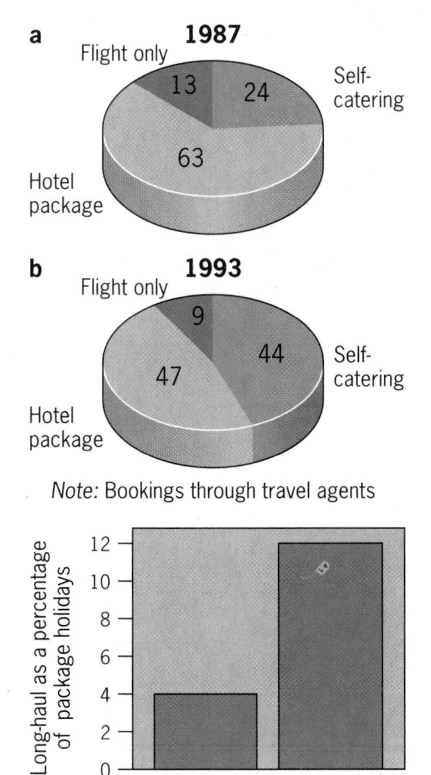

Figure 10.15 People want more independent holidays, and more go on package trips to long-haul destinations

The pleasure periphery

This idea of tourism as a fashion industry, constantly seeking new experiences, helps to explain the concept of the **pleasure periphery**. This depicts the boundaries of tourism as a tidal wave surging ever outwards across planet Earth from major tourist-generating regions (Fig. 10.16). At the outer edge of this surge, in 1992, around 6000 tourists spent an average of £4000 each to visit Antarctica.

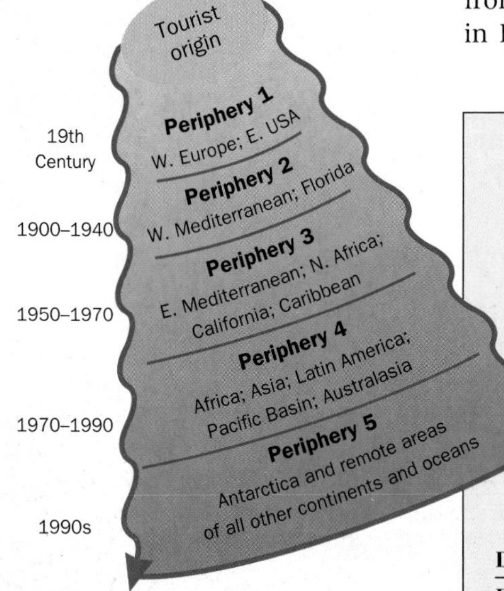

Figure 10.16 The pleasure periphery

ANTARCTICA

Even today, after so many years of exploration, Antarctica still remains a world apart, a majestic last frontier surpassing even the most jaded of travellers' expectations.

Until you have been there yourself, there are virtually no words that do Antarctica justice. This most southern of continents, this desert of ice, is so unique and uncommon to man's experience that even the best of photographs are mere attempts at describing the sheer magnitude, the awe, the beauty and wonder that is more appropriately felt rather than defined.

THE ITINERARY

Day 1 Fly London to Santiago via Buenos Aires.

Day 2 Santiago Arrive and stay 1 night.

Day 3 Fly Santiago to Port Stanley in the Falkland Islands, arriving the early afternoon. Excursion around Port Stanley prior to embarking on the IB *Khlebnikov*. Sail in the evening.

Day 4 Sailing in the Drake's Passage.

Day 5 During our voyage south we will spot numerous ocean birds including the graceful albatross. Our naturalists on board will assist you with their identification as well as giving the first of a series of informative lectures. Arrive at Elephant Island in the afternoon.

Days 6, 7, 8, 9, 10 & 11 During the next 6 days we shall make several landings on the Antarctic Peninsula. We will aim to cover a wide cross-section of the many highlights of the area. Taking into account, on a daily basis, the prevailing weather and ice conditions, we will schedule our programme with a strong emphasis on wildlife viewing. There will also be visits to areas of superb scenery along the coastal terrain, the icebergs and glaciers and indeed the very best that the Peninsula has to offer. With the long days available during the Austral summer, we will have the opportunity to spend many hours ashore using the helicopters or Zodiacs as determined by the conditions. We will also experience crashing through the ice *en route* to islands such as Paulet and Snowhill in the Weddell Sea and travelling much further south than usual to visit the British Base on Margarite Island. The list of visits should include Hope Bay, King George Island, Livingstone Island, Deception Island, Paradise Bay, Lemaire Channel and Cuverville Island.

Figure 10.17 At the outer edge of the pleasure periphery. Advertising a 'voyage of discovery' to Antarctica (*Source*: Noble Caledonia Ltd)

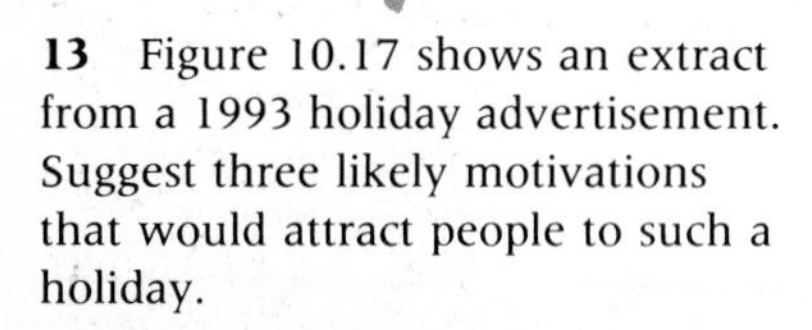

13 Figure 10.17 shows an extract from a 1993 holiday advertisement. Suggest three likely motivations that would attract people to such a holiday.

14 As an environmentalist, give three reasons why tourism should *not* be developed in Antarctica.

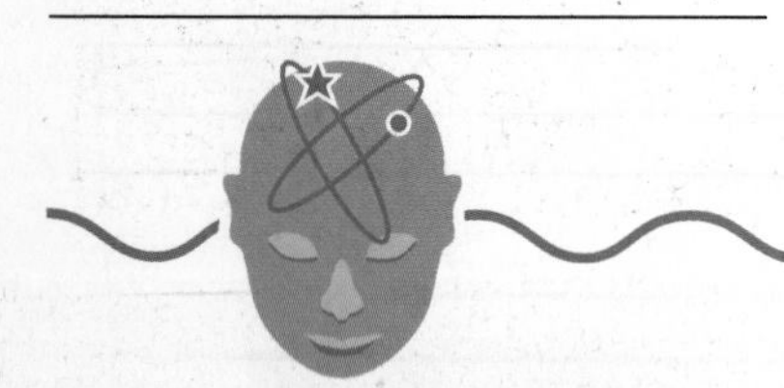

The product cycle

The understanding of travel and tourism as constantly seeking fresh resources leads to the claim that it is an essentially *exploitative* industry. It exploits the resources of a region while they remain in demand, before moving on to new source regions. A crucial outcome of this process is that any specific destination may experience a **product cycle**, comparable to that common in primary extractive industries such as mining and forestry. Figure 10.18a illustrates this product cycle over time for a single tourist destination.

It is also possible to locate different destinations upon the model at a particular moment in time, as in Figure 10.18b. The situation in the early 1990s is set out in Figure 10.19A–D. Thus, Alaska was at the emergent stage, the North Queensland coast was experiencing explosive growth, southern California and

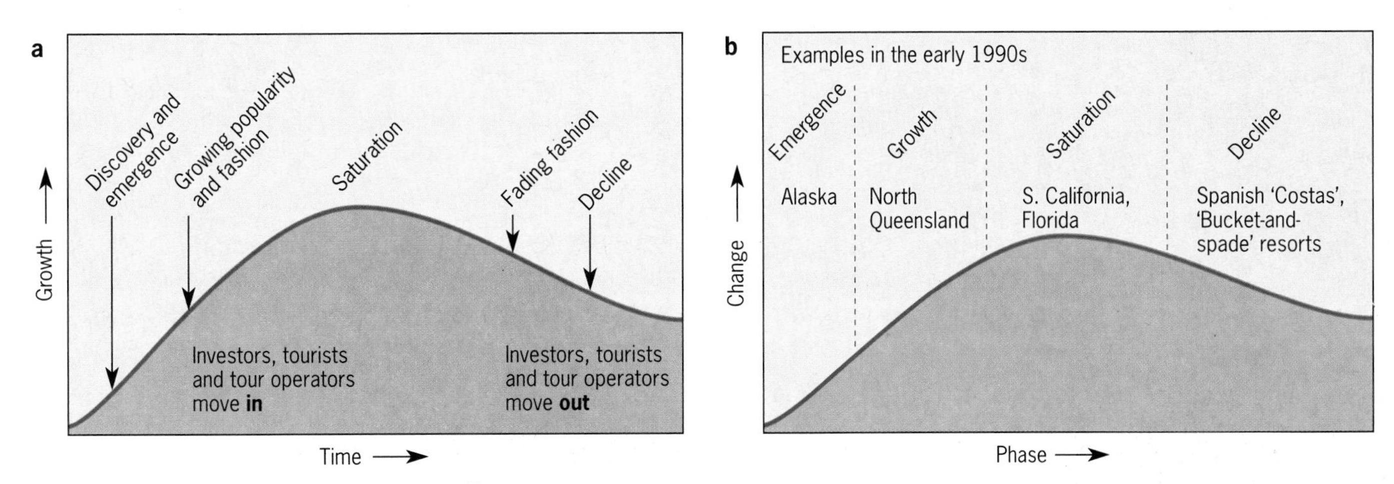

Figure 10.18 Tourism and the product cycle

A

B

Figure 10.19 The tourism product cycle in the early 1990s

A Emergent: Alaska. While cruises to the southern coasts of Alaska and visits to Denali National Park are well-established, the tourism potential of the wild, remote resources of this vast state are just emerging. Glaciers, wetlands and forests are being opened up by both the public sector (National Park and National Forest Services) and private sector specialist tour operators (hunting, wildlife watching, photography, backpacking).

B Growth: North Queensland. The tourism industry and the tourists have discovered the wonderful assembly of high-quality natural resources along the hundreds of kilometres of the North Queensland fringe: sun, sea, sand, rainforests, coral reefs, all currently 'unspoilt' and 'uncrowded'. Thus, in 1990, along a 40km. stretch of coast near the Whitsunday Islands, there were at least 18 planning applications for resorts/marinas, worth more than A$ 40 million. Japanese investors and tour operators are applying the greatest pressure.

C Saturation: Southern California and Florida. They remain powerful magnets for millions of American 'snowbirds' who flee the harsh North American winters, as well as international tourists. But you can drive the 300km from north of Los Angeles to the Mexican border south of San Diego, and the only open stretches of coast are military bases and State Parks and Reserves. Florida too, has used up its 1500km of coast between Tampa on the west and Jacksonville on the east, except for the Everglades National Park, the Kennedy Space Centre and some State Parks.

D Decline: the Spanish 'costas'. Between 1989 and 1992, bookings by British tourists to the Spanish *costas* declined by 25 per cent. The positive image of cheap and guaranteed sun–sea–sand–sangria–sex is being replaced by negative images of pollution, crowding, crime, poor accommodation and over-packaging. The quality of the built environment and the remains of the natural environment – the beaches and the sea – are perceived as deteriorating.

C

D

The product cycle

Florida were still popular but had utilised all their prime coastal resources, while the Spanish 'costas' and many British 'bucket-and-spade' resorts were struggling to avoid the slippery slope of decline (see Chapter 9). In any tourism case-study analysis you do, it is helpful to place your chosen destination within this model, and to justify your placement.

As a resort or destination region passes through the product cycle, so all aspects of the tourism system change – the destination, the tourists and the impacts. Figure 10.20 follows this transformation from the time a few adventurers 'discover' an area, to the time when mass tourism dominates the social, economic and physical environment.

?

15 For any resort or tourist destination region you have visited, place it on:

a The product cycle model.

b The evolutionary model of Figure 10.20.

Give reasons for your placements.

16 Study Figure 10.21 carefully.

a Summarise the key social, economic and environmental issues.

b Place the area on the models in Figures 10.18 and 10.20.

17 Essay: Outline the concept of the product cycle and assess its usefulness for the study of tourism in a destination region. Use examples to illustrate your answer.

Type	**Explorers** discover a destination	**Off-beat adventurers** penetrate a region	**Elite** wealthy status-conscious groups arrive on expensive tours	**Early mass** middle-income groups on organised hotel or villa rental packages and tours	**Mass package** tourists on fully standarised packages
Number	Very few	Small numbers	Limited numbers	Steady flow	Massive numbers
Expectation and impacts	Accept local conditions	Revel in local conditions	*Either* demand Western amenities or 'rough it in comfort'	Look for Western amenities	Expect Western amenities
Example	Scientists and travel writers	Student backpackers	Social elites	Professional families	Wide range of social groups

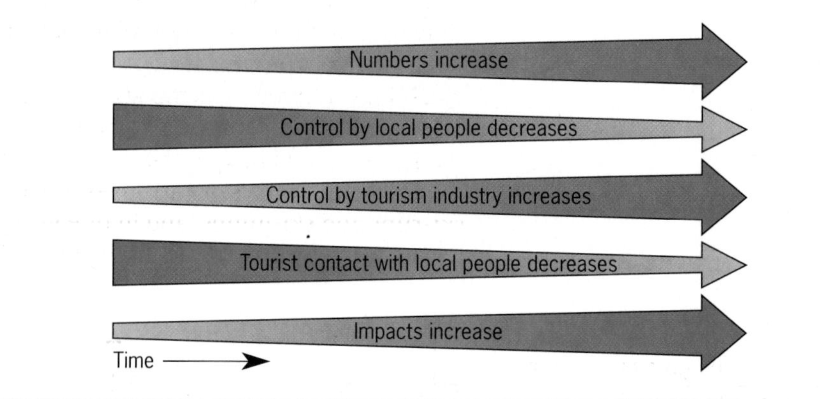

Figure 10.20 The change in types of tourist over time

Figure 10.21 Newspaper report on 'paradise lost in Goa' (*Source*: *The Independent*, 27 January 1993)

THE WORDS and imagery are persuasive: they speak of dream holidays, friendly local people, an unspoilt, palm-fringed paradise. But the reality is drug abuse, child prostitution and widespread environmental destruction.

The Indian coastal state of Goa was singled out yesterday as a lesson in how mass tourism to 'exotic' locations has gone badly wrong. According to the pressure group Tourism Concern, Western tour operators are causing much of the damage but are 'washing their hands' of responsibility.

Goa, which became a Western tourist destination after being discovered by hippies in the 1960s, is now the scene of acid parties, raves and increasing child prostitution. Tourist buses have been pelted with rotten fish and cow dung, and police mount drives against drug-taking Westerners.

Women protest at their portrayal in tourist literature – at how 'they and events like the local carnival are being commoditised at the expense of their dignity and culture'. Children skip school to peddle drugs to Western tourists, who affront the morality of villagers by sunbathing in the nude.

Many local groups are also angry at the special treatment tourists receive, according to a Tourism Concern survey. Hotels, many foreign-owned, receive subsidised water and electricity. Yet one five-star hotel consumes as much water as five villages and one 'five-star tourist' consumes 28 times more electricity per day than a Goan.

THE CONFLICTING VIEWS

The place	The image: *What the brochures say*	The criticisms: *What local people say*
Taj and Fort Aguada holiday complexes	'Relaxed . . . laid back . . . beautifully and peacefully positioned.' (Inspirations India)	Local people denied beach access and access to water pipeline
Leela Beach Hotel	'Walk about in the extensive grounds and the predominant noise is birdsong' (Inspirations)	Refuses to rent out coconut trees to tappers, damages trees, illegal wells built, villages displaced from land, beach access denied
Cidade de Goa Hotel	'Lovely, beachside setting . . . comfort, elegance and friendly service' (Cosmos)	Beach access denied by wall, sewage dumped, court orders taken out against it
Dona Sylvia Hotel	'Excellent location . . . alongside a wonderful beach' (Sunworld)	Illegal fence built, dunes damaged to give guests seaview.

10.7 Is there life after tourism? The search for sustainability

A tourist destination faces two nightmares as the product cycle evolves: first, growing awareness among the indigenous population of the social stresses and environmental changes occurring, and second, that the tourists might stop arriving. Even many of those who dislike the tourist hordes realise that they need the income from tourism. The destination has several options:

1 It may invest some of the income from tourism in other sectors of the economy (i.e. use tourism as one phase in the development process and so diversify the economy in preparation for the time when tourism declines).

2 It may modify its tourism product (the supply) to meet the changing demand (e.g. compete for a different segment of the market).

3 It may attempt to plan and control the tourism development more firmly in order to *sustain the quality and productivity of the attractive resource base over time.* This resource base includes the natural and built environment, the character of society and culture, and the economic basis of life.

Effective development planning is likely to involve elements of all three options.

There is little doubt that, today, all three components of the tourism system (tourists, destinations, the industry) accept the desirability of strategies for **sustainability** rather than exploitation in tourism development (Fig. 10.22). This sounds fine, but key problems lie in the sheer scale, complexity and the dynamism of the industry (Fig. 10.23). Each of the many forms of tourism has its distinctive resource demands and impacts – economic, social, environmental. For instance, preparation for the 1992 Winter Olympics caused a huge amount of environmental damage. Protected forests and rare marshland were violated. A million cubic metres of earth was moved from the mountains for the various ski-runs and ski-jumps, and in one village residents were issued gas masks because of fears of toxic leaks of ammonia from a bobsleigh run!

?

18 Which of the graphs in Figure 10.22 best reflect the concept of sustainable tourism?

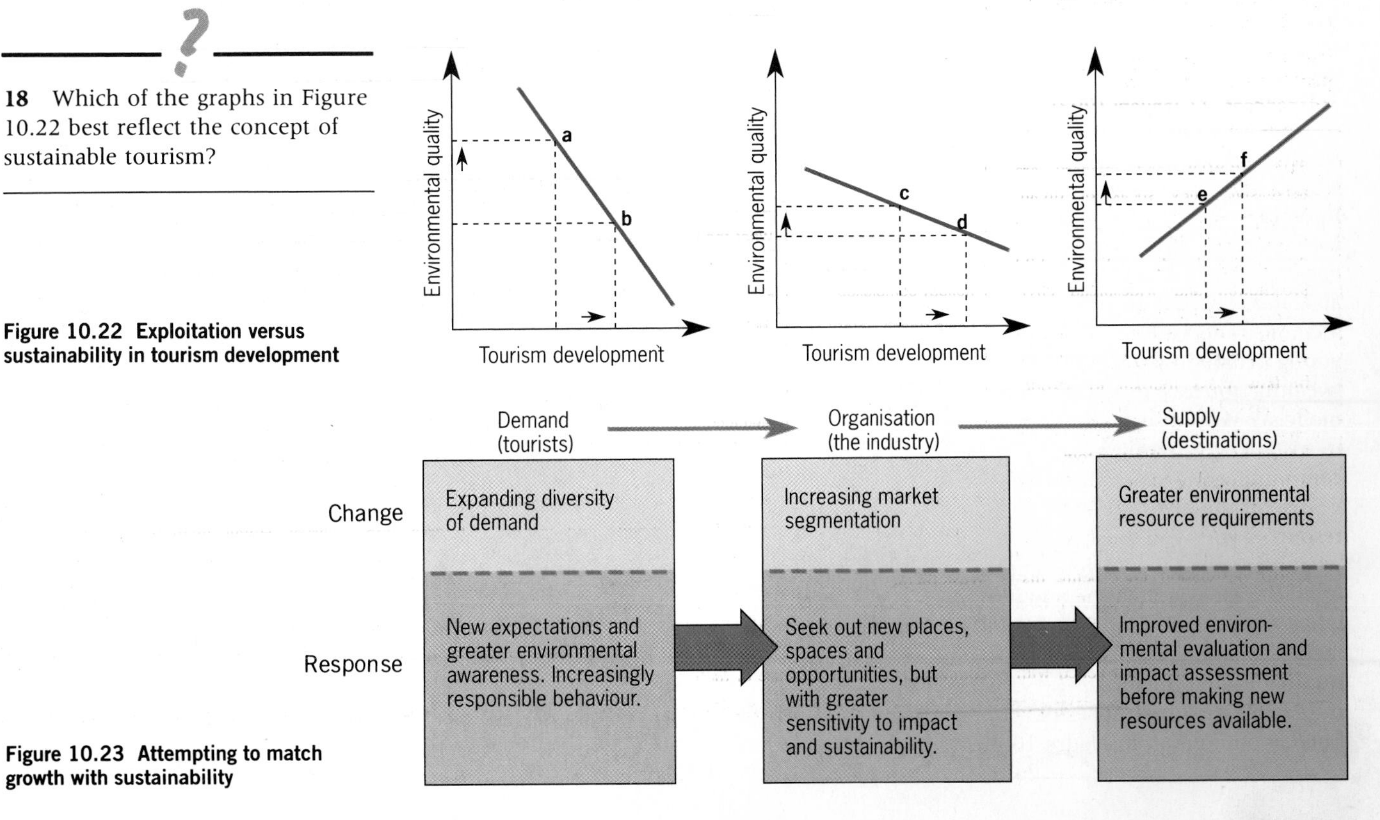

Figure 10.22 Exploitation versus sustainability in tourism development

Figure 10.23 Attempting to match growth with sustainability

Figure 10.24 Sunlust → enclave → concentrated → packaged tourism. The sunlust tourist seeks facilities and amenities that are *better* than at home. All aspects of the holiday are tightly organised by the tour operator – transport is from airport to airport to the resort enclave, where all the tourist's time is spent. There is little contact with the local society or environment, except the beach and sea. The tourist exists in an 'environmental bubble'

?

19 Look at Figures 10.24 and 10.25. Describe an example of:

a A sunlust holiday.

b A wanderlust holiday.

(Draw on your own experience or use tourism advertising literature to help you.)

20 Assess each of the types of holiday in terms of:

a Spending patterns: what you would spend money on; who would get your money; is it likely that your spending would benefit, i.e. sustain the local economy over time? (Think of the elements: accommodation, food and drink, travel, entertainment, activities.)

b Making contact with local people: on what terms (formal or informal); where you would come into contact; with whom; what effect your behaviour and appearance would have (e.g. the 'demonstration effect' whereby young people in particular see 'wealthy' tourists as desirable role models)? Would such contacts help to sustain or to weaken local communities?

c Use of the environment: what resources you would use and in what way; what would your impact upon the environment be and in what ways might your presence make sustaining **environmental quality** more difficult?

d Place each of the types of holiday on a graph in Figure 10.22.

Figure 10.25 Wanderlust → touring → penetrative → dispersed → semi-independent travel. The wanderlust traveller seeks something *different* from the home, moves through and within the destination region, likes to make personal or small-group decisions and enjoys frequent contact with local society and the environment

Figure 10.26 Ocean cruising holidays

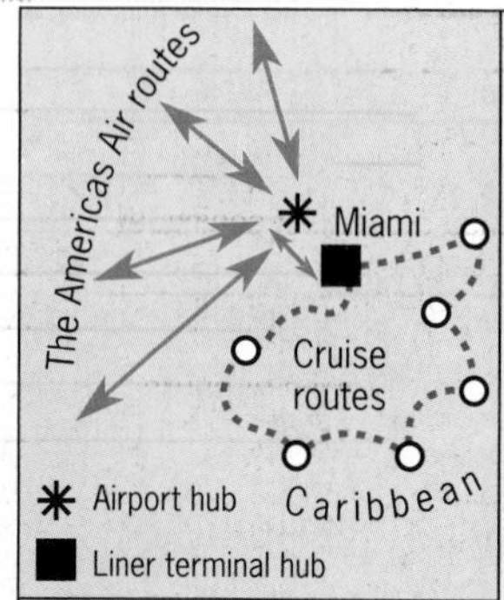

Airlines and cruise lines operate the 'hub' system – collecting customers into a few major terminals and then redistributing them. Miami is an excellent example: a major hub for the North and South American airline networks and highly accessible for the Caribbean tourist destinations, with easy transfer from airport to liner terminal.

The cruises visit a variety of islands, with stopovers ranging from a few hours to two days to allow shore visits, shopping and excursions. Accommodation and most meals are taken aboard the ships. Cruise itineraries have considerable flexibility, and companies can alter routes and stopovers from year to year according to popularity and fashion.

21 Essay: Figure 10.26 sums up the spatial structure of ocean cruise holidays. Discuss the hypothesis that such tourism assists social and environmental sustainability but may be less economically profitable for destinations.

Sustainability and alternative tourism

Sustainability is an idea central to emerging forms of tourism generally grouped under the umbrella of **alternative tourism**, which means alternatives to existing mass tourism. Terms such as 'green tourism', 'soft tourism', 'ecotourism', 'responsible tourism', 'agrotourism', **rural tourism** are increasingly common. We see the signs in the growing numbers of specialist tour operators who organise environmentally sensitive trips to distant and exotic locations. These types of tourism attempt to achieve a better balance between **conservation** values and development values. Increased sensitivity is being shown too, within the mainstream industry, although as the scale of tourism increases so it becomes more difficult to limit impacts and to sustain resources over time (Fig. 10.27).

Six main themes are important in policies for sustainable tourism:

1 Planning and control of the spatial distribution and the character of tourism developments – where they will be and what they will look like.

2 Surveys of resource evaluation and impact assessment *before* development takes place.

3 Integration of tourism into other aspects of regional planning (e.g. where new transport routes are to go).

4 Increasing involvement and control by local and regional communities.

5 Identification of the type of tourism appropriate to the resources and environment.

6 Establishment of a **carrying capacity** that balances conservation and development values.

The following case study and examples illustrate these themes and the problems involved, especially as the scale of the developments increases.

World Expeditions 1993

During the past season we have taken sight-impaired trekkers, from the Guide Dog Association, to trek the Annapurna foothills. Inspired by Peter Hillary, we have pioneered a 'Youth To Everest' programme, in which Australian high school students travel to the Sherpa homelands and work on community projects, as well as having their first taste of trekking. And we've initiated the first group bicycle tours of Vietnam; an enormously enjoyable, free-wheeling adventure.

There are two commitments at the heart of our success: using local staff, and preserving the environment through which we travel. Long ago we pioneered the policy of training local trek leaders in the Himalaya. As we have extended this policy to other countries, our groups too have benefited from the sustained interaction with skilled local guides and their culture.

World Expeditions has long been mindful of preserving the fragile environments that are our worldwide 'turf'. In 1986 we introduced a 'no wood cutting' policy in Nepal; instead, we carry our own cooking kerosene. And everywhere we strive to not 'rubbish' the pristine landscapes our groups are so fortunate to encounter.

This season, we're doing more of the same, and we plan to do it even better. In South America, Antarctica, Asia, Australia and the Pacific, World Expeditions is right in there, on the high road to adventure.

We look forward to you joining us.

KUONI 1993

Kenya is home to some of the most spectacular game parks in the world – it is here that many of our client's experience the thrill of seeing, at first hand, wildlife roaming free.
But if the parks and the wildlife they support are to survive, the Kenya Wildlife Service needs help. The Game Parks and Reserves of Kenya are under intensive pressure from a rapidly increasing human population and unless they can be proven to be worth saving, they will be forced to yield to this pressure. We believe that tourism can help stop this disaster from happening.

In conjunction with the registered UK charity **Friends of Conservation**, Kuoni supports the joint projects of Friends of Conservation and the Kenya Wildlife Service, under the personal management of Dr Richard Leakey. A donation of £2 on behalf of every passenger travelling on safari with us to Kenya will be our 1993 contribution to the Kenya Wildlife Service.
This enables us to support the following projects:

* Wildlife Protection Unit. This unit's tasks include anti-poaching activities, rescuing injured animals, monitoring of tourist vehicles relative to animal harrassment and care of wildlife.
* Rhino Translocation and Wildlife Veterinarian Programme – support for veterinary expertise and the translocation of endangered rhinos into protected sactuaries.
* Community Conservation and Educational Projects – support for local conservation groups and the production of educational material for use in schools.

Should you wish to make an additional contribution to the Kenya Wildlife Service, more information is available from:

Friends of Conservation
Sloane Square House
Holbein Place
London SW1W 8NS
Telephone: 071 730 7904
Registered Charity No: 328176
(Patron: HRH The Prince of Wales)

... Thank you for your help in supporting Kenya's Wildlife.

Figure 10.27 Concerns for sustainability from two tour operators, World Expeditions and Kuoni

Balancing conservation and recreation values: Fraser Island, Queensland, Australia

Fraser Island lies 250km north of Brisbane, and 15km offshore from the town of Hervey Bay (Fig. 10.28). The island is 120km long, up to 25km wide (larger than the Isle of Wight), and composed entirely of sands: both bedded sandstones and white oceanic sands blown into dunes by the wind. There are three main landscape and ecosystem types:

1 Coastal environments – beaches, dunes, rocky headlands, estuaries.

2 Inland environments – eucalyptus forests and heathland.

3 Water bodies – 40 inland lakes and freshwater swamps.

Visitors have arrived by ferry from Hervey Bay and by their own boats since the 1930s, for fishing, wildlife viewing and camping. As recently as 1975, the annual total was only 20 000. By 1990 the numbers had exploded to more than 200 000. This was caused by (*a*) the introduction of vehicle ferries in 1968; (*b*) the development of four-wheeled recreational vehicles; (*c*) increased awareness and fashion. Thus, access and accessibility were both increased.

Although the island was managed by the National Park Service (Great Sandy National Park in the north of the island) and the Forest Service (Fraser Island State Forest), there was no overall **management** plan. As a result, the increasing numbers of four-wheeled vehicles and visitors were causing damage to the beaches, forests and lakes. For these reasons, in 1988 the island was designated as the 'Fraser Island Recreation Area', with one decision-making body.

A management plan was drawn up, based on **zoning** for different carrying capacities (shown on the map). The most fragile and precious resources are zoned for lowest-density use, while more accessible and less sensitive resources are zoned for higher carrying capacities. Thus, the precious and popular lakes and patches of original forest in the centre of the island are zoned for 'primitive' use (i.e. no vehicles, no developed campsites, no marked trails). In contrast, areas near the ferry landing, beside the graded tracks and along the attractive eastern beaches are zoned for more intense use. Visitor totals are to be restricted to 250 000 a year, and 'roads' will not be surfaced, in order to restrict traffic to four-wheeled vehicles. Notice, therefore, that the carrying capacity and the distribution of visitor use are both strongly controlled in the plan.

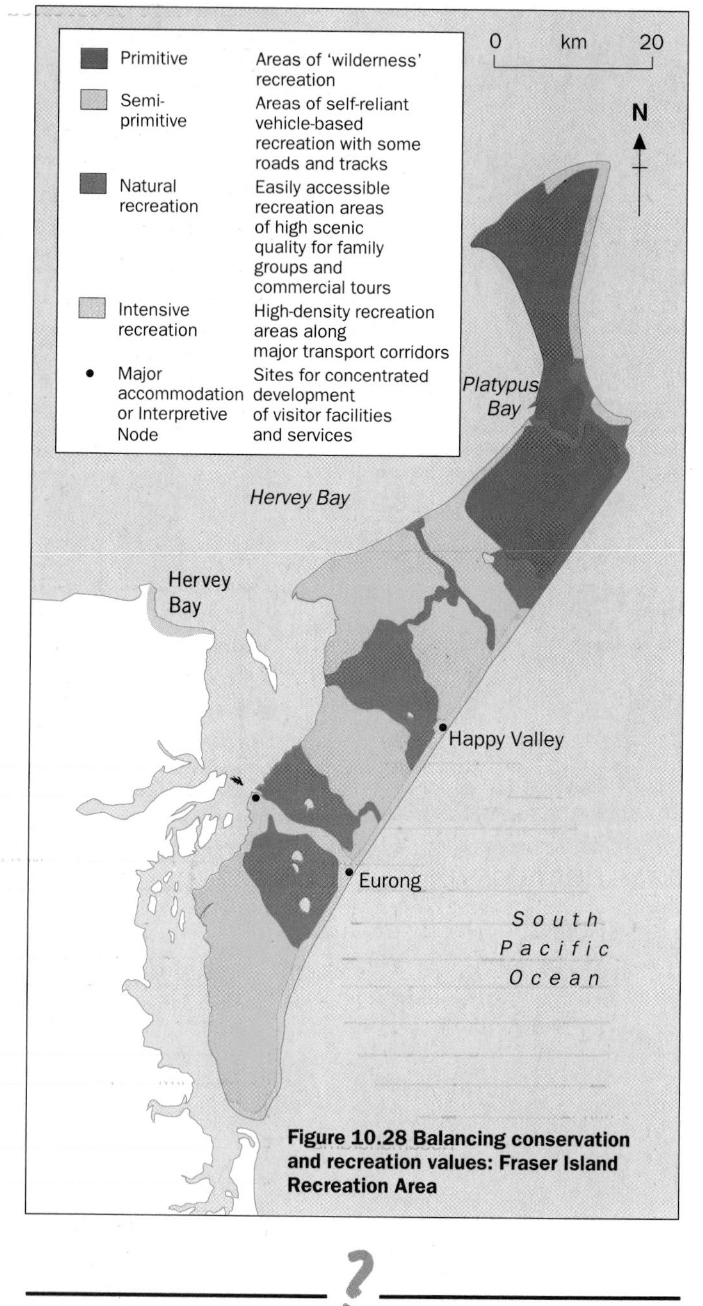

Figure 10.28 Balancing conservation and recreation values: Fraser Island Recreation Area

?

22 Explain why increasing access and accessibility on Fraser Island increased the quantity but decreased the quality of recreational experiences.

23 Illustrate how access and accessibility are used in the Fraser Island management plan to manage carrying capacity.

24 Essay: To what extent does the Fraser Island management plan fall within the six themes for sustainable development set out on page 119?

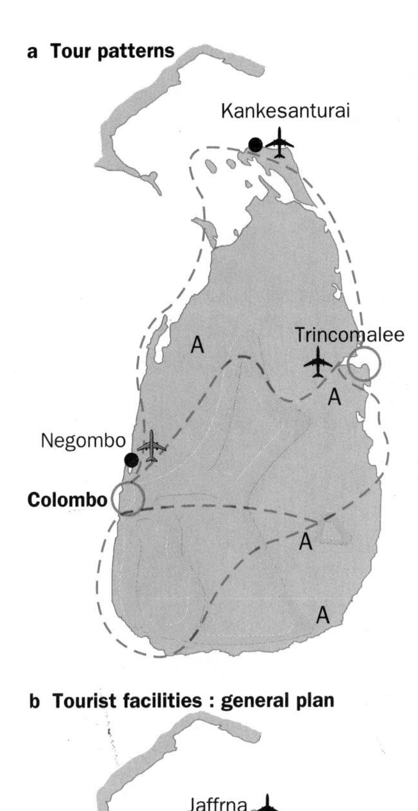

Figure 10.29 Regional planning for tourism in Sri Lanka (*Source*: Baud-Bovy and Lawson, 1977)

Approaches to the search for sustainability

1 Integrated regional planning

Since the early 1970s Sri Lanka has based its tourism development upon the plan shown in Figure 10.29. Sri Lanka is a tropical island of over 64 000sq.km, with a core of forested mountains in the south and lower country towards the north of the island. The 1991 population was 17.2 million and there is a long and varied cultural history. During the 1980s, tourism grew steadily to reach 300 000 arrivals by 1990, but political unrest has been creating problems.

The tourism plan identifies three key resource areas, each with a distinctive tourism potential: coasts with beaches; forested hill country; and areas of historic cultural interest. These attractive resources are made available in two main ways. First, through **enclave tourism**, which is based on accessible resorts centred on attractive cultural and natural resources (e.g. at Colombo, the capital and site of the main international airport, and Trincomalee). Second, the three resource areas and the resort enclaves are connected by a series of corridors along which access and facilities are concentrated. This 'cores and corridors' approach provides a range of tourism experiences while protecting other parts of the island from tourist impacts.

2 The enclave approach – modern resorts

One solution to the problem of maximising economic benefit while limiting social and environmental impacts is to concentrate investment and visitors in a small number of resort enclaves. The best-known example in Europe of enclave development is in southern France. In contrast to the uncontrolled disasters of the Spanish 'costas' (Fig. 10.30), six planned resorts, called *unités touristiques* have been built along the Languedoc–Roussillon coast, with a capacity of 350 000 visitors.

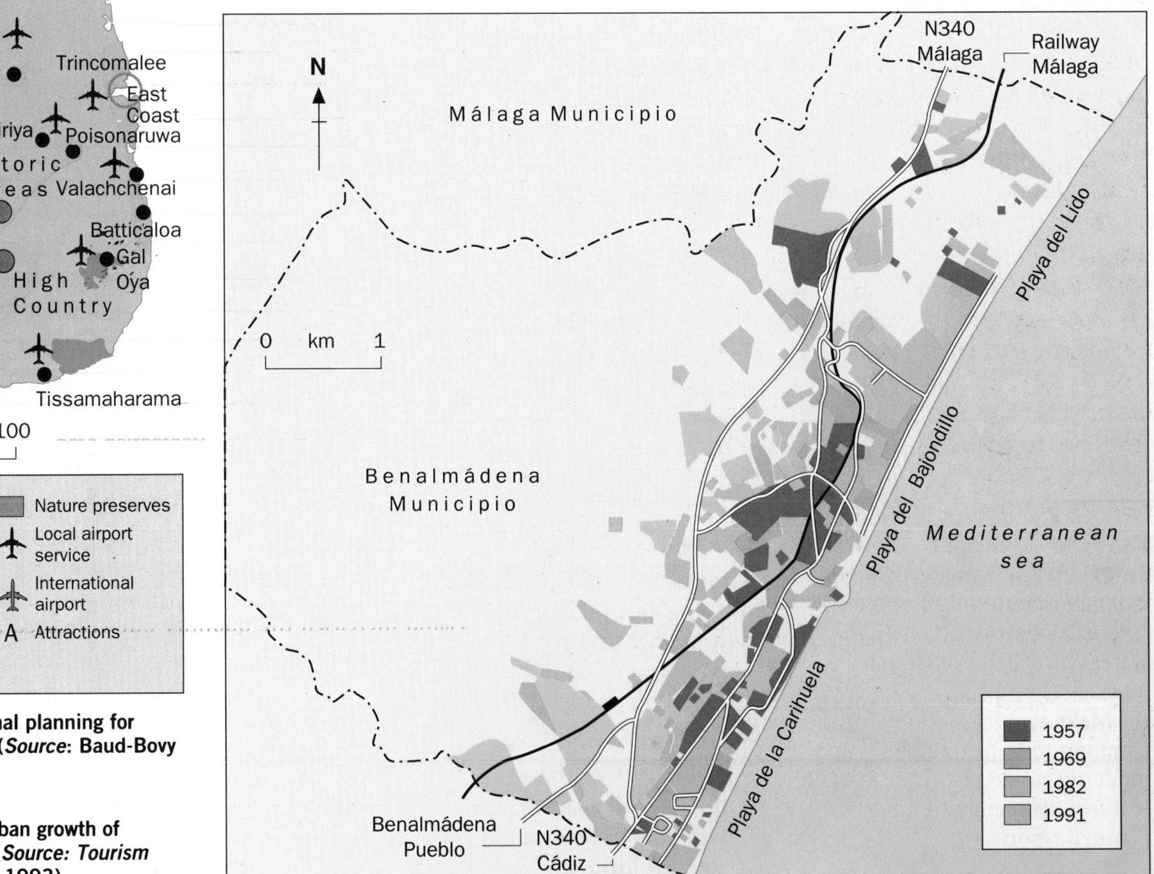

Figure 10.30 The urban growth of Torremolinos, Spain (*Source: Tourism Management*, August 1993)

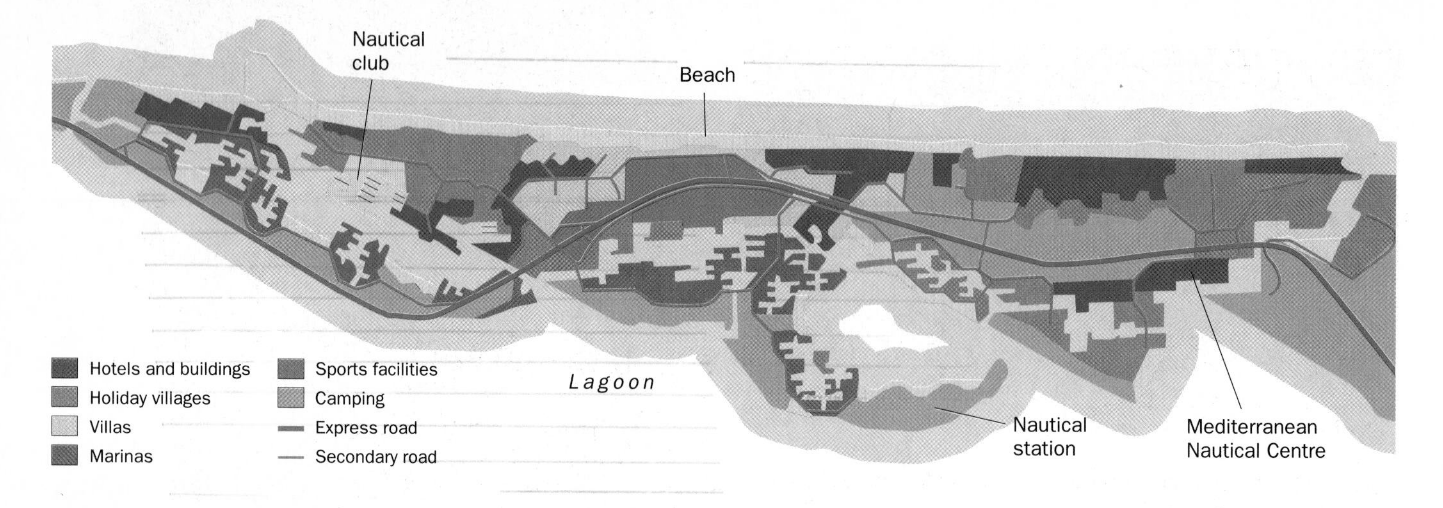

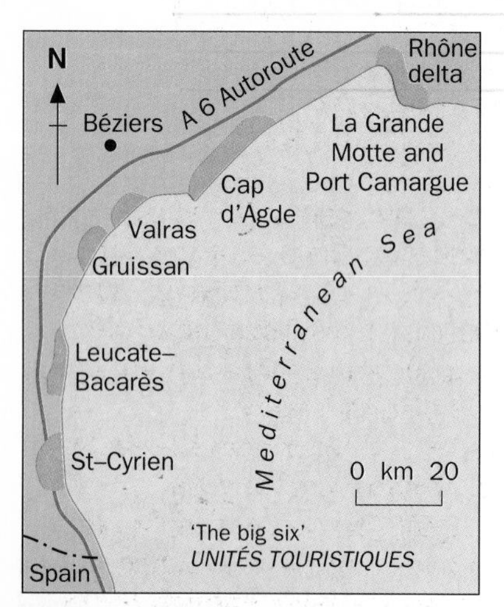

Figure 10.31 Tourism planning in southern France. The six *unités touristiques*, with the resort of Port Leucate-Bacarès in detail (*Source*: Baud-Bovy and Lawson, 1977)

Port Leucate-Bacarès is one of the six *unités* and shows clearly (Fig. 10.31) that the modern resort is very different from the traditional 'bucket-and-spade' resort (Fig. 9.6a). As ever, the aim is to maximise access to the beach and sea. However, the accommodation, the range of facilities and, above all, the transport network are distinctive. The map shows clearly how the resort is built around the spinal road that runs the length of the sand spit. The environment of this spit is totally transformed, but the impact is highly concentrated. None the less, the extensive area required, the increasing quality and range of facilities and attractions demanded by such planned **integrated resorts** require huge capital investments.

3 Ecotourism – sustainability via remoteness and inaccessibility

The essential attractive resources in ecotourism are natural or semi-natural ecosystems (e.g. rainforests) and high-profile species (Fig. 10.32) especially when threatened with extinction (e.g. mountain gorillas). Clearly, sustainability is crucial in this type of tourism – no gorillas, no tourists!

The first problem is that many of these attractive ecosystems and species are found in areas where the local populations (i.e. the resource owners) do not necessarily see the value of conservation, or the potential for tourist income. For example in Belize, in Central America, as population has been growing, so communities have been removing rainforest to extend their cropland. This has reduced the habitat of a number of species, including Howler monkeys.

In one area the villagers, with the encouragement of the government and the WWF (Worldwide Fund for Nature), have been persuaded to support a wildlife reserve. This means that they leave sufficient forest habitat to support colonies of monkeys, and gain income by accommodating tourists and guiding them on trails to see the monkeys. The crucial principle is the involvement of the local people as stewards of their precious resources – they must see that conservation is worth their while. This idea of stewardship and economic benefit is being introduced on a larger scale into the safari tourism industry in countries such as Zambia and Zimbabwe.

The second problem centres upon carrying capacity and numbers. The type of tourist who seeks an 'authentic' experience tends to be crowding-sensitive and expects small numbers, not mass tourism (Fig. 10.33). Furthermore, the attractive resources themselves are often fragile and sensitive to impacts, e.g. coral reefs, and have a low carrying capacity. The most obvious way to control visitor numbers and impacts, and so to sustain the quality of both the resource and the experience is through remoteness and inaccessibility. This approach uses the time–cost–distance factor as the control mechanism – you have to travel a long way and it is expensive in terms of time and money.

25 Study Figure 10.31.
a Describe the morphology of the Port Leucate–Bacarès resort.
b What range of accommodation types can you identify and what activities can be enjoyed?
c Give examples of how the layout maximises access to the water. (Labelled sketch maps will be useful.)
d Make two lists – one of features common to both traditional and modern seaside resorts and one of features distinctive to modern planned resorts.

Figure 10.32 Putting across the conservation message in Mossman Gorge National Park, Queensland

Figure 10.33 Ecotourism – a guided rainforest walk in the Mt Kinabalu National Park, Sabah, Malaysia

Figure 10.34 Location and route to Amazon Lodge

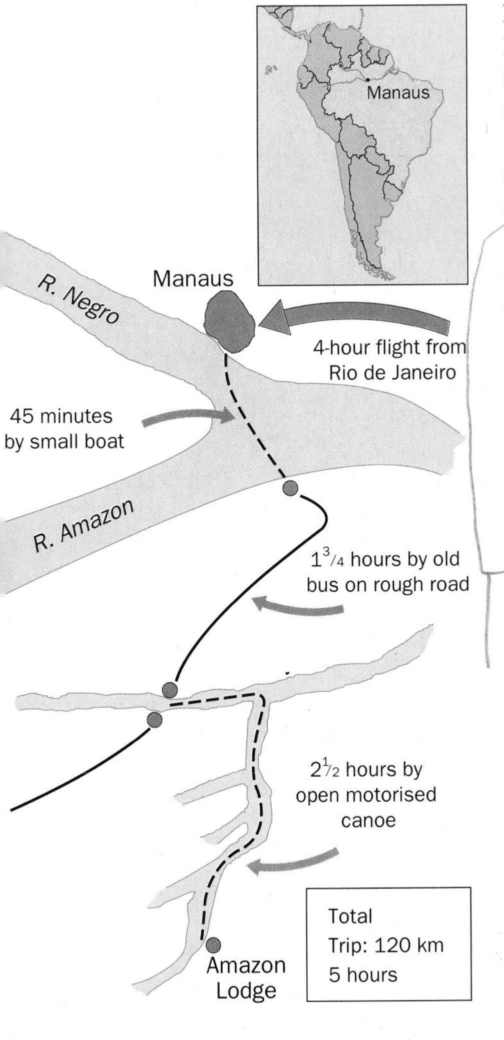

Ecotourism in Brazil

Figure 10.34 illustrates the remoteness control used by a commercial company in Brazil. The tropical rainforests of Amazonia and the communities who live there are attractive to tourists. The main starting point for such trips is Manaus (population 1.5 million), and tour operators offer easy trips from the comfort of city hotels. However, tourists seeking a closer association with 'the jungle' and its inhabitants are catered for at several more distant lodges.

One such operation is Amazon Lodge (Fig. 10.35) where the tour operator and lodge owners sustain the experience and the environment by (*a*) restricting the lodge capacity to 25 guests, (*b*) keeping the lodge 'simple', e.g. no air conditioning or hot water, (*c*) making the five-hour journey adventurous rather than comfortable. For instance, water surfaces are wide enough to use float aircraft, which would reduce the journey to 30 minutes. The lodge is run on ecological principles, e.g. solar power is used; all wastes are taken away in containers; local food is used wherever possible. Trips are made by small boats using low-emission outboard motors and are to different locations to reduce impacts. Tourists are taken to visit local families, but no one family is visited regularly, which again minimises impact (Fig. 10.36).

The Amazon lodge has been operating since 1979, and its programme seems to be sustainable on two counts: in terms of the destination resources and the quality of experience for the tourist.

Figure 10.35 Amazon Lodge: this small, floating lodge is made of local materials, sleeps 25 guests and employs 14 local people

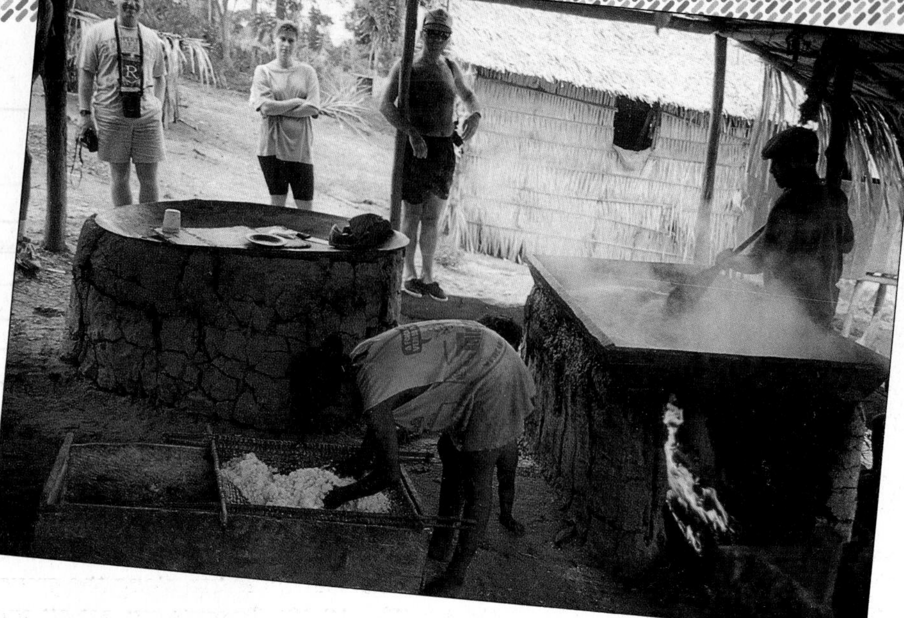

Figure 10.36 A *caboclo* (settler) family preparing their staple food, manioc flour. Groups of visitors never number more than ten and are brought infrequently. They stay for up to one hour. Preparing manioc is not a 'staged' event, but part of the family's day-to-day life

Ecotourism in Alaska

At a larger scale, a government agency, the US National Parks Service, operates an accessibility control policy in the Denali National Park, Alaska. In this example you should remember that (*a*) the area has very few human inhabitants and (*b*) the US government owns the land, making the management of the resources straightforward.

The centrepiece of Denali National Park and Preserve (2.43 million hectares) is Mt McKinley, at 6194 metres the highest point of North America. 'The park exemplifies Alaska's character as one of the world's last great frontiers for wilderness adventure' (Park Handbook). The central unit of this huge area is the Denali Wilderness (Fig. 10.37) and, although it contains the park headquarters, visitor centres, the only campsites and road, it is primarily a wildlife refuge (e.g.

Figure 10.37 Location and features of the Denali National Park Wilderness, Alaska, USA

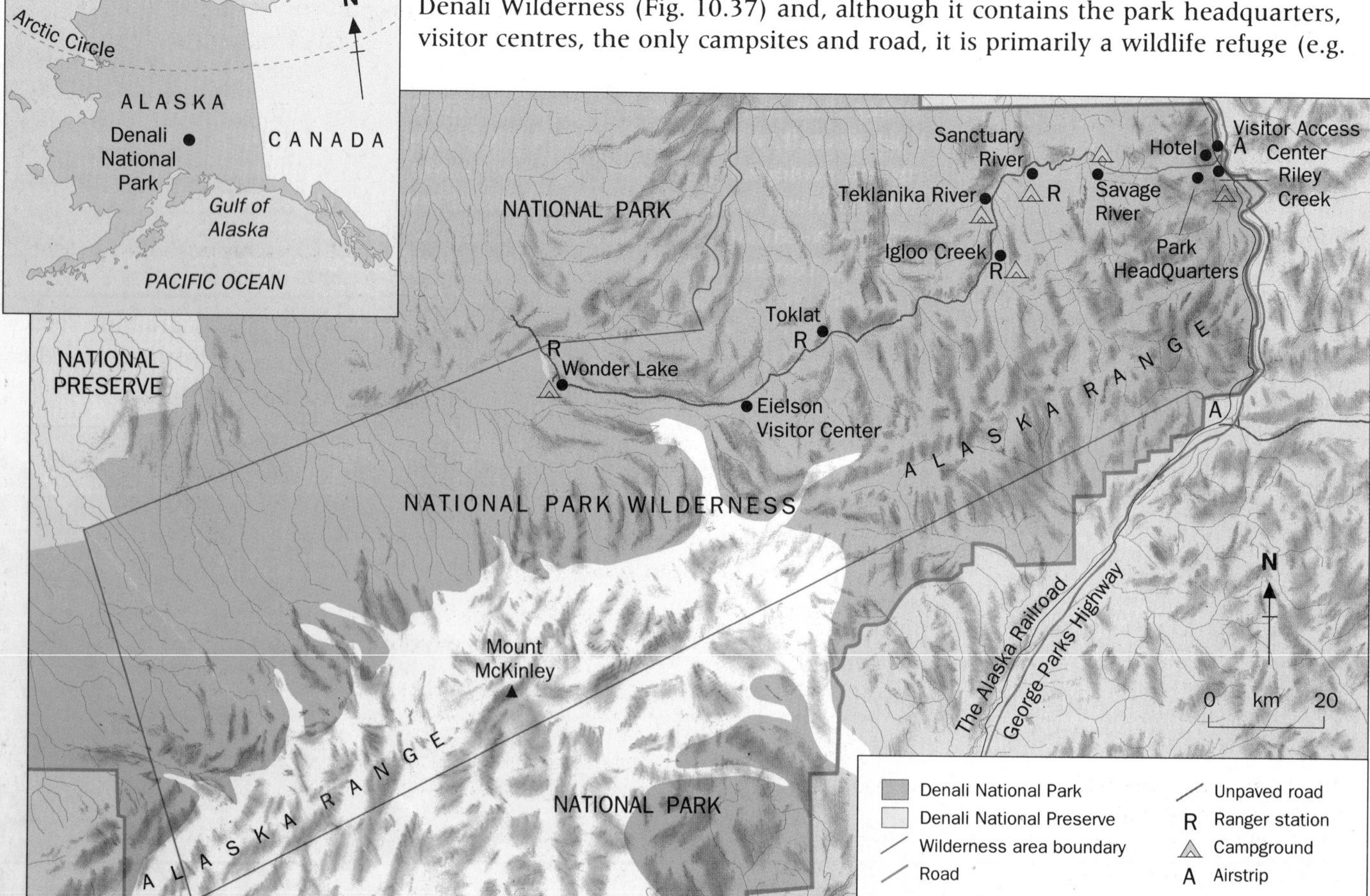

Figure 10.38 The Eielson Visitor Center, looking south towards the Alaska Range

Figure 10.39 The variety of visitor types at the Eielson Visitor Center

bears, caribou). Private vehicles of the 90 000 visitors a year must be left at the park entrance unless the group has a special camping permit. Shuttle buses take visitors on a four-hour trip along the gravel road, 100km to the Eielson Visitor Center (Fig. 10.38). Tourists can get off and pick up the buses at any point, but there are no marked trails across the tundra. From Eielson, reached by 60 000 visitors each year, there are magnificent views to Mt McKinley. Thus, the 'car-and-stroller' visitors experience 'the wilderness', while serious walkers and climbers can disperse for weeks for *their* perceived 'wilderness experience'. Figure 10.39 shows this diversity at Eielson. Thus, the carrying capacity of this fragile environment is strictly controlled by restricted access and remoteness.

Alaska illustrates well the difficulties of controlling tourism and sustaining resources and visitor satisfaction. The combination of transport technology, the popularity of 'the wilderness experience' and the nearness of the huge, affluent North American and Japanese markets bring ever more visitors. This growth is putting increasing stress upon the fragile forests, tundra, wildlife, glaciers and rivers, as well as threatening the quality of visitor experience.

?

26 If the owners of Amazon Lodge (Fig. 10.35) doubled its capacity to 50 guests, suggest what the impacts (positive and negative) would be upon the destination area. Include economic, social and environmental impacts in your answer.

27 You are going to be interviewed on television about sustainable tourism. Prepare for the interview:

a Define 'sustainability' in tourism.

b List the criticisms that your interviewer will put to you.

c Illustrate the points you want to make by using Brazil and Alaska as examples.

28 Essay: Can 'alternative tourism' projects, which aim at sustainability, cope with the problems of mass tourism?

Summary

- People travel for many reasons.
- A holiday involves travelling for pleasure and staying away from one's normal home for at least one night.
- The scale and growth of tourism are making very large demands upon natural and human resources in all parts of the world.
- Tourism is the world's second largest industry and is constantly changing in character.
- Most countries are attracted to tourism because they believe it will generate foreign exchange, investment, income and jobs.
- The economic benefits from tourism may be reduced by 'leakage' and be further affected by social and environmental costs.
- Ownership and control are vital factors affecting who benefits from tourism. Many economically developing countries have found it difficult to gain this control.
- In many countries, tourism has been developed as an exploitative industry, and so passes through a product cycle of growth followed by decline.
- A 'pleasure periphery' has surged outwards across the world from tourist-generating regions during the twentieth century.
- Increasing efforts are being made to encourage tourism developments that are sustainable rather than exploitative.

Glossary

Access The right to visit and use a resource or facility. This right is dependent upon the terms under which the resource/facility owner makes them available.

Accessibility 'Relative opportunity of interaction and contact' (Johnston, 1990). The ease with which people can reach and use a site or attraction in both locational and economic terms.

Alternative tourism A general term used to cover forms of tourism set up as alternatives to existing mass tourism with the primary aim of achieving an acceptable balance between conservation and development values. Examples include 'green tourism', 'soft tourism', 'ecotourism', 'responsible tourism', 'agrotourism' and 'rural tourism'.

At-one-time capacity The maximum number of people that a site or facility can accommodate at one time.

Attitudes Sets of beliefs that predispose a person to perceive and act towards people, environments or situations in a particular way.

Central Business District (CBD) The main commercial, professional and entertainment core of a town or city, containing an assemblage of high-order facilities.

Country Park An area created under the provision of the Countryside Act 1968 to provide urban dwellers with increased opportunities for informal outdoor recreation in country surroundings. Key features are free access and easy accessibility, with the supply located close to demand (i.e. usually within 15km of a town or city).

Carrying capacity The maximum level of use that a site, facility or resource can support without suffering significant environmental deterioration (ecological capacity) or before the quality of visitor experience begins to decline (perceptual capacity). *See* Physical carrying capacity.

Catchment area The area from which users are attracted to a particular resource or facility.

Commercial sector The component of private sector supply whose primary motivation is to sustain profit levels.

Conservation The management of environmental resources and the built environment in such a way as to ensure their sustainability for future generations.

Critical mass The proposition that in order to survive and thrive, a traditional resort must attain a certain 'mass' which can be measured by the quantity, range, character and quality of its attractions.

Demand People's desire for a product, facility or experience and their ability and willingness to pay for it.

Demand-based A term used to describe a facility or attraction that has been located close to the origin of consumer demand.

Dual-use The provision of a leisure facility for both educational and leisure purposes. A dual-use facility is shared by students and the community, and is often funded jointly from local authority education and leisure services budgets.

Economically developed country A country that has achieved a high standard of living and GNP by developing the primary, secondary and tertiary sectors of its economy.

Economically developing country A country with a relatively low standard of living and GNP, and that is attempting to move towards a developed status by enlarging and broadening its industrial base.

Enclave tourism A form of tourism where the tourism experience is concentrated at one location, usually a resort or hotel complex.

Environmental quality This term has two possible meanings: (a) the quantifiable conditions of a resource or resource set, e.g. water or air quality; (b) the level of value that is placed on an environment, e.g. beauty, variety, rarity etc.

Facility An indoor or outdoor amenity or attraction that is provided for leisure use and enjoyment.

Footloose industry An industry that is not constrained in its choice of location by factors such as resource location, transport availability or market source, and thus can operate profitably in a wide range of locations.

Gross National Product (GNP) The total value of the goods and services produced by a country, including the value of its investment abroad.

Heritage tourism A form of tourism whose primary product and attraction is the historical legacy of a destination, e.g. industrial heritage.

Honeypot An especially attractive site or facility which, because of its popularity, is likely to experience high-intensity use and significant environmental impact.

Integrated resort A planned assembly on one site of all the resources, facilities and attractions – accommodation, restaurants, entertainments, transport infrastructure etc. – necessary for the total touristic and recreational experience.

Investment The process of putting money into an enterprise with the aim of making a profit (private commercial sector), or of improving the quality of life for a group or the whole community (voluntary and public sectors).

Leakage The proportion of tourism income that is lost from a destination country and from which it therefore does not benefit, e.g. repayment of foreign loans, payment for imported goods, non-national workers sending money home etc.

Leisure Relatively freely-chosen activity and experiences which take place in time free from work and other obligations.

Management The rational allocation and control of resources and facilities according to a pre-determined set of criteria or objectives, e.g. to make a profit; to conserve an ecosystem.

Manufacturing industry An industry that involves the production of usable goods from raw materials and partially completed components using industrial processes.

Market segment A specific category of consumers, identifiable by their possession of a distinctive set of attributes, interests and spending patterns, e.g. 'Dinkies' – 'double income, no kids'.

Multiple use The management of a given set of resources and facilities for a variety of purposes.

Multiplier effect Spending in one area that produces a greater level of spending in many other areas. The multiplier effect can be a negative chain reaction (decreases in spending) or a positive reaction (increases in spending).

National Park An extensive area of countryside that has been given a special status because of the perceived quality and rarity of its environment, and so is managed in such a way as to conserve this quality. (NB this is an informal definition only. Formal definitions are given in the text on page 79).

Newly-industrialising country A country that has undergone rapid and successful industrialisation within the last 30 years.

Physical carrying capacity The maximum number of users that a facility or site has been designed to hold at one time.

Pleasure periphery A concept that depicts the boundaries of tourism as a tidal wave surging outwards across the world over time, progressively incorporating new, more distant tourist destinations.

Private sector The component of the economy that is made up of privately-owned enterprises. *See* Commercial sector and Voluntary sector.

Product cycle The life cycle of tourism at a destination over time, from 'discovery' to 'decline'. The product cycle model depicts tourism as an exploitative industry comparable with mining – using an attractive resource while it lasts or is in demand, before moving on to exploit another location.

Public sector The component of the economy that consists of government-owned enterprises.

Pull factors The perceived attractive features of a recreational site or holiday destination that draw people to it.

Push factors The perceived negative features of the home environment that motivate people to 'get away' from that place.

Quality of life The social and economic well-being of a community or an individual and their perceived levels of happiness, satisfaction etc.

Recreation Leisure time activity that does not take place within a formal setting of rules and that may or may not involve travel away from the home environment. (Contrast with sport, which is enjoyed within a framework of rules and possibly formal competition.)

Resort An urban settlement whose primary purpose is the provision of leisure experiences. Resorts have distinctive locations, forms and functions.

Resource-based A term used to describe a leisure attraction or facility that is located at the site of the attractive resource (supply-based), e.g. a rockface for climbing; a natural ski slope.

Rural tourism A form of tourism that promotes the attractiveness of the natural and cultural resources of the countryside. It gives high priority to sustaining rural economies and to developing the conservation values of the visitor, and so is an example of the trend towards 'responsible tourism'.

Secondary industry An industry that produces goods using raw (i.e. primary) materials. *See* Manufacturing industry.

Service industry An industry that provides services rather than manufacturing or assembling goods.

Supply The amount of a commodity that is made available.

Supply-based *See* Resource-based.

Sustainability Maintenance of the quality and productivity of an attractive resource base over time. This resource base includes the natural and built environment, the character of society and culture, and the economic viability of the communities.

Sustained yield The use of resources in such a way as to sustain their quality and quantity over time and so sustain the amount of visitor satisfaction, i.e. quality (yield) of visitor experience.

Tertiary industry An industry that involves providing services for other people or industries. *See* Service industry.

Theme park A large leisure facility that is built around a distinctive and focused theme, that charges some form of all-inclusive fee, and offers a broad enough range of facilities and attractions to occupy a family for the whole day.

Throughput capacity The maximum number of users a site or facility can accommodate in a given period of time. It is the relationship between the physical design capacity and the length of individual/group/team participation time, e.g. if a car park at a beauty spot has a physical capacity (at-one-time capacity) of 10 vehicles, is open for 12 hours a day, and the average length of stay per car is 20 minutes, then the throughput capacity is 360 cars per day.

Tourism Activity/experience for business or pleasure that involves travel and temporary stay away from the home environment for at least one night.

Transnational company A large corporation that has subsidiaries in a number of different countries.

Values Enduring beliefs that a particular mode of conduct or way of living is personally or socially preferable to alternative conduct or ways of living.

VFR 'Visiting friends and relatives', a significant component of travel and tourism.

Voluntary sector A sub-group of the private sector whose primary motivation is the provision of social and recreational benefits for individuals and communities. It incorporates a wide range of self-run organisations, e.g. drama societies; sailing clubs; the Caravan Club.

Zone A defined area whose resources are allocated and managed to provide specific kinds of recreational activity and experience, appropriate to the environmental character of the area, e.g. water-ski zone; wilderness zone.

Zoning A management strategy for the spatial differentiation of recreational activities/experiences according to the character of the environmental resources.

Index